Fiction and the Ways of Knowing

Fiction

and the Ways of Knowing

Essays on British Novels

By Avrom Fleishman

University of Texas Press, Austin & London

Library of Congress Cataloging in Publication Data
Fleishman, Avrom.
    Fiction and the ways of knowing.
    1. English fiction—History and criticism—Addresses,
essays, lectures. I. Title
PR823.F57   823'.03   78-4896
ISBN 0-292-72422-5

FOR J. HILLIS MILLER

In utrumque paratus

Contents

Preface

Of the critical essays presented here, about half have previously appeared in books and periodicals; the others were written expressly for this volume. The subject of each essay is customarily an individual English novel of the nineteenth or twentieth century. Their arrangement is roughly chronological rather than historically continuous, for my main aim is to experiment with a criticism drawing on the scholarship of the so-called human sciences. No *vade mecum* of critical method will be found here, only a series of practical efforts to explore fiction's wide range of reference in the culture of ideas, facts, and images.

The variety of scholarly resources on view has been invoked of necessity, not by prior design; I have had to seek them out when faced with specialized questions by the novels themselves. Certain texts make it clear that the author is informed on matters beyond the normal reader's range; one had best follow suit. Some works are only to be grasped in an awareness of the cultural lore tacitly distributed in their own time; one struggles to share in their telling anachronisms. Other works can be understood to say things which their authors cannot have "known," in the sense of systematic thinking, but which they did seize in ways that reason does not know; such knowledge may be set out in a parallel, heuristic fashion without positing doctrinal equivalence or authorial prescience. Among the following studies, about one-third may be classed with research of the first sort, an equal number with the second, and the remainder with the third.

To investigate the matters of fact and belief which make up the designated meanings, the intellectual contexts, and the speculative parallels in these three classes, I have had to undertake a more liberal education than I initially bargained for. In most cases, a novel came to be understood in light of one of the sciences—primarily the social and historical but also including philosophical and religious studies—which may together be described in the current French grouping, *sciences humaines*. The heterogeneity of these contextual materials may be partially compensated by a number of consistent assumptions about the mutual bearings of literature and other ways of conceiving the world, which it is the purpose of the introductory essay to underwrite. The introduction concerns the esthetic status of references to reality in literature and places fiction and other ways of knowing on a commensurate plane where they can supplement each other, but no epistemological generalizations about science and the humanities are offered. I defer to the views of Ernst Cassirer, Jean Piaget, and Michel Foucault in these matters.

My chief presuppositions have been that the hospitality of literature is great enough to welcome even the most arcane and recalcitrant of ideas, symbols, and other *disjecta membra* of civilization; that fiction in particular, though never a mirror of reality, is shot through with realities and takes part in the real; and that an inquirer may be informed by hard data while taking the lively pulse of art, without inexorably reducing it to an investigative formula.

The following have kindly granted permission to reprint: the Johns Hopkins University Press, for "The Socialization of Catherine Morland" (*ELH*, 1974) and "Woolf and McTaggart" (*ELH*, 1969); *Studies in English Literature*, for "Master and Servant in *Little Dorrit*" (1974); the Macmillan Press Ltd, for "Speech and Writing in *Under Western Eyes*," in *Joseph Conrad: A Commemoration*, edited by Norman Sherry (London, 1976); *Contemporary Literature*, for "Science in 'Ithaca'" (1967); *Criticism, a Quarterly for Literature and the Arts*, for "Being and Nothing in *A Passage to India*" (1973); and *Journal of Modern Literature*, for "*The Magus* of the Wizard of the West" (1976). I have lightly revised these articles but resisted the temptation to rework them into a systematic coherence they do not—and need not—claim.

A number of specialists, pre- and postdoctoral, have graciously given consultations: Michael Ryan on Derrida; Laurence J. Victor on modern physics; Peter Petre on Balzac's Melmotte; Ronald Schleifer on Conrad's language teacher; Edward Alexander on nineteenth-century thought; Arthur Budick on Hebrew; David Bergman on Gnosticism. As he has long done (even before I knew him), Arnold Stein set a lofty but beckoning standard of imaginative rationalism for my critical prose.

I have received broader clarification on subjects outside my field from many colleagues at my university—one's closest access to universal mind. My greatest intellectual debt is declared in the dedication, with a recognition that his assent to so referential a view of literature is by no means assumed—although it will be circulated in his Möbius strip.

"Samsara and Nirvana are only words, Govinda.
Nirvana is not a thing; there is only the word Nirvana."
   Govinda said: "Nirvana is not only a word, my friend;
it is a thought."
   Siddhartha continued: "It may be a thought, but I
must confess, my friend, that I do not differentiate very
much between thoughts and words.
   "Quite frankly, I do not attach great importance to
thoughts either. I attach more importance to things."
                                    —HESSE on Buddha

And sometimes it is as a row of little silver cups that
I see her work gleaming. "These trophies," the
inscription runs, "were won by the mind from matter,
its enemy and its friend."
                                    —FORSTER on Woolf

Fiction and the Ways of Knowing

1. Introduction: Fiction as Supplement

*T*HE theory of literature, trafficking in verbal artifice and trammeled by passing tastes, exhibits so keenly the spirit of diversity, if not of negation, that one values any sign of consensus on its central issues. Estheticians as various in their philosophic roots as Roman Ingarden, Susanne Langer, Käte Hamburger, and Jacques Derrida—to cite four leading figures among recent practitioners—are well agreed that literature presents neither a copy of the real world nor a fully real world of its own but has instead an intermediary mode of existence, which it is their labor to define. For Ingarden, struggling to keep his phenomenology from slipping back into the idealism which is its constant threat, the literary work of art is a species of "purely intentional objectivity . . . an objectivity that is in a figurative sense 'created' by an act of consciousness or by a manifold of acts or, finally, by a formation (e.g., a word meaning, a sentence)."[1] For Langer, seeking to bring Cassirer's symbolic forms down to the concrete expressions of artistic media, the esthetic realm is a shadow world: ". . . the space in which we live and act is not what is treated in art at all. . . . Like the space 'behind' the surface of a mirror, [artistic space] is what the physicists call 'virtual space'—an intangible image."[2] Hamburger, after much aggressive floundering (which produces important contributions to our understanding of narrative tenses in fiction along the way), upholds another form of fictionality: ". . . a sentence occurring in a novel has a different character from the very same sentence when it stands in a letter. It is part of a scene, of an independently existing fictive reality. . . . In other words, whereas a real reality is because it is, a fictive reality 'is' only by virtue of its being narrated. . . ."[3] And Derrida, in the most sophisticated effort to describe the world of signs as distinct from the so-called real world (an effort which appears to leave the real world as fictional as the verbal one), locates literary space neither in the world nor in its symbols but in the play of differences among them—an extension of the process by which verbal symbols are fashioned from the differentiations of the linguistic code. I shall return to each of these theories of literature for special illumination and for particular disagreements, but it is impressive to contemplate for a moment their broad agreement that, whatever it is that appears in literature, it is not the "real" world.

Yet, what is our experience when we open a novel and read:

When the lands and goods of Ivar Gjesling the younger, of Sundbu, were divided after his death in 1306, his lands in Sil of Gudbrandsdal fell to his daughter Ragnfrid and her husband Lavrans Björgulfsön. Up to then they had lived on Lavrans' manor of Skog at Follo, near Oslo; but now they moved up to Jörundgaard at the top of the open lands of Sil.

Lavrans was of the stock that was known in this country as the Lagmandssons. It had come here from Sweden with that Laurentius, Lagmand of East Gothland, who took the Belbo Jarl's sister, the Lady Bengta, out of Verta Convent, and carried her off to Norway. Sir Laurentius lived at the Court of King Haakon the Old. . . .[4]

A sample quotation followed by an *ad hominem* argument is the chief method of much esthetic theorizing and will, by itself, prove no more effective than usual here in winning truth rather than assent. But it does raise the question, how do we respond to works which themselves insist on their reality function, which tie themselves closely to historical time and geographical space, which mix invented names with the names of actual persons, and which refer to objects that are observable in the inhabited world? It would be a reader of a special sort—narrowly committed to the intentional, virtual, subjective, or differential character of literary language—who could restrain all curiosity to know which of the proper nouns in Sigrid Undset's paragraphs were historical and which invented. Nor is this a matter of idle curiosity, for a comfortable orientation to this novel will require some discrimination between its historical and its fictional elements—otherwise one would read like the book-club member who subscribes for the "love interest" and perceives only the romance portion *or* like the historical-minded devotee who reads only for information about medieval Norway. Now, if discrimination between the factual and the invented is not only desirable but possible, it suggests that literature has more than one way of intersecting with the external world, that not all its sentences lie on the same derealized plane, that (to use ordinary, imprecise language) some of the things literature talks about are evoked as *things* more than are others, and literature can be said to communicate *with* as well as *about* them.

One need not echo Dr. Johnson or Brooks Atkinson to speak up for the common reader, the naïve fellow so much abused in theoretical literature, who asks improper questions and receives spurious satisfactions from works of art; who wants to know not whether Lavrans and Lavransdatter really existed but whether the lands of Norway are indeed laid out as beautifully as they are described in the novel, and whether life in the Middle Ages was quite like that—i.e., who wants to know to what extent the author is emulating or deviating from what is otherwise observable. Nor are we defending merely the addict of historical fiction, for many a novel, save the unrelievedly fantastic, has its worldly inquirer who will pore over the accurate maps that accompany the better editions of Hardy and Dostoyevsky or the critical biographies of Proust and Conrad. When Faulkner adds such a map to *Absalom, Absalom!* while declaring himself "sole owner and proprietor" of its domain, such readers will be quick to note the proximity of Yoknapatawpha to Oxford, Mississippi, and other intersections of the real and the fictional worlds. And then there is the author of *Ulysses*, who urgently strove to verify every sentence referring to his native city in his novel; he failed to satisfy such readers as R. M. Adams, who rechecked every fact and found some erroneous, but Joyce still stands as the artist of the factual, making his fictional world out of the real *and* the imaginary.

From the plains of windy Troy, and since Aeneas came from Troy "to Italy and the shore of Lavinium," to *The Armies of the Night* and *Slaughterhouse-5*, literature has asserted the privileges of impurity, blending the real and the imaginary, starting from facts and working up fictions, mixing memory and desire. The notion that literature is made of words and that there are no lumps of matter between the covers of a book (other than paper and print) is by now familiar enough for critical examination. What does it mean to say "made of words," when words are entangled in reality to an extent beyond the mind of man to state but which only the aphasiac fails to grasp? Although the structural character of language can be pressed to deliver a version of literature *sui generis*—as pure as the euphony of Mallarmé's disembodied words, like *cellar door*—there is at least one class of linguistic terms that cannot so easily be defined by reference to the code rather than to the world. I speak, to be sure, of *proper nouns*.

One might, of course, claim that when Undset writes "Oslo" she does not produce a reference to the actual city but appropriates the name for a fictional, quasi-real, virtual, differential city existing only in literary space.[5] There is an even more radical way of dealing with proper nouns: since every use of the word "Oslo" refers to a mental concept of some ultimately unknowable entity, an entity constantly changing and thus different from what it was at the time of the word's use, there can be no neatly congruent reference to the things of this world. And, obviously, proper nouns can be used for purely imaginary entities, like Lavrans and Lavransdatter. Yet—to employ differential analysis for our own purposes—the argument which shows the nonreferentiality of "Lavrans" and the argument which affirms the nonreferentiality of "Oslo" are not the same. This suggests that, even considered as modes of nonreferentiality, these terms are different in kind and that literature is remarkable not for its reduction of all elements to a common plane but for its heterogeneous mélange of the real and the imaginary. We still have to deal, however, with the reality elements or, as Ingarden calls them, the "represented objectivities," whose nature deserves more attention than it has been given.

What is needed, it seems, is a rhetoric of the modes in which real objects, persons, places, and times are represented by name in literary works. Among the distinctions that would be required are special terms for the various genres—e.g., for the mode of representing Blackfriars Bridge in *Daniel Deronda* and for that of Westminster Bridge in Wordsworth's sonnet—as well as distinctions within the subgenres to mark off, among others, the functions of historical names in Shakespeare's chronicle plays from those in his tragedies. Beyond these generic variations, there remains a nest of tangled problems in the genre that most estheticians, for very good reason, evade: fiction, particularly the novel.

A start in this direction has been made in a punctilious study by Kathleen Seidel,[6] which assesses the proper nouns of several Trollope novels in an effort to discover which of them represent real entities and which do not—by no means an obvious distinction for the modern reader. Even more problematic than the basic identifications are the verbal forms in which persons, places, and things are introduced: they appear to be as diversified as the forms of most other narrative techniques. Thus we have fully named or surnamed historical persons (Reverend Arabin "sat for a while at the feet of the Great Newman" [*Barchester Towers*]), those alluded to only by their first names, coupled with an invented surname (Reverend Grantly's sons, named for three powerful contemporary bishops, in *The Warden*), and others indicated by their positions or titles alone (The Prime Minister, the Poet Laureate, etc.). More complicated cases occur when an actual family is given an invented member (Beauchamp Beauclerk in *The Way We Live Now*), when a fictional character is placed in a real position (Mrs. Hurtle's husband is reported to be attorney general for Kansas, in the same novel), and when real persons are mixed with fictional ones in the same sentence ("You remember how completely [Sir Abraham Haphazard] put down that scoundrel Horseman about the Bishop of Beverley's case . . ." [*The Warden*]: Edward Horsman being an M.P. critical of the established church, the Bishop of Beverley being nonexistent). Similar mixed cases occur when fictional characters are said to possess real objects (Tom Towers' paintings by Millais in *The Warden*), when such persons are said to live at actual addresses (almost all the London set of *The Way We Live Now* is situated by streets or squares), and when characters move from fictional places to real ones (Barsetshire is invented but its inhabitants are constantly traveling to and from specific parts of England). It becomes, indeed, possible to point to the precise place where the geographical world ends and the fictional begins. In *The Way We Live Now*, that spot is "a mile or two from Norfolk," as we follow the novelist's directions to the imaginary Carbury Hall by real place-names, until we reach it amid a white space of unexplored territory on the map.

I leave the most pungent details of this investigation to the eventual readers of Seidel's essay, but it is clear that no simple rubrics exist for classifying the myriad forms of ascertainable references to reality in works of fiction. Until an orientation toward these references is reached, we literally don't know where we are in the fictional world of a novel. But readers make up for their disorientation as those lost in a foreign country do: they fill in gaps by loosely held assumptions, they make a tacit map of the realm based on prior and ongoing experience, they act *as if* the fictional were a real world and experimentally project what is required to get about in it. It has been suggested that the true root of the Aristotelian concept of mimesis lies in establishing this worldlike self-consistency, rather than in directly imitating external reality. It may perhaps better be said that the locus of fiction lies in the shifting combinations of the known and the unknown, the real and the imaginary.[7]

Before proceeding to this constructive reality-illusion of fiction, let us see how the four theories cited at the outset dispose of the phenomena. For Hamburger, the problem is simple: "The date [e.g., one stated in Hermann Broch's *Sleepwalkers*] plays a role no different from that of any other characterization of a day in a novel. It is nothing other than a piece of the raw material furnished to literature by reality, and in fiction it is just as fictive as house and street, field and forest, as the cities Mannheim and Cologne. . . . For as soon as time and place constitute the field of experience belonging to fictive persons, i.e., as soon as they render the field of fiction itself, they no longer possess any character of 'reality,' even though the field of fiction may exhibit some constituents that originate in a more or less familiar realm of reality."[8] Like a shaman weaving a spell over an object, magically transforming the profane into the sacred, this esthetician endows —or claims that the novelist endows—any named object with a purely fictional existence at the moment of its inclusion in a certain kind of text. Yet the concluding phrases of Hamburger's statement suggest a fundamental insecurity in this transubstantiation: the fictive object is constantly in danger of slipping back into the real world whence it came (as "raw material"—a technological or a sacramental metaphor?). The theorist is led to guard her defenses by disclaiming the relevance of any antecedent reality: "For a geographically uninformed reader, someone on another continent, let us say, the names 'Cologne' and 'Mannheim' can just as little refer to the reality of these cities as the generally unfamiliar name of some village existing somewhere. . . ." And this is how, in fact, many uninformed readers do respond to fictional scenes of which they have no experience. But that is hardly a response to be held up as appropriate for the elaborate specifications of time, place, and history deployed in a novel of intensely modern Continental experience like *The Sleepwalkers*.

A more subtle discrimination between the fictional and the public world is offered by Langer's theory. While strident in its assertion that "the events in a novel are purely virtual events, 'known' only to equally virtual people,"[9] it goes on to consider the problematic case of autobiographical novelists, taking up their almost invariable failure to properly mingle fact and fiction: "They have the autobiographical gift, but not the fecund imagination of a real novelist, to whom his own life is only one theme among many. The barely fictionalized self-story then bears the marks of its origin: for the incidents are not consistently projected into the mode of memory. They are variously tinged with that modality, depending on whether they spring from real memory, available records, or invention filling the gaps of recollection. In the hands of a true novelist, on the contrary, his own story is entirely raw material, and the end product entirely fiction." Although a full appreciation of this passage rests on Langer's theory of literature as "virtual history . . . in the mode typified by memory," we have enough here to indicate the strengths and weaknesses of her proposed solution to the scandal of fact in fiction. It is to be seen that Langer's criterion of success and failure in autobiographical fiction is Procrustean, instancing as successes only Joyce's *Portrait* and Tolstoy's *Kreutzer Sonata* and omitting the long chain of complex personal accounts from Boethius' *Consolation* to Herzog's bellow. Yet the mere argument that pure transpositions of fact into fiction are rare suggests that the more frequent literary phenomenon is the impure and mixed work, which holds data from the real world in loose suspension in a literary text.[10] This is in fact the case, and it remains for the critic to discriminate not between pure and impure fictional worlds but between more or less fully assimilated appropriations of worldly resources.

The most formidable apparatus for including all the manifold elements of a literary work has been designed by Roman Ingarden, who systematically describes it as a "polyphonic harmony" [read: organic unity] of esthetic qualities arising from the content and interrelation of a number of literary *strata*. These include the stratum of verbal sounds and phonetic formations; the stratum of semantic units (sentence meanings); the stratum of represented objects; and the stratum of schematized aspects, in which the represented objects "come to appearance" (or what may be called the stylistic register—established by diction, metaphor, etc.—in which experience is rendered).[11] There is yet another level, which Ingarden does not distinguish as a stratum, of "metaphysical qualities [essences]," akin to categories like tragic, ethical, ideal. It is with the third stratum, of the various objects portrayed in literary work, that we have to do here, and it is to Ingarden's enduring credit that he has made so secure a position in his magisterial account of the literary work of art for this neglected but inescapable level of literary function. Yet his extended discussion of represented objects reveals the intractability of the problem for even the most patient of inquirers:

> . . . in a literary work, the ontic character present in the content of represented objects undergoes a correlative modification. If in a novel, for example, there are people, animals, lands, houses, etc.—i.e., clearly objects whose type of existence is *real* existence—they then appear in

the literary work in the character of reality, even though the reader is usually not explicitly conscious of it. This character of reality, however, is not to be fully identified with the ontic character of truly existing real objects. In represented objectivities there is only an *external habitus* of reality, which does not intend, as it were, to be taken altogether seriously. . . . If the represented objectivities are apprehended in their peculiar essence, then—according to their content—they do indeed belong to the type of real objectivities; but nevertheless, from the outset, they do not belong there as if they were "rooted" in the real world and as if they could find themselves *of their own accord* in real space and real time, i.e., quite independently of whether a conscious subject performed an act directed precisely at them. A peculiar modification of the character of reality takes place here, one which does not remove it, yet almost reduces it to a mere claim to reality. . . . [This modification] is rather something so unique that it can hardly be adequately described.

One can sympathize with this noble admission of failure—for that is what the passage amounts to—in quest of a solution to some of the most profound and persistent cruxes of art. I have omitted some of Ingarden's qualifications—the difference between the work itself and its "concretizations" in the reader's experience, the multiplied distinctions of his concluding ontological chapters, and more—but already the argument teeters like a seesaw between the tendencies to objectify and to subjectivize the literary object. The represented objects are real and quasi-real, they share the "character of reality" with the objects they represent but are not fully identified with them, they have an *"external habitus"* of reality, but do not exist in the real world, they are independent of "explicit" consciousness but cannot be located in space and time without the conscious act of the reader. They make a "claim of reality," but that claim is distinguished from the "claim to truthfulness" of scientific statements (to be discussed below). Ultimately, Ingarden's detailed elaboration of the *"habitus* of reality" of represented objects seems sketchy and hollow, and the last sentence quoted bespeaks a need for other hooks to grapple with this unique and elusive mode of existence.

Consider the case of a novel in which a scene is placed on Oxford Street, London, or Charles Street, Baltimore, or any street with which the reader happens to be familiar. The conditions of universality for works of art require that this novel be comprehensible to readers without such personal knowledge—although it may be doubted that a reader totally unaware of the existence of London or Paris would be able to understand certain British or French novels. But no one (with the possible exception of Käte Hamburger) would deny that the setting on Oxford Street makes for a novel different from one in which the same scene is placed on a street with a fictional name in a fictional city. Moreover, informed readers—that is, those with experience of Oxford Street—stand in a relation to the narrative different from those without such experience, since they are required to bring their other sources of information into relation with the rendering given in the fiction. This reference to real space does not make the space of the novel real, nor does it allow direct transfers from the real to the fictional realm —one does not walk from Oxford Street into the novelistic world or from the novel into Oxford Street. But the choice of an originally referential sign rather than a purely imaginary one is an available option for the novelist, and it sets up special activities in the novel's working. Existing within the fictional work, referential signs maintain their original operation while acquiring a new one: they continue to refer to a real world while they are brought into play with entirely new terms in the text. Just as purely fictional place-names exist side by side with referential ones in a novel, so do other fictional objects—persons, things, situations—exist in tandem with the names of real beings, with which they enter into relations that determine the specific character of each work. The represented objects of fiction are thus not all of the same make, and in the striking juxtaposition of its unlike materials lies the special quality of fiction's estheticizing process.

It is a paradox of our time, in which the "fictionality" of fiction has become a watchword of literary pundits, that many currently approved fictional works have incorporated pieces of the real world in an increasingly self-assured way. While estheticians and linguists argue the pure formality, intentionality, or ideality of literary language, contemporary writers have behaved rather in the manner of Andy Warhol, if not of Walter Cronkite. The novel-of-history or history-as-novel of Capote and Mailer, the collage or garbage dump of the literal and the fantastic in Barthelme and Pynchon, all conspire to belie the ideal of esthetic purity in the fictional world.[12] Moreover, this state of affairs is by no means new: the novel is preeminently the form that arose out of nonliterary works and that has never had a classical model, canonical theory, or fixed tradition to regulate it. Journalism, confessional autobiography, travel books, scandal sheets—all these factual and semifactual reports went into the novel's birth and, like the picaresque figures who have often been its protagonists, the genre has never been of pure lineage, though like them it may have bragged of it. Theories which purport uniformity are usually suspect in literary history, but those of the novel's pure fictionality show up with high definition as prescriptive exhortations rather than as descriptive generalizations. The novel has, like Cleopatra, charmed by its inconstancy; its only rule is freedom, and it assimilates chunks of the real world, often without troubling overmuch to digest, transform, or transubstantiate them. The locus of fiction is the unruly jostling of all the objects of culture—of the real with the illusory, the found with the imagined, the irreducible with the artificial.

The theory of literature—or, rather, of writing—which most readily encourages an appreciation of fiction's roguish irregularity is that of Jacques Derrida. Like Ingarden's, Derrida's concerns derive from Husserl's "painful question," the question of "how subjectivity can in itself bring forth . . . formations that can be rightly accounted as ideal *Objects* in an ideal 'world.' —And then (on a higher level) the question of how these [subjective] idealities can take on spatio-temporally restricted *existence*, in the cultural world (which must surely be considered as real, as included in the spatio-temporal universe)."[13] And, we may add, existence as literary objects, surely another portion of the cultural world which proceeds from subjective to objective existence. Unlike Ingarden's, Derrida's tendency is toward reduction rather than multiplication of operational categories, although his fecund imagination proliferates new terms to cover extended functions of his root concepts. Ultimately, it may prove that Derrida's prolific writings on philosophy, linguistics, literature, psychology, and other disciplines have produced a panoply of engaging ideas which derive from one radical insight: since there is no direct contact with reality (he rejects the concept of perception), men institute systems of deferred substitutions for the being which they lack, so that reality is constituted as a system of differences. By this insight it may be possible to trace the workings of reality in fiction, which other theorists have rendered obscure by positing a radical distinction between them; it may also be possible to push a step further and discover the relation of literature to other differential systems.

Derrida's way of putting his thesis is undoubtedly more accurate than the above formulation: ". . . what is supplementary is in reality *differance*, the operation of differing which at one and the same time both fissures and retards presence, submitting it simultaneously to primordial division and delay. . . . [the concept of *differance*] designates this function of substitutive supplementation [*suppléance*] in general, the 'in the place of' (*für etwas*) structure which belongs to every sign in general."[14] Taking this negative, delaying, and nonpresent strain as characteristic of all symbol systems, Derrida suggests a sketch for a history of culture: ". . . we shall designate by the term *differance* the movement by which language, or any code, any system of reference in general, becomes 'historically' constituted as a fabric of differences" (p. 141). Taken as a characteristic of history and consciousness (though these traditional concepts are themselves put in question), the root idea of *differance* spawns an important offspring: "The living present springs forth out of its nonidentity with itself and from the possibility of a retentional trace. It is always already a trace" (p. 85). Life itself, then, rather than standing juxtaposed to its representations as the immediately experienced to the equivocally figured, is here to be seen as obeying the same laws of differentiation as the symbol systems which offer to represent it. Objects and their literary signs are not relegated to separate realms of being: they function similarly and move freely from one realm to the other.

There is much to be gained by following Derrida over this shadowy ground. His root idea permits us to see the objects encoded in the proper names used in fiction as surviving the attempt to reduce them to purely esthetic entities—because their presence is already delayed, inscribed in a system of differential signs. This thought encourages us to see their operation in literary works as a continued "play of differences"—this time, between the cultural code and the work's renewed activation of it. But the idea also tempts us to lose sight of the irreducible individualities latent in names, of their persistent, deviant self-presentations (as must inevitably befall any presence, in Derrida's view). As he puts it, ". . . there is every reason to believe that representation and reality are not merely added together here and there in language, for the simple reason that it is impossible in principle to rigorously distinguish them" (p. 49).[15] This puts literature and life, signs and objects so equably on the same plane that they enter the night in which all cats are grey.

However similar and interpenetrating are the differentiating processes within the world of cultural systems and within the literary work into which they penetrate, the world of cultural codes was there before the work—which follows it as a discourse of its discourses, a second-level representation. (Piqued by Derrida's highly sexed terminology, one might add to his affirmation of the Nietzschean "freeplay" of the world the necessity of its foreplay.) What is left in the work is a trace of that prior and never fully present world, deposited in its words: those proper nouns that are themselves traces of absent things. Following Derrida's thought, we may find that the cultural signs with which fiction is filled are themselves empty of presence—that the signified is "always already in the position of the signifier"[16]—and yet they provide that which literature traces. Like all good philosophies, this leaves things as they were, but it leaves them *in writing*, showing how they came to be—indeed, for their survival, needed to be—written into literary texts. Despite (or because of) the ultimate differences between life and art, fictions declare the traces of an evanescent existence in their words, especially their proper nouns—this declarative property marking the continued life, not the derealization or esthetic reduction, of things.

The fictional trace is, as a mark of identity which presupposes a difference, as fragile as it is irrepressible. Any assertion of realistic representation quickly breaks down into a recognition of difference—as the word is not the thing, the work is not the world. Yet the effaceability of literature's traces not only confesses to its ultimate defeat as representation but also makes a grudging testament to what is before and after it—the cultural world. The widely proclaimed self-referential or self-deconstructing—but not self-destroying—tendency in literature is its admission of a supplementary, but necessary, relation to the world. Literature is always something extra, added to objects for whatever social and personal uses, inevitably confessing its marginal standing and its ultimate illusoriness, but confirming its permanent vocation in the very record of its defeat.

Literature supplements not only the primary cultural world of language, belief, and behavior but second-level systems as well, which like it attempt to discourse of those discourses. As in the human sciences, which have been shown to operate by conceptual schemes tantamount to fictions, the role of literary fictions is to locate us in our human world, to contrive for us a securer perch in reality by all the arts at its disposal. To determine how literature does this, by comparison with the fictions by which the human sciences confront reality, will help us toward the special virtue of fiction as a genre, toward its supplementary and invaluable contribution to the cultural world. But, first, a brief sally into the arena where philosophers set scientific writing against literary writing, only to observe the prearranged victory of the former in the quest for truth.

In a chapter of *The Literary Work of Art*, Ingarden considers the "borderline case" of "the scientific work: the simple report." This is one of the few places in philosophy (outside the work of Derrida)[17] in which the comparability of these kinds of writing is acknowledged before an attempt is made to distinguish them. Ingarden's distinction between the literary and the scientific work—even as later elaborated in *The Cognition of the Literary Work of Art*—will not satisfy us but may point the way to a finer accommodation. The phenomenological grounds of his distinction are clear enough:

1. Sentences that appear in a scientific work are almost exclusively *true* [i.e., genuine] *judgments*. They may be true or false, but, whatever the case, by their very essence they lay claim to truthfulness. . . .

2. The structure of a scientific work naturally consists of purely intentional sentence correlates (almost exclusively states of affairs) and represented objectivities. But since sentences are here predominantly true judgments, the directional ray of the contained meanings passes through the content of the purely intentional sentence correlates so that the sentences refer to objectively existing states of affairs or to objects contained in them. . . .

3. In a scientific work, in both the stratum of phonetic formations and the stratum of units of meaning, there may appear properties which, viewed in themselves, contain aesthetic value qualities and which, in conjunction with corresponding elements of other strata, produce a polyphony of value qualities. But while this, too, is not precluded in a scientific work, it is not at all necessary; for a scientific work, it is a dispensable luxury.[18]

Though this may seem well for a "simple report," as soon as we recall that "scientific work" here is to include many forms of nonliterary writing, such as philosophy, the social sciences, and history, both the bravado and the renunciations of this account seem Spartan. Not only would the arts of Plato be found "dispensable," in this view, but even the esthetic qualities implicit in a grand rhetorical performance like Spinoza's *Ethics* would become inessential to its vision of the world—as they assuredly are not. On the other hand, the referential function of scientific works is allowed enough loopholes here so that literature could slip into many of the same functions—if not essentially and exclusively, at least occasionally and saliently.

For it can be seen that Ingarden's second distinction hinges on the notion that the sentences of the scientific work are judgments, that is, statements about reality that can be shown to be true or false. It is this verifiability claim that differentiates the scientific sentence from the "purely intentional" sentences of literature (or, as Ingarden artfully says of science, "the directional ray of the contained meanings passes through" to objects). In the first distinction, truth judgments are described as having an essence, but if so they would reveal their character not only by their content but by their structure. It may be possible to show, as Hamburger has attempted to do, that certain sentence structures are unique to literary works, but it is not possible to limit judgment sentences to scientific works by their form alone. Context (e.g., the appearance of the sentence in a scientific journal) is another criterion, a legitimate but insufficient one. A scientific sentence can appear in a literary work without losing—often, indeed, roundly proclaiming—its truth, for $E = mc^2$ remains true when stated in a novel, although $E = mc^3$ may appear also, as a speculative variation. Similarly, science, which tries to include true statements, can also illustratively contain false ones if clearly labeled (as in history and psychology). Thus, only a tautological and strangely voluntaristic ascription remains to distinguish scientific sentences—"they lay claim to truthfulness." But, if wishes and claims come into account, what is to limit the power of literary sentences in their dealings with reality? Artists have been guilty of megalomania in many forms, and one may scorn their claims to reveal truth where others fail, but the mere fact that they make such claims would on this criterion class them among the scientists.

An interesting extension of the issues at stake here has recently been made in a pair of articles by certain American followers of the Oxford school of speech-act theorists. John R. Searle, writing on "The Logical Status of Fictional Discourse,"[19] proposes a demarcation of fictional statements from genuine assertions along lines similar to Ingarden's: assertions involve a commitment to truth, while the sentences in stories are *pretended* representative acts, not "serious" in their relation to truth; they evoke a stance of pretense in the writer and reader comparable to that at work in charades and other games. Although this bald summary of Searle's account of fiction makes it sound trivializing and therefore trivial, his essay must be taken as a thoughtful effort to establish fictional discourse as a going concern, rejecting excessive claims for its burden but describing accurately what it does. Moreover, Searle is acutely aware of the areas of overlap to which I have pointed: the fact that there are no essential linguistic features distinguishing fictional from nonfictional utterances, and the fact that fictional works may contain nonfictional elements along with invented ones, e.g., references to real places such as those discussed above. After duly acknowledging these grey areas, Searle rests on a naïve intentionalism similar to that revealed at the base of Ingarden's analysis: genuine assertions are "sincere," involving the belief of the speaker, presumably in his literal, word-for-word truthfulness—a rare form of monomania. Meanwhile, fictions generate "horizontal conventions" to cut across the "vertical conventions" relating real references to objects: these horizontal conventions are not detailed but seem to imply the reader's abandoning any demand for the writer's sincerity, adopting instead an intention only to be told a story.

In an incisive critique of Searle's paper, Stanley Fish has pointed out the ways in which "pretended reference" applies not only to fiction but to "discourse in general," showing the ultimate conventionality of even truth assertions and the fields, like history, which depend on them. I shall not repeat the arguments that tend to break down any rigid distinction between historiography and historical fiction,[20] but these are only a special case of the difficulties incumbent on prescriptive definitions of fiction and scientific writing. There *is* a difference, no doubt, that leads librarians to shelve books in various ranges of their storehouses, but they would probably be the first to surrender all but the most pragmatic reasons for their actions. At the other, the theoretical, extreme, one need not subscribe to a theory of knowledge that puts all human thinking on the same plane, whether of symbol formation (Cassirer) or of structurality (Lévi-Strauss). Instead of arguing the likeness or unlikeness of literature and science, we might consider their *supplementarity*, and here a new potentiality in Derrida's idea of the supplement is opened up. While he considers *differance* within philosophy, literature, and other systems, we might go on to consider the differences among them as an indispensable aspect of their working.

Whatever it is that fiction, among other literary forms, says, it is presumably something that nonliterary writing doesn't say—fully, exclusively, or satisfactorily. It is quite possible that fiction doesn't say this fully, exclusively, or satisfactorily either, but the measure of its success or failure is often made by reference to other forms of statement—sociology, psychology, history, etc.—with varying degrees of sophistication. Whatever fiction says, it seems to be said at the margins of other enterprises, overlapping them and, as it were, pirating their resources whenever available, appropriate, or opportune. Fiction lives on history, biography, psychology, sociology, philosophy, and every other thought that has been thought about the world—the history of ideas and other interweavings of literary and non-literary texts will testify to that.

If novels from Apuleius' to Pynchon's delight in citing facts, recounting theories, and traversing the civilized world in their range of reference to contemporary affairs, what can we say of the relation between literature and science as it is enacted in this particular genre? The key word is "enacted," for the materials of the human sciences—persons, places, and all the paraphernalia of living—are here put into action together with imaginary elements, like fictional characters and situations. In reading, we observe the difference this conjunction makes: the scientifically described world is no longer left standing in its own realm but confronts other ranges of experience and becomes illuminated by that confrontation; facts are still facts but show a new side when placed with fictions—sometimes revealing their own fictional elements in the process. A novel is, then, a field of differences between fact and fiction, art and science, and among the sciences severally: it is constituted neither by being purely representational nor purely imaginary but by its associative and differentiating processes. If fiction has this peculiarly differential working, it can make a special claim to stand as the supplement of the human sciences. It is, as it were, their horizon, the space where they pass over into what is beyond science. Boldly reversing the direction of Hegel's dictum, we may say that fiction is the borderland where science passes into art.

I submit three texts by way of illustrating the differential and supplementary operations of philosophy, history, and fiction:[21]

A

We ought thus to examine closely . . . all that Freud invites us
to think concerning writing as "fraying" [*effrayage*] . . . : opening up of
its own space, effraction, breaking of a path against resistances, rup-
ture or irruption becoming a route (*rupta, via rupta*), violent inscription
of a form, tracing of a difference in a nature or a matter which are think-
able as such only in their *opposition* to writing. The road (*route*) is
opened in nature or matter, forest or wood (*hylé*)[,] and institutes a
reversibility of time and space. We should have to study together,
genetically and structurally, the history of the road and the history of
writing. We are thinking here of Freud's texts on the work of the mem-
ory-trace (*Erinnerungsspur*) which, though no longer the neurological
trace, is not yet "conscious memory" . . . , of the *itinerant* work of the
trace, producing and not following its route, of the trace which traces,
of the trace which frays itself its path. The metaphor of the frayed
path, so frequent in Freud's descriptions, is always in communication
with the theme of the *supplementary delay* and the reconstitution of

meaning through deferment, after a slow mole-like advance, after the subterranean toil of an impress.[22]

B

An expansive Mississippi politician once said that the Natchez Trace was the oldest road in the world, made by animals and the Indians long before the Romans built the Appian Way. Political oratory has not always required documentation in Mississippi. The Trace's age is still a matter of guesswork for historians as well as politicians. It is certain that as white men after De Soto knew it, it was a road which flourished greatly and swiftly and, like many men upon it, died young too.

The Natchez Trace wore that name only briefly. It was sometimes called the Chickasaw Trace and sometimes, at its southern end, the Path to the Choctaw Nation. Amazingly it was even labeled the Path of Peace. When officials in Washington decided on its necessity as an improved route for the mails and the military from frontier Nashville to Natchez, then the most distant American outpost, they pompously christened it the Columbian Highway.

That was a name too fancy for either its character or its travelers. By those who moved over it, it was often simply called the Natchez Road or the Nashville Road, depending upon which direction they were headed. Its lasting name was finally fixed in the history and the folklore of the West by those veterans of the Battle of New Orleans who, upon this path, also gave Andrew Jackson his nickname of Old Hickory. Long afterwards, when these once valiant fighters had become garrulous gaffers, the Natchez Trace ran through many of their tallest tales.

The death of the old road can be more definitely dated. It was in effect doomed in a year which for more reasons than one was called the *annus mirabilis* of the Mississippi Valley. That was the year in which Indians were called most eloquently to retake the lands of their fathers. Even more important, the first steamboat proved its power to meet the Mississippi's currents and end the necessity of overland travel homeward. And nature seemed to celebrate both events with a trembling earth and a flaming sky.[23]

C

Coming upon the Trace, he looked at the high cedars, azure and still as distant smoke overhead, with their silver roots trailing down on either side like the veins of deepness in this place, and he noted some fact to his memory—this earth that wears but will not crumble or slide or turn to dust, they say it exists in one other spot in the world, Egypt—and then forgot it. He walked quietly. All life used this Trace, and he liked to see the animals move along it in direct, oblivious journeys, for they had begun it and made it, the buffalo and deer and the small running creatures before man ever knew where he wanted to go, and birds flew a great mirrored course above. Walking beneath them Audubon remembered how in the cities he had seen these very birds in his imagination, calling them up whenever he wished, even in the hard and glittering outer parlors where if an artist were humble enough to wait, some idle hand held up promised money. He walked lightly and he went as carefully as he had started at two that morning, crayon and paper, a gun, and a small bottle of spirits disposed about his body. *(Note: "The mocking birds so gentle that they would scarcely move out of the way.")* He looked with care; great abundance had ceased to startle him, and he could see things one by one. In Natchez they had told him of many strange and marvelous birds that were to be found here. Their descriptions had been exact, complete, and wildly varying, and he took them for inventions and believed that like all the worldly things that came out of Natchez, they would be disposed of and shamed by any man's excursion into the reality of Nature.[24]

The first assessment to be made is of the multiplicity of languages in the A text: Latin, Greek, French, German, and English (if the translation be included) form stages of a series in the effort to define a term—*Bahnung*, in Freud's terminology—that is to serve as the basis of a concept, the "trace," which is to be identified with an activity, writing in general. The equivalent series in the B text is not of conceptual terms in various languages but of proper names for the same object, a road in Mississippi; translation from other tongues also plays a role, to be sure, in the English equivalent of what must be an Indian designation, "the Path to the Choctaw Nation." But primarily these names are functions not so much of differential language codes as of varying beliefs and activities—sometimes the names change according to the direction of movement on the road, while at other times they may be called on to put in play a wish ("Path of Peace"), an event (Jackson's establishment of Federal dominance in the area), or a myth ("the oldest road in the world"). The sequence in text C is less homogeneous, including as it does reports of geographical phenomena (similar soil in Egypt), statements about biological activity ("all life used this Trace"), and other references to matters of fact and problems of interpretation. The C text also involves a repeated indication of perceptual activity on the part of a human subject: "he looked . . . he noted . . . he liked to see . . . he remembered how he had seen . . . he looked with care . . . he could see . . . he took them for inventions and believed. . . ." The last term in this series is the most complex, involving a perception of others' perceptions of the Natchez Trace (the reports of Natchez denizens, which are called "exact, complete, and wildly varying"), so that a greater degree of openness to false report and thus a greater indeterminacy settle upon this text. Although confident generalization from a few texts to a theory of discourse would require greater support, we may intuit from these features that philosophic writing about a trace involves tracking the concept through a comparative examination of various languages; that historical writing about a place named "trace" involves distinguishing this name from a number of other names given to that place by various groups in the course of time; and that fictional writing in which that place-name appears may involve both of these series and some others.

A second stage of assessment may be reached by following the internal movement of these series. Text A begins with an equivalence: "writing as 'fraying'" (to which the translator adds the French word he has approximated: *effrayage*, Derrida's substitution for Freud's term, *Bahnung*). This verbal association is then given connotative definitions: opening a space, breaking a path, becoming a route. These activities are then associated with terms in Latin and Greek which name elements of the activity (route: *via rupta*; through matter: *hylé*)—a number of these have complex careers in the history of philosophy. The process is not simply one of verbal or conceptual association, for two conjoint enterprises are urged on us: we are to think about how roads are made and about how writing is done, together. But the implication of this movement of thought, and the terms which convey it, is that road making and writing are equally human activities and that shifts from one to the other involve no loss of articulation, not to speak of prestige. Writing is, then, an energetic activity, on a level with tree felling, earth moving, and rock blasting; indeed, there is a certain joy in contemplating the penetrative and scoring functions of the pen. The tendency to assimilate the act of writing to other human acts—especially those which involve conflict with matter, where physical energy is at work—is to be found in the theories of Freud from which Derrida takes his departure. Freud's well-known physiological side, his tendency toward materialist reductionism, is apparent in this review of his theory of memory as the graving and repassing of traces through the neurological system. The A text moves easily between the physical and the interpretive modes of tracing: the trace's intermediary level of unconsciousness (neither neurological nor conscious), the work and productivity of the tracing ("producing and not following its route"), and the measurable deferral time involved in recovering the trace—these are instances of human activity being placed on the same plane with changes in states of matter. *Differance* as deferral is here imagined as a "slow mole-like advance" through "subterranean" depths. Indeed, the cumulative procedure of the A text—typical of Derrida, and perhaps of philosophic writing generally—is to wear away a track in thought by adding on names, clauses, concepts, and metaphors of similar disposition and deep-graven effect.

The movement of historical writing down its road is not less wearing than that of philosophical writing. The B text begins and ends by recording myth—from the hyperboles of political oratory to the religious awe of natural events which occur simultaneously with historical changes. In between, as we have seen, is a series of names for the geographical phenomenon under examination, each of them connoting a manner of using the road in various historical periods. The B text also employs a number of organic metaphors in tracing the career of the path, e.g., it is said to die at a certain point—although not finally, since we are later informed that it has been revived under the New Deal as a W.P.A. project and is now called the Natchez Trace Parkway. Similarly, its birth is as indefinite as its death, beginning as it does, even before the animals and the Indians, as a geological formation: "The lands were fertile, made of an easily cut and cultivated soil composed of the dust of old glaciers blown by the river winds. When cut the roadbanks stood like a sliced cake." The inevitable use of metaphors in historical writing stands out vividly here both in the submerged organic assumptions and in the most explicit domestic allusions. Moreover, the subtle figures of personification suggest that the road is treated *with humanity*, that is, with the respect one pays to human beings. But the humanity of good historical writing goes further, engraving a sense of persistent and repetitive human life, which is the sum of continued experiences and varied projects in limited spaces (as in Fernand Braudel's Mediterranean world). The road has, like history itself, no clear-cut beginning or end, and it opens up infinite layers of discovery for the people who record its traces —those stratified layers which are retained in their writing. Comparable to the movement of philosophical writing, that of history builds up the successive strata of artifacts, names, recorded events that have layered our roads, our world.

With C we come to the most complex text: the fictional account of a historical person, John James Audubon, as he moves along the Natchez Trace looking for birds to kill, paint, and add to his would-be complete ornithological collection. It will not do to say that this is a derealized version of Audubon, divorced from his true historical existence; in the midst of the fictional text is embedded an approximate quotation from his journals—as, elsewhere in the story, the words and deeds of two other historical persons are also used in the course of their characterization.[25] Although the literary text was written before the most complete history of the Natchez Trace (of which B is an excerpt), Eudora Welty knew enough about the road to describe it by way of those who traveled it, employing many of the historian's legends and facts. She includes in her story the varied personal activities which have left their traces in the earth and in human report—like the brigandage of James Murrell and the evangelism of Lorenzo Dow, who are, with Audubon, the story's protagonists.

Beyond its historical accumulation, much of "A Still Moment" is taken up with an exposition and a comparison of three versions of the philosophical concept of totality: Dow's desire to save all souls, Murrell's aim to kill all others, and Audubon's ambition to paint all birds. Moreover, just as Audubon's activity is a mixture of science and art, his point of view as taken up in the narrative is a synthesis of the esthetic and the pragmatic. It includes psychological aspects (the use of "imagination" in "calling up" the memory of birds), philosophic generalizations ("the reality of Nature"), and a patient listing of objects of praxis—the artist providing himself not only with crayon and paper but with whisky bottle and gun. We may tentatively conclude that the fiction writer's activity is the most inclusive of the three here described, involving not only conceptual terms and their relationships (as in A), together with facts drawn from a number of time frames (as in B), but also a synthetic activity that incorporates these and many other series. There is, moreover, one further element of the story which neither A nor B can claim, and in this lies fiction's special power to supplement the data it receives.

The movement toward a significant conclusion, or a final term in the sequence, breaks down in the fictional more readily than in the philosophical and historical texts. There is reported progression along a road and a series of observations—that is, notations in the text of observations by various consciousnesses—but little progress toward a determined conclusion. Similarly, in the story as a whole, there is a sequence of monologues rendered in free indirect style but no strong plot impulse—although some suspense is generated by James Murrell's project of killing Lorenzo Dow as he rides to preach his gospel. Instead, at the place where the dramatic climax or focal event of many a historical (and fictional) narrative occurs, the writer places a represented object: a single, motionless white heron, described with all the majesty of similar birds in Yeats' poetry. All three totality-seeking personages in the story see the bird, are arrested by the vision, and interrupt for a moment their intense conceptual and practical efforts. Although the artist, Audubon, is first to recover movement—killing the bird and preparing another esthetic/scientific conquest—the story and its characters have been held in what the title calls "a still moment."

Eudora Welty has indicated the inconclusiveness—that is, the inexhaustibility—of her venture: "Why, just to write about what might happen along some little road like the Natchez Trace—which reaches so far into the past and has been the trail for so many kinds of people—is enough to keep you busy for life."[26] And indeed she has located her stories and novels along this road, from the early *The Robber Bridegroom* to the recent *Losing Battles* (which does not name but further adumbrates the road). We might conclude from the inconclusiveness of the chosen paragraph, of the story itself (though this would require extended demonstration), and of the author's lifework that there is something characteristic of literary activity in this mixture of repeated activity and ultimate stasis. The text involves transactions with the historical and philosophical worlds; it is made up of a tissue of the languages by which people have named their relations to those worlds but in addition it suspends its movement of tracing events and their designations, content for a while merely to contemplate those series while all but ceasing its own serial flow.

Yet, if we are to believe some of the sentences in C with at least part of our minds, life is like that, too: "All life used this Trace, and he liked to see the animals move along it in direct, oblivious journeys, . . . and birds flew a great mirrored course above." Not only beasts but men pursue their course up and down the trace, over their roads in both directions, but they also delight in contemplation of themselves, in their mirrored movement along figured paths. The movement of words in science and philosophy traces the incessant motion of body and mind in the world; but the supplement of stasis in literature also responds to a momentary phase of human existence, its occasional removal from action, praxis, and tracing—its eddying into still moments before renewing its headlong course. To these moments the novelist, like the poet, addresses himself, and in this story Audubon is the type of the artist: "He looked with care; great abundance had ceased to startle him, and he could see things one by one."

Fiction is the supplement of historical and philosophical writing—and perhaps of the human sciences in general—in that it is the place where concepts and facts are allowed a moment of rest and contemplation in their own right, before continuing their energetic careers. Like the forms of thought which confront reality more directly, fiction is itself dynamic in its inner processes—the tensions of the words within the work. It may also have rhetorical effects which extend its activity beyond the text, whether affectively, cognitively, or pragmatically. But—bastard child that it is—this impure art contains not only things in verbal form, and the movements of things, but also still moments. "A Still Moment" can stand as the paradigm for the inclusiveness and supplementation of fiction.

Yet, if fiction supplements other writings, it also needs them for its sustenance. And the critic of fiction needs them, too, by way of comparison, information, and differentiation. Fiction is defined by its supplementation of and difference from other forms, and one cannot glory in its uniqueness without frequent forays into other ways of knowing and writing the world. The critic of fiction will have to know as much as one can about the human sciences and their presence in fiction—about things and words and their differences.

2. The Socialization of Catherine Morland

And as to most matters, to say the truth, there are not many that I know my own mind about. —CATHERINE MORLAND

VERY schoolboy knows Catherine Morland as an innocent who goes out to discover the world as romance and finds instead the harsh realities of the social nexus in which she lives. In the satirical plan of *Northanger Abbey*, the naïf finds that she has made up her mind not, like Elizabeth Bennet and Emma Woodhouse and Anne Elliot, on the basis of insufficient evidence but on the wrong kind of evidence altogether—Gothic romance proving no appropriate model in a country neither medieval nor romantic. Yet, like that greater naïf whose mind was turned by reading high-flown romances and who found them inapplicable to his time, the heroine—even in her mediocrity—reflects the grand ironies of human experience in the structure of her perceptions. Catherine, like the Don, is matched against not one or another of the antagonists encountered in the course of her travels but against the entire network of tacit assumptions and habitual behavior which constitutes the individual's cultural milieu. How she learns to make her way in the world by acquiring the cultural forms under which its members order their own thought and conduct—this is the universal drama which *Northanger Abbey* instances.

The realm of literature is the most obvious exception to Catherine's disclaimer, quoted above;[1] in literary matters, she knows her own mind. Without her reading, which gives her a set of terms by which to order—erroneously, as it happens—some of her perceptions, she might not be aware of herself at all, much less know the external world in even a rudimentary way. It is not alone her scanty store of social facts but her flimsy equipment for grasping such facts that Jane Austen develops in the opening account of Catherine's difference from the heroines of romance. After detailing her superficial training and ineptitude in music, gardening, and other subjects, Austen says: "What a strange, unaccountable character!—for with all these symptoms of profligacy at ten years old, she had neither a bad heart nor a bad temper . . . she was moreover noisy and wild, hated confinement and cleanliness, and loved nothing so well in the world as rolling down the green slope at the back of the house" (i, 14). Austen will, of course, neither exult in the glories of childhood innocence nor prefer this variant of the natural to civilized corruption. Instead, she will trace the stages by which this tomboy is made, not simply into an approximation of a heroine or a marriageable young lady, but into an adequately functioning member of her society. What Catherine does in the course of the action is to *make up her mind*, that is, to furnish it with the abstractions, symbols, and patterns of understanding by which we are made distinctively human in the process of cultural formation. The story of this young lady's development is distinguished in the tradition of the *Bildungsroman* by its systematic exploration of the variety of forms which culture provides to constitute the individual mind—a culture including not only literature and moral dicta but esthetic norms, historiography, language, and several kinds of rhetoric. It is as if Austen had rewritten the tale of Tom Jones or Wilhelm Meister while holding a copy of Cassirer's *Philosophy of Symbolic Forms*.[2] But Jane Austen did not need a philosopher to support her in establishing her vision of life as lived *sub specie cultūs*.

Austen refers facetiously to Catherine's development as her "training for a heroine" (i, 15), but the materials of her training conspire rather to confirm her in an isthmus of a middle state, destined to fill an ordinary social role among the lower or middle gentry. She is encouraged to make this adaptation by timely exposure to literature, the arcanum of her tribe: by Gray's churchyard maxim recalling the "flower . . . born to blush unseen" (quoted: i, 15), supported by sympathetic thoughts of the poor beetle who "feels a pang as great / As when a giant dies" (misquoted from *Measure for Measure*). In both cases, encouragement is given to accept one's middling lot, while claiming an inner life of sentiment equal to the greatest. Additional models for forming one's expectations of life and postures of response are provided; she is told of Pope's unfortunate lady, who "bear[s] about the mockery of woe" (quoted: i, 15), as contrasted with the less extravagant but equally artificial stance of the woman in love who seems "like Patience on a monument / Smiling at Grief" (from *Twelfth Night*). Catherine is here instructed in attitudes of resignation and emotional restraint, based on pictorial images for their bodily expression. Individuality is, on the other hand, given some scope by the application to her own youthful impulses of Thomson's lines on teaching "the young idea how to shoot" (from "Spring"; quoted: i, 15). Catherine's ideas can hardly be considered flowering, but such authority provides a sanction for the romantic impulses that emerge in her taste for the Gothic. In general, we can say that the unshaped mind picks up the formulas available to it in the literature of its social milieu but selects and emphasizes according to the apparently fixed dispositions of age and temperament, i.e., there is a natural element at work amid the cultural process.[3]

In line with her acquisition of appropriate emotional stances by which to greet the eventualities of love and life, Catherine is provided with a smattering of moral attitudes by her authority figures. Her home supplies her with apt ethical reflections drawn from collections of maxims like Thomas Moss' *Poems on Several Occasions* and Henry Mackenzie's *The Mirror*. When Catherine finds herself aflutter over the prospect of dancing with Henry Tilney at a Bath cotillion, Austen mimics the moralizing strain which has been imparted to Catherine: "What gown and what head-dress she should wear on the occasion became her chief concern. She cannot be justified in it. Dress is at all times a frivolous distinction, and excessive solicitude about it often destroys its own aim. Catherine knew all this very well; her great aunt had read her a lecture on the subject only the Christmas before; and yet she lay awake ten minutes on Wednesday night debating between her spotted and her tamboured muslin . . ." (x, 73). Moral dicta thus must compete with natural impulses, but they provide the forum of decision and the limits of conduct.

Catherine's chaperone, Mrs. Allen, makes efficient use of moral dicta to assuage her disappointment at the neglect with which she is met at Bath: "This sentiment ['how pleasant it would be if we had any acquaintance here'] had been uttered so often in vain, that Mrs. Allen had no particular reason to hope it would be followed with more advantage now; but we are told to 'despair of nothing we would attain,' as 'unwearied diligence our point would gain'; and the unwearied diligence with which she had every day wished for the same thing was at length to have its just reward . . ." (iv, 31). Meeting an old acquaintance, Mrs. Thorpe, may be accounted some reward for Mrs. Allen's patient hope, but the annoyance to Catherine and the misery of her brother which the Thorpes bring in their wake come to seem less than a providential "just reward." Yet such are the theology-laden terms by which the men and women of Austen's world define their feelings, expectations, and fulfillments.

A more general way to describe such formulations would be to say that events, both social and psychological, hardly exist without a language to enunciate them. It is in keeping with this premise that much of Catherine's education consists of instruction in rhetoric. In one of the first conversations with Tilney, the subject of style is raised when Catherine confesses that she keeps no diary. He replies in his arch manner: "Not keep a journal! . . . How are the civilities and compliments of every day to be related as they ought to be, unless noted down every evening in a journal? . . . it is this delightful habit of journalizing which largely contributes to form the easy style of writing for which ladies are so generally celebrated" (ii, 27). Henry makes two points here: the events of the day cannot—for the experiencer —fully be said to have happened until they are transcribed, and the habitual activity of transforming experience into language gives its peculiar cast to the feminine style. Henry goes on to characterize that style as "faultless, except in three particulars[:] A general deficiency of subject, a total inattention to stops, and a very frequent ignorance of grammar"–but these satirical barbs are less profound than his grasp of the relation between the language of young ladies and their modes of assimilating experience.[4]

Henry is, to be sure, something of a pedant on young ladies' deficiencies, and when he catches Catherine up for a colloquial use of "nice" his sister reports on his frequent badgering of her for "incorrectness of language" (xiv, 107). But he does not confine himself to noting the sillier traits of feminine style and looks instead toward a standard of intelligible and honest communication, from which the ladies' mannerisms are often a concerted deviation. It is striking that he finds his norm best represented in Catherine herself. When he chastises her for her naïveté in interpreting motives, she replies, ". . . I cannot speak well enough to be unintelligible" (xvi, 133). For Catherine's language, despite or because of her novice status in the arts of social relationship, represents a frank intelligibility–to the point of plain-dealing bluntness. She has already established as much with Tilney when, during the contretemps over their broken date, she names the anger his facial expression reveals. Henry tries to mask not so much his feelings as the naming of them: "I angry! I could have no right." But Catherine frankly declares the evidence: "Well, nobody would have thought you had no right who saw your face." Henry's response is the mark of her victory and affirms the principle to which he himself subscribes: "He replied by asking her to make room for him, and talking of the play" (xii, 95). That is, he is embarrassed into silence on the subject but also more than ever attracted to Catherine for her rhetorical excellence.

The inclusion of ethical and linguistic norms in the educational activity of *Northanger Abbey* proceeds as a matter of course; rules for speech and social conduct are the first to be taught in any society. More specialized kinds of information are soon provided Catherine in her orientation to adult society–particularly in the realms of historiography and esthetics. The former is introduced in the course of discussing the novice's own special interest, fiction. Her preference leads her to make a sweeping rejection of works of history: ". . . history, real solemn history, I cannot be interested in . . . The quarrels of popes and kings, with wars or pestilences, in every page; the men all so good for nothing, and hardly any women at all–it is very tiresome: and yet I often think it odd that it should be so dull, for a great deal of it must be invention. The speeches that are put into the heroes' mouths, their thoughts and designs–the chief of all this must be invention, and invention is what delights me in other books" (xiv, 108). Catherine's naïveté allows her to make two telling points about eighteenth-century historiography, which is most directly implicated: that its subject matter is restricted to affairs of state, with a corresponding absence of cultural activities and with a predilection toward the so-called "crimes and follies" of historical personages; and the apparently paradoxical point that, for all their preference for the factual, historians tend toward ideal reconstructions of states of mind, speeches, and even situations for which precise data are lacking. Catherine is here expressing more than a girlish preference for the romantic as opposed to the brute facts of life, or for fictional best sellers rather than the nonfiction shelf of current reading. Her criticism implies a desire for an image of life that is larger than the proceedings of statesmen and the movements of armies; she wants a picture of the actual life lived by men and women, the world of manners and morals that was later assimilated into historiography by nineteenth-century *Kulturgeschichte*.

The Tilneys, brother and sister, take up the argument in defense of history, but their assumptions do not deny those of Catherine. Eleanor defends the role of "embellishment" or imagination in historical writing, pointing to the success of Hume and Robertson in creating idealized speeches for their historical figures, but this is consistent with the desire for human interest—Catherine would doubtless welcome imaginative heightening if it did not pose as literal fact. Henry, meanwhile, grants the failure of lesser historians to fulfill the "higher aim" (xiv, 109) of history, which the more distinguished achieve. In his well-trained neoclassical parlance, the higher aim of history is "to instruct," but this moralistic abstraction might well accommodate the truthful picture of human life for which Catherine hungers. The close relationship between these ideas of history is never fully revealed to the participants in the debate, but there is an underlying fund of agreement on the need for both the revelation of human truths and the creation of an esthetically satisfying formulation of the past. Catherine is not yet of a mind to adopt historical instruction as a complement to her other modes of orientation to the world around her, but it remains a potentiality of her subsequent marriage to Tilney—in which the anticipated modification of her taste for the Gothic would bring about a more sophisticated awareness of the past.

The social value of esthetic tastes imparted by a girlish education may seem as meager as that of historiography, but the late eighteenth and early nineteenth centuries were as insistent as our own times that a young person should be up-to-date about the arts. Landscape, architecture, and painting or drawing were clearly matters of concern for the well-bred, and there are discussions throughout the Austen canon on these matters.[5] Landscape design does not play an important role in *Northanger Abbey*, where the focus of discussion is on architecture. The inspiration for such discussion usually stems from Catherine herself, as she responds to townscapes and buildings with the imagined structures of Gothic romance in mind. Her interest in the unfortunate excursion to Blaize Castle with John Thorpe largely derives from anticipation that it is "like what one reads of" (xi, 85); similarly, her view of the spectacle of Bath and its surroundings is in accord with "what I have read about" (xiv, 106). The fullest image of what a medieval building *should* be is, of course, her conception of Northanger Abbey: ". . . she was to be for weeks under the same roof with the person whose society she mostly prized—and, in addition to all the rest, this roof was to be the roof of an abbey!—Her passion for ancient edifices was next in degree to her passion for Henry Tilney—and castles and abbies made usually the charm of those reveries which his image did not fill" (xvii, 141). There is a strong suggestion that not only her anticipation of a social visit but her sexual vibration, too, is given its form in her mind—its "image" in her "reveries"—in the framework of the architectural models provided by her reading. Here is another indication of the power of acquired notions of form to shape even one's image of the beloved.

We are given a detailed account of the country house as Catherine explores it, first with General Tilney for a guide and then on her own. The rooms are oppressively modern, the pre-Reformation cloister has become a mere "court," and only the original kitchen proves "rich in the massy walls and smoke of former days" (xxiii, 183). The genuine mystery of English country house architecture—its mixture of medieval and classical elements and the roots of this mixture of styles in the tangled religious history of the country—all this is lost upon "the well-read Catherine." She is reduced to a simple target of satire as she builds up a mystery around the furniture of her room, according to the prescriptions Henry has set out for her; and she discovers a provocative document that proves to be a laundry list (chapter xxi). In general, Catherine's expectation is of the obscurity associated with antiquity and barbarism, and she takes this association literally enough to be disappointed when the abbey proves not obscure but open to the light of day: "To be sure, the pointed arch was preserved—the form of them was Gothic—they might be even casements—but every pane was so large, so clear, so light!" (xx, 162).

Architectural taste, as often happens, leads to architectural principle, and Catherine is enlisted in the camp of the preservationists who have, for over two centuries, opposed the alteration (and sometimes the restoration) of the monuments of the past: "Catherine could have raved at the hand which had swept away what must have been beyond the value of all the rest [of the building], for purposes of mere domestic economy . . ." (xxiii, 184). As the visit proceeds, however, she comes to sense that personal comfort and contemporary style may be virtues, too: "They took a slight survey of all; and Catherine was impressed, beyond her expectation, by their multiplicity and their convenience" (xxiii, 184). There is, in fact, a process of social as well as architectural enlightenment at work during her stay at Northanger, which culminates in the revelation of the general's avarice and tyrannical manners. The heroine is engaged in a sequence of discoveries about the life lived in country houses, the relation of that manner of life to the visible structures, and the relationships that obtain between esthetic and ethical values. While Catherine is disabused of her belief in medieval models for men like General Tilney, she learns that a light and airy modern mansion may be the preferred domain of a man who can be crudely inhospitable to a suddenly unwanted guest.

Besides her grand ideas of architecture, Catherine has been urged to try her hand at drawing—". . . she did what she could in that way, by drawing houses and trees, hens and chickens, all very much like one another" (i, 14). But she is unable to appropriate visual models for the shaping of her personal life, particularly for her projection of a desirable lover: "Her greatest deficiency was in the pencil—she had no notion of drawing—not enough even to attempt a sketch of her lover's profile, that she might be detected in the design" (i, 16). This lack of a technique by which to form a conception of a lover is equaled by her lack of a terminology by which to see the countryside around her: the Tilneys "were viewing the country with the eyes of persons accustomed to drawing, and decided on its capability of being formed into pictures, with all the eagerness of real taste. Here Catherine was quite lost. . . . The little which she could understand however appeared to contradict the very few notions she had entertained on the matter before. It seemed as if a good view were no longer to be taken from the top of an high hill, and that a clear blue sky was no longer a proof of a fine day" (xiv, 110). If any confirmation be needed that cultural symbols can make rain and fine weather, we have it here: not only a good view but a fair day depend for their existence on what we expect them to be. While Catherine is facetiously granted an advantage in being able to attract a lover by her naïveté ("Where people wish to attach, they should always be ignorant"), her best weapon is her capacity to see the world as she is taught to see it: ". . . a lecture on the picturesque immediately followed, in which his instructions were so clear that she soon began to see beauty in every thing admired by him . . . Catherine was so hopeful a scholar, that when they gained the top of Beechen Cliff, she voluntarily rejected the whole city of Bath, as unworthy to make part of a landscape" (xiv, 111).

The most explicit acknowledgment that cultural forms determine the structure of reality for Catherine emerges from her discussion of flowers with Henry:

"What beautiful hyacinths!—I have just learnt to love a hyacinth."

"And how might you learn?—By accident or argument?"

"Your sister taught me; I cannot tell how. Mrs. Allen used to take pains, year after year, to make me like them; but I never could, till I saw them the other day in Milsom-street; I am naturally indifferent about flowers." . . .

"At any rate, however, I am pleased that you have learnt to love a hyacinth. The mere habit of learning to love is the thing; and a teachableness of disposition in a young lady is a great blessing." (xxii, 174)

Two broad implications may be drawn from this dialogue: the fairly obvious one that the judgment of beauty and value is a product of education, involving relationships with other people and invoking their perceptual models; and, second, that "nature" plays a role in addition to the powerful force of culture but that this role seems restricted to an openness to cultural influence, "a teachableness of disposition," rather than an inclination in a given direction. Catherine is "naturally indifferent," but this lack of disposition can be hostile to influence, preferring to be left neutral, or it can welcome instruction (especially if Henry's) and eventually acquire the "habit of learning to love." Human nature is seen here as best employed in opening itself to cultural formation—the virtue of naturalness lying not in effusions of pure feeling or freedom from artificial embellishments but in enthusiasm for such acquired sensibilities as the love of flowers.

A further esthetic debate takes place in the novel on the question of representation in painting, particularly of likeness in portraiture. The subject is the dead Mrs. Tilney's portrait and the general's attitude to it—heightened, of course, by Catherine's suspicions of its Gothic role in bearing witness to his presumed crime. The discussion opens before Catherine is shown the picture: Eleanor explains that her father was "dissatisfied" with it but that she has hung it in her own room—"where I shall be happy to shew it you;—it is very like" (xxii, 181). Catherine's inference immediately follows: "A portrait—very like—of a departed wife, not valued by the husband!—He must have been dreadfully cruel to her!" She focuses on the likeness as the mark which should recommend it to Tilney as a primitive substitute for the departed; yet it is precisely that likeness which she comes to question. After seeing the monument to Mrs. Tilney at church on Sunday, and marveling at the general's coolness in facing up to this testimony to his presumed misdeeds, she confronts the portrait in Eleanor's room:

> It represented a very lovely woman, with a mild and pensive countenance, justifying, so far, the expectations of its new observer; but they were not in every respect answered, for Catherine had depended upon meeting with features, air, complexion that should be the very counterpart, the very image, if not of Henry's, of Eleanor's;—the only portraits of which she had been in the habit of thinking, bearing always an equal resemblance of mother and child. A face once taken was taken for generations. But here she was obliged to look and consider and study for a likeness. (xxiv, 191)

Catherine fails to confirm her previous inference that the general's dismissal of a "very like" representation of his wife indicates his culpability, for the portrait is not to her mind representative of a Tilney face. But this defeated expectation leads her to go over the grounds of judging likeness.[6] She recognizes in herself a tacit assumption or desire that the portrait will resemble the man she loves (the latter itself a shorthand term for a complex cultural symbol and a term which Jane Austen uses sparingly). This assumption depends in turn on previous experience, most of the portraits she has seen having been done on the principle that parents and children must resemble each other—"A face once taken was taken for generations." The esthetic or commercial conventions of a certain type of artist—probably of a social rank inferior to those whom the general and the higher gentry would employ—are thus found to be the determinants of her "habit of thinking." Yet they fail to act as determinants in this case: Catherine is honest and perceptive enough to find the likeness to her beloved absent; she is being introduced to the norms of another school of painting, in which the sitter's individuality is at a higher premium than confirmation of family unity. To sum up, she has transcended both her easy assumption that the portrait resembles Mrs. Tilney, and is therefore an indicator of the general's guilt, and also her assumption that the portrait resembles Henry and will therefore call forth the adoring responses she gives his appearance. Instead, she values the painting with a purer esthetic response, although touched by personal feeling: "She contemplated it, however, in spite of this drawback, with much emotion; and, but for a yet stronger interest, would have left it unwillingly" (xxiv, 191). We cannot say for sure, but she seems to respond to the human values of the portrait—perhaps to the image of Mrs. Tilney's individual being.

Another domain of cultural formation in which the heroine is given some training in getting through the world is that of politics. There are no elements of political theory, or even generalizations about political behavior, in the course of her education. But in a remarkable conversation—frequently quoted at length in the critical literature on this novel—a number of symbols are imparted by which Catherine may learn to make perceptions of contemporary affairs. The subject emerges from one of the debates on literature and, although punctuated by an amusing misunderstanding, the talk of politics becomes linked to the system of fictions which structures the heroine's world. Catherine looks forward to the next Gothic novel to "come out in London," which is to be "more horrible than any thing we have met with yet" (xiv, 112), but Eleanor takes her to mean a "dreadful riot" in actual life. Henry quickly perceives the double entendres on "come out" and "horrible" and elaborates them into a joke on government: "'Government,' said Henry, endeavouring not to smile, 'neither desires nor dares to interfere in such matters. There must be murder; and government cares not how much.'" The play on words becomes a play on concepts, the most directly implicated being that of laissez-faire—government noninterference in private affairs is now extended from publication about murder to murder itself. When Henry explains his little joke, he only complicates it by bringing recent history into evidence:

"You [Catherine] talked of expected horrors in London—and instead of instantly conceiving, as any rational creature would have done, that such words could relate only to a circulating library, she [Eleanor] immediately pictured to herself a mob of three thousand men assembling in St. George's Fields; the Bank attacked, the Tower threatened, the streets of London flowing with blood, a detachment of the 12th Light Dragoons, (the hopes of the nation,) called up from Northampton to quell the insurgents, and the gallant Capt. Frederick Tilney, in the moment of charging at the head of his troop, knocked off his horse by a brickbat from an upper window." (xiv, 113)

The perhaps unconscious irony of Henry's satire on girlish exaggeration is that there is no exaggeration here: his account picks up the chief events of the Gordon riots of 1780—within the lifetimes of the characters, assuming a setting contemporary with the writing of the novel. Moreover, as Dickens was to point out in his version of the riots in *Barnaby Rudge*, one of the chief horrors was the ineffectuality of a government taking the laissez-faire stance in the midst of a near holocaust.

In effect, Henry's ridicule of his sister's revolutionary fantasies anticipates his later disclaimer of Catherine's literary fantasy vis-à-vis his father's presumed crime. In both cases the assumption that "it can't happen here" in enlightened, modern England rings a bit false. One of the best commentaries on this subtler note is that of A. Walton Litz: "The ironies of this misunderstanding are directed at complacent sense as well as exaggerated sensibility . . . Gothic violence is not impossible in English society, only repressed and rigidly controlled."[7] Although Henry in both sessions provides Catherine with a full set of the favored pieties of English political mythology, he fails to overcome the strong influence of the Gothic symbols of underlying social crime. Indeed, his account of the riots, together with his parodic predictions of her terror at visiting the abbey, may provide indirect support for her sense of the comparable horrors of life and literature.

In this context, the celebrated satire of Gothic fiction in *Northanger Abbey* becomes but one phase—the decisive phase, to be sure—in a process of socialization. Catherine's enthusiasm for romantic novels is by no means a personal idiosyncrasy to be removed by education; she is at the crest of the wave of public taste—especially for girls of her age and class. On the other hand, an exclusive attention to exotic scenes—let alone extraordinary situations—may tend to unfit the novice for playing roles in the social world. The heroine must therefore be instructed in the approved way of taking her literary experiences: not as simple schemes for perceiving the world around her but as highly charged symbols whose forms add shadow and depth to the prosaic. In the end she must learn to take the Gothic novels not as alternatives to the given but as enrichments and articulations of it. As Lloyd W. Brown writes, in making a similar point:

The abbey has been endowed with its own individual personality, and the primary function of this identity lies in its stubborn resistance to the patterns of Gothic meaning that Catherine tries to force upon it. Simultaneously, the aura of imaginative splendor which overexcites Catherine serves to rebuke the crass materialism of the building's owner. In effect, Northanger Abbey is a satiric projection of the highly subjective nature of the symbolic process itself. Particularly in the cases of Catherine and General Tilney, it is emblematic of the way in which means of communication like symbols can also be psychological and moral experiences.[8]

A review of the heroine's use of her fictional experience in forming judgments is in order, before approaching her confrontation with the abbey. While she does not indulge in Isabella's conventional effusions on true love—"Every thing is so insipid, so uninteresting, that does not relate to the beloved object!" (vi, 41)—Catherine does take a view of marriage along storybook lines; when Henry attempts a witty comparison of marriage and dancing, she objects: "People that marry can never part, but must go and keep house together. People that dance, only stand opposite each other in a long room for half an hour" (x, 77). Similarly, when the first indications of Isabella's infidelity to her brother emerge, Catherine refuses to believe in the existence of deviations from plighted troth—when Henry sarcastically replies, "I understand: she is in love with James, and flirts with Frederick," she rejects the reality: "Oh! no, not flirts. A woman in love with one man cannot flirt with another" (xix, 151). Yet at hearing of Mrs. Tilney's death "Catherine's blood ran cold," in the appropriate literary phrase; "Could it be possible?—Could Henry's father?—And yet how many were the examples to justify even the blackest suspicions!" (xxiii, 186–187). How can we account for the shift in Catherine's notions of what is morally possible—from the conviction that "a woman in love with one man cannot flirt with another" to the assurance that her "blackest suspicions" are simple truth?

The answer would seem to lie not in the realities but in the symbols involved in these judgments of the possible. The belief that sexual indiscretion is impossible in a respectable girl derives not from generalizations about the conduct of others but only from a sense of what is conceivable in literary convention. Although wider experience of the world may lead her to modify her sexual conceptions, Catherine limits her view of the possible according to the select range of fiction in which such peccadilloes are inadmissible. In the matter of wife murder, on the other hand, Gothicism can widen her conception of the possible. In effect, all such conduct takes place for Catherine in a fictional realm, and it is to one corner of that realm that she consigns General Tilney. There is no great danger of wronging him because her judgment is less a moral than a literary one; her perceptions of his features are not judgments of ethical worth but of literary genre. In this way, she invests him with considerably more intensity and interest than he initially possesses; just as Catherine's visit to Northanger Abbey is heightened by Gothic associations, her image of its proprietor is given vigor and color by her literary sense.

When Catherine comes to reflect on Henry's explanation of the limited applicability of Continental depravities to the sceptered isle of England, she grasps a point about human nature that is far more convincing than his reliance on "the laws of the land, and the manners of the age." "Among the Alps and Pyrenees [she muses], perhaps, there were no mixed characters. There, such as were not as spotless as an angel, might have the dispositions of a fiend. But in England it was not so; among the English, she believed, in their hearts and habits, there was a general though unequal mixture of good and bad" (xxv, 200). Catherine is here in line for promotion in literary as well as ethical discrimination, for she is able to preserve her illusions about Latin extremes of character yet accepts the Anglo-Saxon as the domain of complex men and women, a fit subject for literary realism. While the complexity of human character was well known to authors before the advent of nineteenth-century realism, it is a firm part of the network of assumptions which determines that literary tradition. In effect, Catherine—with Jane Austen—opts for the conventions of realism in dealing with English life, whatever grotesques of romanticism may be appropriate to Romance lands.

The climax of Catherine's development is no volte-face from romance to realism but a strengthening of her powers of discrimination by combining the variety of modes of interpretation in which she has become practiced. Her inclination is not to remove the guiltless general from moral scrutiny but to refine her evaluation of him: "Upon this conviction [cited above], she would not be surprised if even in Henry and Eleanor Tilney, some slight imperfection might hereafter appear; and upon this conviction she need not fear to acknowledge some actual specks in the character of their father, who, though cleared from the grossly injurious suspicions which she must ever blush to have entertained, she did believe, upon serious consideration, to be not perfectly amiable" (xxv, 200). Given this mode of perception, she is capable of judging the genuine moral horror of his rough treatment of her—though its abruptness makes it a shock nonetheless. And when Henry tests her in her responses to Isabella's jilting of her brother, according to the literary models of feeling to which she might previously be expected to subscribe, she displays an accuracy of introspection that matches her newly acquired ethical sophistication. "'You feel [he suggests] that you have no longer any friend to whom you can speak with unreserve; on whose regard you can place dependence; or whose counsel, in any difficulty, you could rely on. You feel all this?' 'No,' said Catherine, after a few moments' reflection, 'I do not—ought I?'" (xxv, 207). Her lingering timidity is quickly rebuked by Henry, who delivers one of Jane Austen's finest affirmations of the Socratic imperative of moral intelligence: "You feel, as you always do, what is most to the credit of human nature.—Such feelings ought to be investigated, that they may know themselves."

In other ways, too, Catherine's literary sense of Northanger is not so much discredited as reworked into another, more complicated pattern. When Eleanor comes to her room to tell of her summary dismissal by the general, the scene is conceived Gothically: ". . . it seemed as if some one was touching the very doorway—and in another moment a slight motion of the lock proved that some hand must be on it. She trembled a little at the idea of any one's approaching so cautiously; but resolving not to be again overcome by trivial appearances of alarm, or misled by a raised imagination, she stepped quietly forward, and opened the door. Eleanor, and only Eleanor stood there. Catherine's spirits however were tranquillized but for an instant, for Eleanor's cheeks were pale, and her manner greatly agitated" (xxviii, 222–223). The first indications of a satirical control shaping this narration imply that the naïve Catherine is again to be reminded—or in this case to remind herself—of the disparity between fact and fiction. Elements of the two realms are melded indissolubly, however: Eleanor's hesitation at the door is motivated by genuine embarrassment and unwillingness to hurt her friend, while her appearance conforms to the melodramatic stance of a fictional character.

Again, the scene itself lends form to Catherine's response to the climactic event: "That room, in which her disturbed imagination had tormented her on her first arrival, was again the scene of agitated spirits and unquiet slumbers" (xxviii, 227). It is true that, as the new disturbance is "superior in reality and substance," Catherine regards the "solitude of her situation, the darkness of her chamber, the antiquity of the building . . . without the smallest emotion"; but it is also true that her "contemplation of actual and natural evil" accords perfectly with such a setting—if not in the Gothic, then in the *penseroso* vein. Finally, the heroine's summation of the general, even after Henry's lucid explanation of his motives, employs her reading to provide a metaphoric construct, rather than a literal description, of his behavior: "Catherine, at any rate, heard enough to feel, that in suspecting General Tilney of either murdering or shutting up his wife, she had scarcely sinned against his character, or magnified his cruelty" (xxx, 247).

When the evidence of this fusion of moral, esthetic, and other perceptual modes is taken together, we are better able to assimilate the artifice in Jane Austen's rapidly sketched denouement. Her facetious remarks and obtrusive presence have called denunciations down from those with expectations of a consistent realist style but, if the novel's traffic with cultural fictions is held in mind, strictures by reference to realist norms seem footless. *Northanger Abbey* moves beyond its initial parodic style into a fairly conventional satire of the beau monde at Bath, finally arriving at a complex comic version of the perceptual illusions involved in all human enterprises—of which a visit to a country house may be taken as a significant instance. In a keen insight into the connection of this mixture of genres with the denouement's artifice, Frank J. Kearful has written:

> The book thus ends by denying the autonomy of the illusion it has presented, as in a Prospero-like gesture the narrator disperses the creatures of her imagination and the world they inhabit. Those who object to the inconsistency of technique and structure in *Northanger Abbey* as well as those who reduce it to univocal form have missed the point of what they have read. . . . [Austen] is, rather, combining elements of all these [genres] in such a fashion as to make us aware of the paradoxical nature of all illusion—even those illusions by which we master illusion.[9]

We may add to this deduction from the novel's mixture of genres a reflection on the varied content of the work: the heroine moves from an unformulated openness to experience, through a naïve notion of the direct applicability of symbols (like those of the Gothic novels) to a more sophisticated use of cultural forms—which she treats no longer literally but metaphorically. When the heroine becomes aware that a literary convention does not predict or determine the behavior of those to whom it superficially applies —and yet that it may be taken as a useful metaphoric construct by which to shape one's response to them, as Catherine does with regard to General Tilney—she has arrived at a peak of cultural self-consciousness, in which one both sees through the artificiality of all cultural symbols and yet remains an active and skillful participant in their processes.

Such playful remarks as those in which the narrative voice accepts the "credit of a wild imagination" (xxx, 243), hastens her characters "to perfect felicity" (xxx, 250), and questions "whether the tendency of this work be altogether to recommend parental tyranny, or reward filial disobedience" (xxxi, 252), expose the author as a participant in the same symbolic processes by which Catherine's mind is formed in the course of the work. Just as the heroine molds the raw data of experience according to the forms provided in her culture, so the novelist forms the raw data of a fictional donnée by manipulating the conventions and expectations of the literary tradition in which she functions. If the latter are shown to be merely arbitrary, we can relish them the more as a special case of the complex cultural forms displayed in the action. We accept the necessity of, and the enrichment offered by, systems of cultural symbols; by the same token, we are invited to appreciate the artfulness of this most fictional of nineteenth-century fictions.

3. *Wuthering Heights*: The Love of a Sylph and a Gnome

"Wuthering Heights" was hewn in a wild workshop, with simple tools, out of homely materials. The statuary found a granite block on a solitary moor: gazing thereon, he saw how from the crag might be elicited a head, savage, swart, sinister; a form moulded with at least one element of grandeur—power. . . . With time and labour, the crag took human shape; and there it stands colossal, dark, and frowning, half statue, half rock. . . .
—CURRER BELL, preface to the "new" (second) edition

THE premise stated in the title of this essay will require provisional justification, although its credibility can only gradually be gained. On its face, the premise is grotesque, and to defend it on the grounds that *Wuthering Heights* is a prime instance of the grotesque would merely engage the fallacy of imitative form in criticism—where grotesquerie has no defense. Although the novel has been exposed to as wide a range of interpretive strategies as exist in modern criticism, there have been, to my knowledge, no esoteric keys to open its mysteries. While it is often said that Emily Brontë was in some sense a mystic, it is tacitly agreed that her cultural resources did not extend much beyond Byron and the Bible.[1] For these reasons, a view of her novel which places it in an intellectual tradition of (even now) shady standing, and which associates it with religious texts of questionable orthodoxy, will run against the rational prejudices of even her less complacent readers.

What can we learn of her sources? Even if the titles of religious commentaries in her father's library were to be examined, no evidence of Emily Brontë's learning in such tomes could be inferred. There are, however, a number of indications in the language of the Brontë milieu of a shared strain of esoteric lore. "I am the Chief Genius Branii. With me there are three others. She, Wellesley, who protects you, is named Tallii; she who protects Parry is named Emmii; she who protects Ross is called Annii. Those lesser ones whom ye saw are Genii and Fairies, our slaves and minions."[2] So speaks a monstrous voice in one of the earliest writings of the Brontë children, "The History of the Young Men," a fantasy largely inspired by Branwell's tastes for the military and the demonic. A number of details of its setting suggest, however, imaginative resources that stand out from its schoolboy associations. Fannie Ratchford, the editor of the juvenilia, summarizes its themes: "The Parsonage, to the tiny mortals in the monster's hand, was a palace of diamonds, the pillars of which were ruby and emerald illuminated with lamps too bright to look upon; and the girls' bedroom, a hall of sapphire with thrones of gold, on which sat the Princes of the Genii [i.e., the children themselves]. The choosing of favorite soldiers [e.g., Wellesley, Parry, Ross] became the Genii's promise of protection and future glory: 'I tell you all that ye shall one day be kings.'" If this be less than true prophecy, it is more than juvenile playacting. Similar decor and terminology are used intermittently in Emily's and Anne's Gondal saga, and the precious stones and metals are brought together in Emily's most difficult poem, "The Philosopher."

A more imposing testimony to Emily Brontë's dealing with esoteric tradition lies in her nonfictional writings. In the remarkable series of French exercises written at the Pension Héger in Brussels, she takes the opportunity of formal composition to set forth what amounts to a Gnostic theology. The essays have often been cited as vigorous expressions of the dark side of orthodox Christian principles; I believe they tend toward heresy of the most estimable sort. In the first, "The Cat," she begins coyly with a moralized character of the animal: "We cannot stand up under comparison with the dog, he is infinitely too good; but the cat, although he differs in some physical traits, is extremely like us in disposition. In truth, there may be people who would say that the resemblance is close only to the meanest human beings, that it is limited to their excessive hypocrisy, cruelty, and ingratitude. . . . I answer, that if hypocrisy, cruelty, and ingratitude are the characteristics exclusively of mean people, this class includes everyone. . . ."[3] How has such a radical corruption of both races, feline and human, taken place? The Fall here is pictured in sweeping terms, suggesting a human debasement of all creation: cats "owe all their wretchedness and bad qualities to the great ancestor of the human race, for surely cats in Paradise were not mean" (p. 10). Yet the dog stands removed from the general debacle, "infinitely too good" for comparison—a domesticated image of the conventional deity?

The present relations of God to his creatures—their radically fallen nature and the tyrannical character of his governance—are disturbingly presented in another essay, "Filial Love":

> "Honor thy father and thy mother—if thou wilt live." In such a commandment God reveals the baseness of man in His sight; for human beings to perform the tenderest and holiest of all duties, a threat is necessary. . . . "Honor thy parents or thou shalt die!" Now, this commandment is not given, this threat is not added for nothing: there may be people who are so contemptuous of their own welfare, their duty and their God, that the spark of heavenly fire within them dies and

leaves them a moral chaos without light and without order, a hideous degradation of the image in which they were created. (p. 13)

From an initial irritability with God for his low estimate of mankind—and a hint of reproach for a deity who rules by strict judgment and chastisement—the essayist repeats the commandment with grudging assent to its implication: there are some (later called monsters) who do merit a god of justice, so radical is their evil. Indeed, they seem to have no chance of redemption under this divine plan: "The time will come when conscience will awaken; then there will be a terrible retribution; what mediator will then defend the criminal whom God accuses? . . . This man has rejected happiness during his mortal life, and by the same deeds has ensured himself torment for eternity. Let men and angels weep over his fate—he was their brother" (p. 14). More startling than the absence of Christ as mediator in this scheme of things is the close connection of the damned not only with other mortals but with angels—they are involved in a common condition, irredeemable perhaps only to some but threatening all.

The most impressive of the essays, "The Butterfly," is well known as a sustained prose poem on that age-old symbol of the soul; it is also the most awesome account of "nature red in tooth and claw" in pre-Darwinian literature: "All creation is equally insane. . . . Nature is an inexplicable puzzle, life exists on a principle of destruction; every creature must be the relentless instrument of death to the others, or himself cease to live. Nevertheless, we celebrate the day of our birth, and we praise God that we entered such a world" (p. 17). The irony of the last sentence questions the praiseworthiness of a God whose creation reflects the mind of its creator—"insane." The essayist shows herself aware of incipient apostasy in invoking an evil god on the Gnostic model: "I threw the flower to the ground; at that moment the universe appeared to me a vast machine constructed only to bring forth evil: I almost doubted the goodness of God for not annihilating man on the day of his first sin" (p. 18). Her apparent shying away from an evil god is coy; God's mercy shows up as a failure to annihilate an evil mankind—as he should do if he were truly good.

This backhanded orthodoxy only generates further flirtations with heresy: "I was silent, but an inner voice said to me, 'Let not the creature judge his creator, here is a symbol of the world to come—just as the ugly caterpillar is the beginning of the splendid butterfly, this globe is the embryo of a new heaven and of a new earth whose meagerest beauty infinitely surpasses mortal imagination" (p. 18). The biologistic doctrine of redemption entailed here has often been rejected in Christian tradition; the chrysalis figure introduces the notion of an inevitable decay of the fallen world and its natural production of a renewed earth. This natural theology underscores the determined stages by which redemption takes place, without benefit of divine intervention or moral agency.

To take these speculations seriously, it is unnecessary to posit Brontë's direct acquaintance with specific religious texts or even a theologically consistent turn of mind. It is sufficient that she mixes a number of personal formulations into her orthodox language and that these deviations approximate a widely distributed fund of doctrine stemming from the Gnostic religion of the early Christian era. As a leading scholar in this field sums up its essential tenets (before tracing its myriad ramifications):

> The cardinal feature of gnostic thought is the radical dualism that governs the relation of God and world, and correspondingly that of man and world. The deity is absolutely transmundane, its nature alien to that of the universe, which it neither created nor governs and to which it is the complete antithesis: to the divine realm of light, self-contained and remote, the cosmos is opposed as the realm of darkness. . . . The universe, the domain of the Archons, is like a vast prison whose innermost dungeon is the earth, the scene of man's life. . . . Equipped with this *gnosis*, the soul after death travels upwards, leaving behind at each sphere the physical "vestment" contributed by it: thus the spirit stripped of all foreign accretions reaches the God beyond the world and becomes reunited with the divine substance. On the scale of the the total divine drama, this process is part of the restoration of the deity's own wholeness. . . .[4]

Emily Brontë supplies no such system of cosmic spheres, each with its psychical and material properties, comparable to those of the alchemical and astrological traditions; nor does she institute a plan of salvation involving traversal of these spheres and reunion with a divine substance so as to reconstitute a lost wholeness. She does adumbrate concepts allied to these, particularly in her sense of the radical alienation of the human soul, manifested in the imagery of imprisonment, and in her sketch of a reunion of the elements or souls themselves. Even more than its Platonic analogues, e.g., the myth of the cave, and going beyond its source in the Manicheans' periodic defeat of light by the realm of darkness, the Gnostic religion expresses a vision of the world as a prison and the human soul as a shackled alien, struggling to be free and whole. It is to this sect of advocates for the imprisoned soul of humanity—and with an intensity unparalleled in English literature, except for Blake and perhaps Lawrence—that Emily Brontë may be said to owe her first allegiance.

The largest category of her poems, according to the (not unchallengeable) arrangement by Fannie Ratchford, is the group called "poems of war, imprisonment, and exile."[5] Though the grouping of these subjects seems lax, it corresponds to the primary matter of the Gondal saga, in which most of the presumed actions, conspiracies, and betrayals are described and lamented by the loser from the standpoint of his prison cell. Titles like "Written in the Gaaldine Prison Caves. To A.G.A.," "From a Dungeon Wall in the

Southern College," and "The Prisoner: A Fragment" make the point in its overt form. Its implications show themselves when well-known poems like "Aye, there it is! . . ." are read with this context in mind:

> And thou art now a spirit pouring
> Thy presence into all—
> The essence of the Tempest's roaring
> And of the Tempest's fall—
>
> A universal influence
> From Thine own influence free;
> A principle of life, intense,
> Lost to mortality.
>
> Thus truly when that breast is cold
> Thy prisoned soul shall rise,
> The dungeon mingle with the mould—
> The captive with the skies. (no. 148)

The "spirit," "presence," "essence," "influence," "principle of life" are none other than the "prisoned soul" itself, the poem being an address by the prisoner to his own unquenchable spirit. Lest this assertion of independence be too easily equated with Stoic or existential ethics of a freedom which lies with the prisoner's will, the final lines demand a more metaphysical interpretation. Not only does the prisoned soul, presumably an aerial element, mingle with the skies but the implied contrast requires that the prisoned body which is left behind be cognate with the dungeon itself. These imprisoning containers, whether body or dungeon, are left behind with "the mould"—either of mortal decay or of earthly matter as such.

The self-liberating power of the free spirit is also identical to the "God within my breast" of "No coward soul is mine" (no. 191), a spirit which not only resembles the traditional deity in being "ever-present," infinite, and immortal but which effectively replaces that deity, as it "Changes, sustains, dissolves, creates and rears . . . Every existence." What is perhaps less clear is the identity of this life principle with Imagination, which acquires in Brontë something beyond the metaphysical attributes ascribed to it in earlier Romantic poetry. "To Imagination" (no. 174) contrasts the inner life with its dark surroundings as a juxtaposition of one world with another:

> So hopeless is the world without,
> The world within I doubly prize;
> Thy world where guile and hate and doubt
> And cold suspicion never rise;
> Where thou and I and Liberty
> Have undisputed sovereignty.

>What matters it that all around
>Danger and grief and darkness lie,
>
>.   .   .   .   .   .   .
>
>But thou art ever there to bring
>The hovering visions back and breathe
>New glories o'er the blighted spring
>And call a lovelier life from death,
>And whisper with a voice divine
>Of real worlds as bright as thine.

This subtly distinguishes the bright, unreal world of Imagination not only from the realm of nature, which is real and dark, but also from the possibility of other worlds, which are real and bright. The function of the inner light is to be a "benignant power" in leading the soul out of its natural prison and on to its true home.

A more complex but equally extreme statement of the soul's power is "The Philosopher" (no. 181; the author's apparent title was "The Philosopher's conclusion," according to the editor's note). The scene seems to involve a visit by a wise man to a prisoner; they compare notes on their vision (or lack of it) of a third being:

>"I saw a Spirit standing, Man,
>Where thou dost stand—an hour ago;
>And round his feet, three rivers ran
>Of equal depth and equal flow—
>
>"A Golden stream, and one like blood,
>And one like Sapphire, seemed to be,
>But where they joined their triple flood
>It tumbled in an inky sea.
>
>"The Spirit bent his dazzling gaze
>Down on that Ocean's gloomy night,
>Then—kindling all with sudden blaze,
>The glad deep sparkled wide and bright—
>White as the sun; far, far more fair
>Than the divided sources were!"
>
>—And even for that Spirit, Seer,
>I've watched and sought my lifetime long;
>Sought Him in Heaven, Hell, Earth and Air,
>An endless search—and always wrong!
>
>Had I but seen his glorious eye
>*Once* light the clouds that 'wilder me,

I ne'er had raised this coward cry
To cease to think and cease to be—

It is not enough to note, with the often illuminating Jacques Blondel, the echoes of "Kubla Khan" and other visionary poems from Blake to Claudel or to offer allegorical equations: "Dans le livre de la Genèse, le sang est identifié à l'âme; le fleuve d'or pourrait être ici l'imagination, et le saphir, la raison."[6] The elements of this vision are significant if taken piecemeal, but their elaboration leads us to open the possibility of Brontë's having imaginative dealings with the tradition of symbols, myths, and topoi for which Gnosticism and its branches provide the speculative underpinnings. For the master spirit stands amid elemental streams, which join where he stands in a general confusion of matter represented by the sea; he can mentally control the flux, associated with darkness, and by his gaze turn it into light—creating value greater than the initial ingredients, the "divided sources." It is not clear whether this "Spirit" or the "Seer" who reports him should be called the "Philosopher"; what seems required is that we see his gnosis as an activity exercised on the elements of nature, combining and transforming them from their dark, imprisoning state to one of light and beauty.

The most pronounced eruption of Gnostic religion into Western literature comes by way of the love feast of the Cathars. Denis de Rougemont has traced this influence from the literature of courtly love down through *Tristan und Isolde* and lists a fair number of nineteenth-century British and Continental novels among its train.[7] In his formulation, the collocation of love and death is based on Gnostic dualism: "Man is not free. He is determined by the Devil. But if he accepts his calamitous destiny *up to the death* which will free him from his body, he may attain to that fusion of two selves who will thereupon have ceased to *suffer* love and will enter upon Supreme Joy." From this pattern of *askesis*, de Rougemont draws the following implications: "the religious and heretical nostalgia for an escape out of this wicked world, the condemnation and simultaneous divinization of sensuality, the strivings of the soul to escape from the fundamental *inordinatio* of the period, and from the tragic contradiction between Good—which must be Love—and the Evil that is victorious over Good in the created world." These are the root ideas of *Wuthering Heights*, and the point has not been lost on critics of the novel: Derek Stanford cites Catharist sources, although without explanation, and the union of love and death informs the most searching readings, from Georges Bataille's seminal essay to J. Hillis Miller's comprehensive account.[8] What is at issue is less the specific source of Brontë's dualistic attitudes toward the world, the torments of love and the escape through death, than the marked presence in the novel of symbolic language and narrative assumptions derived from the wider Gnostic tradition, including its alchemical offshoots.

The most ample exposition of the nature of reality in *Wuthering Heights* is provided by the discourses of Catherine Earnshaw Linton. While she supplies the keys to the metaphysics and symbolism of the novel, she is not always a reliable expositor, being an adept who desires a condition she has not yet attained at the time of her death. The Catharist Cathy first sketches a psychology; in answer to Nelly Dean's question, "where is the obstacle" to her marrying Edgar Linton, "'*Here*! and *here*!' replied Catherine, striking one hand on her forehead, and the other on her breast. 'In whichever place the soul lives—in my soul, and in my heart, I'm convinced I'm wrong!'"[9] The physical correlations are perhaps deliberately vague, since the seat of the soul either in the bodily mind or the heart must be a temporary one, at best a matter of indifference, at worst imprisonment. A similar indeterminacy attaches to Cathy's account of the soul's origin and journey: "I was only going to say that heaven did not seem to be my home; and I broke my heart with weeping to come back to earth; and the angels were so angry that they flung me out, into the middle of the heath on the top of Wuthering Heights; where I woke sobbing for joy" (ix, 99–100). More striking than the vivid account of alienation from a heavenly realm is the attribution of demonic agency to "the angels." It is not necessary to identify these with the Archons who rule the orders of the fallen universe to see these angels as instruments of a hostile system at odds with the soul's desires. Yet, curiously, this alienation from heaven is a fortunate fall, for it brings Cathy to "the middle of the heath," where she cries for joy. What sort of heaven and earth can these be, to evoke such reversed feelings?

A hint of an answer is given in the concluding sentence of the same paragraph: "Whatever our souls are made of, [Heathcliff's] and mine are the same, and Linton's is as different as a moonbeam from lightning, or frost from fire" (100). The primary assumption of this proposition is that souls are made of substances akin to material elements. Cathy then goes on to claim that her soul and Heathcliff's are of the same substance—that she is originally of the *earth* and wants to "come back" to it. It is this claim which is shown to be mistaken in the event. The novel will dramatize the more accurate view that Cathy is a creature of *air* who is nevertheless (and inexplicably) not at home in heaven, which in this context means primarily the region of air. She falls (or is pushed) to earth—to the very "middle" of the heath, at the "top" of Wuthering Heights—where she finds herself suddenly happy. She there encounters the manifestation and foremost inhabitant of the earth, whose name derives from the heath itself; and so strong is her affinity that she claims identity with him. But they must each undergo an *askesis* in which their differing natures are transformed, so as to be miscible or permeable to each other.

That Cathy exhibits the well-known fallacy of leaping from similarities to equations is evident not only from the analogy of moonbeam and lightning, frost and fire, with which she discredits her relation to Edgar. She goes on, in the grand finale of her famous speech, to make this precise jump from metaphor to identity: ". . . my love for Heathcliff resembles the eternal rocks beneath—a source of little visible delight, but necessary. Nelly, I *am* Heathcliff . . ." (ix, 101–102). She is not, of course, but very much wants to be, and the remainder of the fiction is the narrative of Heathcliff's efforts to approximate himself to her, while she hovers in the air and earth about him, till their final union, in which they are distributed in "the soft wind breathing through the grass" as "sleepers in that quiet earth" (xxxiv, 414). From this point of view, the novel is metaphysical not only in its landscape—as set out in the definitive essay of Lord David Cecil—or only in its values, encouraging an embrace of death in order to transcend the lesser world of the Lintons, Thrushcross Grange, and ordinary human life. It is metaphysical in its dramatic action, which traces an alchemical transformation of the elements, a creature of earth and one of air transforming themselves so as to realize their union in a substantial medium—not simply by way of death or in some vague beyond-the-grave but in their physical/spiritual existence.

To describe this transformation, it is not necessary to correlate the characters with the *Book on Nymphs, Sylphs, Pygmies, and Salamanders, and on the Other Spirits* by Theophrastus von Hohenheim, called Paracelsus.[10] It is equally unnecessary to specify the chief characters' propensities by reference to the widely shared temperamental psychology of the humors, with their substantial and ethical correlatives: air with sanguine temper and the vices of "Lechery and perhaps Envy," earth with melancholy and avarice.[11] Instead, we may follow the development of character in this novel as we do in most others, by stages and in context, though with an awareness that the general concept of "character" here is less that of modern psychology than that of the humors tradition and its alchemical variants.

Such thinking underwrites the imagery of earth that is consistently used for the hero's characterization; Cathy tells us that "Heathcliff is—an unreclaimed creature, without refinement—without cultivation; an arid wilderness of furze and whinstone" (x, 126). Later, on her deathbed, Cathy goes through a number of dream images which have teased commentators out of thought—the alien, unreturned lapwing, the fairy cave under Penistone Crags, and the black clothespress with its mirror. More decisively, however, it is at this juncture that Cathy enacts her fundamental impulse toward air; before throwing the window open to contract her death, or breath of life, she says: "Oh, if I were but in my own bed in the old house! . . . And that wind sounding in the firs by the lattice. Do let me feel it—it comes straight down the moor—do let me have one breath!" (xii, 151–152). She then expounds the subsequent events of the plot in what seems like delirium: "It's a rough journey, and a sad heart to travel it; and we must pass by Gimmerton Kirk, to go that journey! . . . I'll not lie there by myself; they may bury me twelve feet deep, and throw the church down over me, but I won't rest till you are with me . . . I never will! . . . He's considering . . . he'd rather I'd come to him! Find a way, then! not through that Kirkyard . . . You are slow! Be content, you always followed me!" (xii, 154). It is not enough, then, that she go into the earth, or even—as we will learn—that he lie next to her there. The "way" is a transformation, and a technique must be found to make it.

Heathcliff's journey, then, is mapped out for him in material terms, though not in precise operations. It remains for Cathy to prepare his *askesis* with an appropriate doctrine, that of the fallen world and the "other" world: ". . . the thing that irks me most is this shattered prison, after all. I'm tired, tired of being enclosed here. I'm wearying to escape into that glorious world, and to be always there; not seeing it dimly through tears, and yearning for it through the walls of an aching heart; but really with it, and in it" (xv, 197). Cathy's spatial designations are crucial; she wants not merely escape from the prison of the world but a relation to the other realm without mediation—neither through the water of tears nor through the bodily forms of the heart. She wants to be *with* it and *in* it, suggesting a compound substance, earth/air. But she also acknowledges that she cannot exist in the other world without uniting first with her lover: "I shall not be at peace" without him, she has just said. The Cathy that Lockwood encounters when he sleeps in her room at Wuthering Heights, at the novel's spectacular opening, is not just a homeless spirit seeking to be "let in" but a creature of air bereft not only of a residing place but of a stable substance.

Heathcliff's task is thus not simply to die but to prepare himself for proper fusion with the lingering departed. First he must locate her; while it is a matter of indifference or confusion to Christians like Nelly Dean whether she is "still on earth or now in Heaven" (xvi, 202), he must be more precise: "Where is she? Not *there* [indicating the grave]—not in heaven—not perished—where? . . . Be with me always—take any form—drive me mad! only *do* not leave me in this abyss, where I cannot find you!" (xvi, 204). The abyss is abstractly defined as the place where he cannot find her, not as earth itself. It is through a recognition that his first investigation was too sweepingly negative that Heathcliff will eventually find Cathy—for she is *"there"* in the earth, and in heaven, considered as air, as well.

The major step in Heathcliff's recovery of Cathy is his discovery of the virtues of his own nature, earth. Throughout the novel, the heights above Wuthering Heights—called with a fine orthography not Penniston but "Penistone Craggs"—resonate with a more powerful mana than that of the heath itself. It is the place of Nelly's legendary fairy cave, it is the goal of the second Cathy's pubescent strivings ("Now, am I old enough to go to Penistone Craggs?" [xviii, 234]), and it is the spot for her meeting with Hareton, foreseeing the eventual rapprochement of the two families and the two houses. The name and its cognates also infiltrate the symbolic diction, as when Cathy declares that her "love for Heathcliff resembles the eternal rocks beneath" (ix, 101). And the pictured landscape, in the conversation of Cathy II and Nelly, generates the sense of awe that attaches not merely to mountains but to high and sacred places:

> The abrupt descent of Penistone Craggs particularly attracted her notice, especially when the setting sun shone on it and the topmost Heights, and the whole extent of landscape besides lay in shadow.
>
> I explained that they were bare masses of stone, with hardly enough earth in their clefts to nourish a stunted tree.
>
> "And why are they bright so long after it is evening here?" she pursued.
>
> "Because they are a great deal higher up than we are," replied I; "you could not climb them, they are too high and steep. . . ."
>
> "Oh, you have been on them!" she cried, gleefully. "Then I can go, too, when I am a woman." (xviii, 233)

The sexual power of this place seems inescapable, yet it would be naïve to limit its import to that. It holds the light (and presumably the heat) of the sun longer than other places on earth and, though there is little earth on it, it may be thought of as earth in a particularly pure state. It is these virtues of earth, and his own identity with it, that Heathcliff discovers in his quest.

Only a growth in self-consciousness can account for his learning the limitations of his grotesque technique of material union—removing a slat of Cathy's coffin in order to mingle his body with hers. In contemplation of being buried next to her, he imagines merely corporeal contiguity: "I dreamt I was sleeping the last sleep, by that sleeper, with my heart stopped, and my cheek frozen against hers" (xxix, 349). But a clue to the actual form of their union comes in the sexton's warning that opening the coffin will change Cathy's composition: ". . . he said it would change, if the air blew on it, and so I struck one side of the coffin loose—and covered it up . . ." (xxix, 349). The more sophisticated project of "dissolving with her, and being more happy still"—called here "transformation"—requires that both natures change to become a new and conjoint substance. Heathcliff gains an inkling of this chemistry in a subsequent reminiscence of his initial leap at direct contact:

> . . . I was on the point of attaining my object [of uncovering the body], when it seemed that I heard a sigh from some one above, close at the edge of the grave, and bending down.—"If I can only get this off," I muttered, "I wish they may shovel in the earth over us both!" and I wrenched at it more desperately still. There was another sigh, close at my ear. I appeared to feel the warm breath of it displacing the sleet-laden wind. I knew no living thing in flesh and blood was by—but as certainly as you perceive the approach to some substantial body in the

dark, though it cannot be discerned, so certainly I felt that Cathy was there, not under me, but on the earth. (xxix, 350)

His awareness of her presence as of a "substantial body" is compounded with a recognition that she cannot be seen; she is of air, a breath "displacing the sleet-laden wind," yet on the earth. This distribution of the elements may be appropriate for the desired union.

Heathcliff's highest gnosis is of the symbolic dimension of these physical embodiments. In his final declaration, he proposes a symbolic view of the universe as a set of physical vehicles, the signs of Cathy's presence: ". . . what is not connected with her to me? and what does not recall her? I cannot look down to this floor, but her features are shaped on the flags! In every cloud, in every tree—filling the air at night, and caught by glimpses in every object by day, I am surrounded with her image! . . . The entire world is a dreadful collection of memoranda that she did exist, and that I have lost her!" (xxxiii, 394). Although pained at perceiving the difference between symbol and reality, Heathcliff is capable of finding the tokens of the soul both in cloud and tree, air and the "objects" of earth. By this awareness of the symbolic properties of his own nature and of Cathy's, he is prepared to merge with her in death—which he readily wills. That this death entails a transformation into a new, fused substance is suggested by their continued presence on and in the heath, as witnessed by "a little boy with a sheep and two lambs," who reports, "They's Heathcliff and a woman, yonder, under t' Nab" (xxxiv, 412)—i.e., below the crest of the hill and/or within it.

There is a sense in which this text may be said to speak for itself. The fact that innumerable critics have written—and written well—on its interpretation belies neither its self-expressive power nor its ultimate uninterpretability. Like most fictions and poems of transcendent worth, *Wuthering Heights* has many meanings, most of them compatible, some of them more urgent than others, the sum of them more persuasive then any one, none of them right when taken by itself. It would be an abandonment of these principles of interpretation to insist on an esoteric reading of the novel that tells a reserved meaning in preference to a public one. Yet, amid all the commentary on this near-sacred text, there should be room for a statement of the alchemical processes engaged in the dramatic action. I submit a selection of topics from a popular but authoritative guide to the subject, by a believer but not a fanatic:

> The essence and aim of mysticism is union with God. Alchemy does not speak of this. What is related to the mystical way, however, is the alchemical aim to regain the original "nobility" of human nature . . .
> The purity of the symbol man must be regained, before the human form can be reassumed into its infinite and divine Archetype. Spiritual-

ly understood, the transmutation of lead into gold is nothing other than the regaining of the original nobility of human nature.

If the elements are listed in the order of their material "fineness" or "subtlety," earth comes lowest, and air highest. . . . Earth is characterized by heaviness: it possesses a downward tendency. . . . Air both rises and extends, whereas fire rises exclusively.

Just like the corporeal *materia*, which manifests itself most readily in the four elements, so the *materia* of the soul, in its deployment, has several mutually opposing tendencies. . . . As applied to the soul, "earth" is that aspect or tendency which causes it to sink into the body and which attaches it to the latter. . . . For the soul, "air," free and mobile, envelops all forms of consciousness.

Alchemically speaking, the hub of the [cosmic] wheel is the *quinta essentia*. By this is meant either the spiritual pole of all four elements or their common substantial ground, ether, in which they are all indivisibly contained. In order once again to attain to this centre, the disequilibrium of the differentiated elements must be repaired, water must become fiery, fire liquid, earth weightless, and air solid. Here, however, one leaves the plane of physical appearances and enters the realm of spiritual alchemy. . . . "This is what is meant by the re-transformation of the elements."

In order to demonstrate that *materia prima* [another name for *quinta essentia*] contains in potency all forms of consciousness and thus all forms of the ephemeral world, the ninth-century Arab alchemist Abu'l-Qâsim al-Irâqï writes: ". . . *materia prima* is to be found in a mountain, which contains a measureless quantity of uncreated things. . . ." The mountain in which *materia prima* is to be found is the human body. . . . The interior of the earth is also the interior of the body, that is, the inward, undifferentiated centre of consciousness. The hidden stone is here none other than *materia prima*.

The marriage of Sulphur and Quicksilver, Sun and Moon, King and Queen, is the central symbol of alchemy. . . . According to some representations of the "chemical marriage" the king and queen, on marriage, are killed and buried together, only to rise again rejuvenated. That this connection between marriage and death is in the nature of things, is indicated by the fact that, according to ancient experience, a marriage in a dream means a death, and a death in a dream means a marriage. . . . On "chemical marriage," Quicksilver take unto itself Sulphur, and Sulphur, Quicksilver. Both forces "die," as foes and lovers. Then the changing and reflective moon of the soul unites with the immutable sun of the spirit so that it is extinguished, and yet illumined, at one and the same time.[12]

These doctrines may be related to *Wuthering Heights* in a sequence of declining specificity. If mysticism aims at union with God, Emily Brontë's work exhibits no mysticism, for there is no God in it apart from the "God within my breast." Indeed, the strong anti-Christian portrayals of the novel (Joseph and, to a lesser degree, Nelly) suggest a concentrated effort to distinguish a religion free not only of moral cant but of a hierarchical deity. If, on the other hand, the doctrine of gnosis and its alchemical enactments aims at purification, retransformation, and recovery of the soul's lost wholeness—and of the ideal of human nature—this tradition seems an appropriate one in which to interpret so heterodox a work. The presence of a consistent imagery associating Heathcliff with earth, the heath and its rocky substructure, and associating Cathy with air, breath and wind, invites us to find the fictional manifestations of these elements freighted with something of their traditional implications. At the least, their opposition in "fineness" or "subtlety" and their divergent directions—contractive/downward and expansive/upward—connote significant character movements. The identification of earth with body and of air with soul will, of course, demand a greater leap of faith, not least because the alchemical theory itself seems to shift its grounds at this point, from seeing the four material elements as having a variety of spiritual burdens to differentiating among those elements their degrees of spiritual intensity—some being more, some less refined. Yet the qualitative connections of air with freedom, mobility, and consciousness (with the breath of life itself, in biblical parlance), and those of earth with attachment to the body, are so widespread as to broadly support a more specific alchemical designation.

At this point, the theories of the alchemists begin to distinguish themselves sharply from the wider Gnostic tradition, and by the same token their application to the novel becomes increasingly problematic. There is nothing in the text to correspond with *quinta essentia* or ether, no scheme for the pairing and rotation of the elements by their opposites, no alchemical wheel, Solomonic seal, or planetary spheres. But there is "spiritual alchemy" or "retransformation" in the fairly explicit intentions and actions of the protagonists, who change their element and fuse with their opposites—earth becomes weightless and air solid, ending the disequilibrium of their differentiation. There is, indeed, a mountain (or crag) that represents vital potency in the imagination of the characters; and the "hidden stone," which is vulgarized as the philosopher's stone in popular legend, appears here in the language of heights, cliffs, eternal rocks, and penis stone—interpretable as the human body manifest, incomplete without the infusion of a finer substance.

Having doubtless lost some of my readers with these assertions, I conclude by acknowledging that the mystic marriage enacted in *Wuthering Heights* involves neither quicksilver nor sulphur, that the imagery of sun and moon is present in the text but not decisive, and that the protagonists' universality as erotic-spiritual king and queen may be suggested but is not imposed. It is enough that their reunion carry with it suggestions of death and renewal, reunion by fusion, love-death and joyous awakening, a restoration of peace after discord and bondage, an extinction of individuality and a recovery of harmony—both within the soul and with the circumambient elements.

4. A Napoleon of Heroines:
Historical Myth in *Vanity Fair*

"That is he," said the black man: "that is Bonaparte! He eats three
sheep every day, and all the little children he can lay hands on!"
—A SERVANT TO THACKERAY, at St. Helena

IVE la France! Vive l'Empereur! Vive Bonaparte!"[1] With
these memorable words, Becky Sharp makes her declaration
of independence from Miss Pinkerton's establishment for the
education of young ladies and from the Establishment at large.
She has already expressed her rejection of the values and authorities of that
institution by throwing back its parting gift, a copy of Dr. Johnson's *Dictionary*—loading that act with a force of symbolic negation equal to the
symbolic virtue with which the book is endowed by Miss Pinkerton. Becky's opposite number in the narrative structure of *Vanity Fair*, the good
bourgeoise Amelia Sedley, reacts to her declaration with appropriate horror,
couched in terms of religious awe: "'O Rebecca, Rebecca, for shame!' cried
Miss Sedley; for this was the greatest blasphemy Rebecca had as yet uttered;
and in those days, in England, to say 'Long live Bonaparte!' was as much
as to say 'Long live Lucifer!' 'How can you—how dare you have such wicked,
revengeful thoughts?'" (ii, 19). The narrator is quick to make a specific
designation of time and place for the interpretation of value-laden language,
as if to suggest that Napoleon was not in fact Lucifer, that we hail and
anathematize historical figures not for what they are but for the effects such
slogans generate, and that others react to these slogans not simply as decla-
rations of political preference but as evocations of the gods—beneficent
or dark, as the case may be. This is to say—as Thackeray himself could
not have said but as he shows himself fully aware—that human behavior,
even on the level of reacting to the loss of a job (as Becky is doing), is historically specific in its choice of archetypal symbols. Becky shows a fine
ear for the language that will at that precise time and place most pointedly
convey her revolt, and the schoolmistresses and schoolgirls confirm her
rhetorical power by their religious horror of her mere words.

The novel in which this symbolic behavior occurs has been widely recognized as having something to do with history, although few would call it
a historical novel.[2] The detailed integument of manners, customs, gossip,
and all the Regency bric-a-brac which the Tillotsons' edition lovingly as-

sembles around the text—all this is an undoubted element of the historicity of *Vanity Fair*, as it is of other great novels-of-history like *Middlemarch* and *Nostromo*. What makes these works fall outside the canons of historical fiction itself is their lack of a point of dramatic intersection of the fictional and the actual, best created when a fictitious and a historical personage are represented in the same scene. The mere report of historical events in which fictional characters participate (as is the case in the reported buildup to the first reform bill in *Middlemarch*) will not quite create the mixture of the real and the imaginary on the same plane of representation. A possible evasion of this difficulty occurs when historical actions are symbolically represented, as in the disguised version of the Panamanian separation from Colombia in *Nostromo*.

There are historical scenes in *Vanity Fair*, of course, and even the non-speaking presence of real personages, as in the presentation of Becky at the court of George IV; but the novel can be considered historical only in a special—though perhaps more profound—sense. It is not the realistic portrayal of early nineteenth-century English society or the eruption of the battle of Waterloo into the ordinary lives of typical characters which makes *Vanity Fair* a great novel-of-history but, rather, its enactment of the processes by which historical events are assimilated into consciousness and behavior. These processes are largely conducted in the forms of language and myth, and the primary mythic presence which orders linguistic responses throughout the novel is the figure of Napoleon.

It has been observed that the structure of the novel, based on intersections and divergences in the careers of two female protagonists (neither of whom is a heroine), is informed by the metaphor of the campaign. As the contents page has it: ". . . Miss Sharp and Miss Sedley prepare to open the Campaign," "Rebecca is in presence of the enemy," ". . . Amelia joins her regiment [and] invades the Low Countries." Less apparent is the close modeling of Becky's campaign on that of Napoleon,[3] with the corresponding invasion of the Low Countries by Amelia a counteraction equivalent to the defensive maneuvers of the monarchical powers. In Amelia's case, the metaphor lends mock-heroic piquancy to her determined efforts to follow and keep her errant husband. In Becky's case, however, the metaphor is based on a wider range of personal and ideological affinities between tenor and vehicle, which modulates its satiric overtones and transforms metaphor into myth.

Like Napoleon, Becky is an outsider in the dominant society—if not Corsican at least Bohemian, in a sense which Thackeray was among the first to introduce into English parlance.[4] Daughter of a dipsomaniac artist and a "young woman of the French nation, who was by profession an opera-girl" (ii, 20)—a code for a semiprofessional prostitute—Becky begins in Soho and occasionally reverts to the demimonde: "She became a perfect Bohemian ere long, herding with people whom it would make your hair stand on end to meet. . . . She went about from town to town among these Bo-hemians" (lxiv, 625). Although of an alien breed, like the Corsican upstart Becky identifies herself with the dominant culture in order to make her conquest. In Napoleon's case, this involved transforming himself and his family into the royal lineage which the revolution has deposed. In Becky's case, assimilation into the dominant culture is a never-ending process (she is last seen as an Evangelical, forsooth), but it begins with her manipulation of a cultural tool, language. Her mastery of French is a curiously ambiguous property, and her handling of it shows up the ambiguity of all historical artifacts. It is an asset in the dominant culture of England, and her position at Miss Pinkerton's academy is owing to her skill in teaching this refine-ment; but French has also about it something suspect, especially in the period following the revolution. Becky is quick to seize upon it as a weapon. When Miss Pinkerton tries to overawe her, Becky hits on the plan of speak-ing to her only in French, "which quite routed the old woman. In order to maintain authority in her school, it became necessary to remove this rebel, this monster, this serpent, this fire-brand . . ." (ii, 23).

Beyond these traits of cultural assimilation and cultural warfare, Becky resembles Napoleon preeminently in her rebellion against the class struc-ture of aristocratic (and also nouveau riche) society. "'What airs that girl gives herself, because she is an Earl's grand-daughter,' she said of one [pu-pil]. 'How they cringe and bow to that Creole, because of her hundred thou-sand pounds! I am a thousand times cleverer and more charming than that creature, for all her wealth. I am as well-bred as the Earl's grand-daughter, for all her fine pedigree; and yet every one passes me by here. . . .' She de-termined at any rate to get free from the prison in which she found herself, and now began to act for herself, and for the first time to make connected plans for the future" (ii, 22). *La carrière ouverte aux talents!* This was the cry which enlisted so many of Napoleon's most vigorous and most compe-tent supporters—the men of ability who had no chance in a class-bound and stagnant society. Like the chief adventurer himself, Becky speaks for all those of intelligence, symbolic skill, theatrical manipulativeness, and the other arts by which rising men and women make their fortunes—if not by overthrowing the dominant classes, then by infiltrating and conquering them.

Becky is quite articulate about her plans, being highly conscious of the class discrimination she faces and the powers she commands: "I am alone in the world. . . . I have nothing to look for but what my own labour can bring me; and while that little pink-faced chit Amelia, with not half my sense, has ten thousand pounds and an establishment secure, poor Rebecca (and my figure is far better than hers) has only herself and her own wits to trust to. Well, let us see if my wits cannot provide me with an honourable maintenance, and if some day or the other I cannot show Miss Amelia my real superiority over her" (x, 88). It is obviously not only her wits but her body that Becky has at her command, and with her realistic sense of these "real" qualities–commodities, tools, weapons, as they variously appear– she is empowered to lay down her challenge to English society, as Napo- leon laid his down before Europe. And so Becky makes her campaign through the class structure, moving upward from the nabobs (Jos) through the gentry (Rawdon) and the aristocracy (Steyne) until presented at court –when follows her Napoleon-like fall.

No one would claim that *Vanity Fair* is an extended allegory of recent European history or that Becky Sharp is either literally or symbolically Napoleon. But the novel acts in a number of other ways to explore social behavior under the impact of symbolic structures we may call mythic. The most readily recognized is the proliferation of forms in which Napoleon appears in the English consciousness, carrying superhuman or more-than- rational force. For the ruined merchant, Amelia's father, Napoleon is not merely an archfiend but the center of a vast conspiracy by the powers-that- be: "And I say that the escape of Boney from Elba was a damned imposition and plot, sir, in which half the powers of Europe were concerned, to bring the funds down, and to ruin this country" (xx, 191–192). For the bluestock- ing Francophile, Miss Crawley, on the other hand, Napoleon is the object of what we know today as radical chic: "She was a *bel esprit*, and a dreadful Radical for those days. She had been in France (where St. Just, they say, inspired her with an unfortunate passion), and loved, ever after, French novels, French cookery, and French wines. She read Voltaire, and had Rous- seau by heart; talked very lightly about divorce, and most energetically of the rights of women" (x, 93).[5] Napoleon's image suffers some diminution with Miss Crawley when the Hundred Days throws a scare into *rentiers* like herself, but her sentiments are renewed after the threat of change has passed.

Her nephew exploits this mystique for his own ends: "When the Coun- tess Dowager of Southdown fell foul of the Corsican upstart, as the fashion was in those days, and showed that he was a monster stained with every conceivable crime, a coward and a tyrant not fit to live, one whose fall was predicted, &c., Pitt Crawley suddenly took up the cudgels in favour of the man of Destiny. . . . And he spoke in terms of the strongest indignation of the faithless conduct of the allies towards this dethroned monarch, who, after giving himself generously up to their mercy, was consigned to an ignoble and cruel banishment, while a bigotted Popish rabble was tyrannis- ing over France in his stead" (xxxiv, 325–326). Pitt is, of course, mouthing the self-generated myths of the *Mémorial de Sainte-Hélène* in an effort to ingratiate himself with his aunt and win her fortune and, though the ef- ficacy of the myth is somewhat diminished, its power over Miss Crawley's mind remains strong: ". . . though, to be sure, the downfall of the Emperor did not very much agitate the old lady, or his ill-treatment tend to shorten her life or natural rest, yet Pitt spoke to her heart when he lauded . . . her idols; and by that single speech made immense progress in her favour."

The final version of Napoleon is his ultimate reduction not simply to a political symbol but to a mythological abstraction, put to the service of religion and education for the moral formation of the young. For Amelia's son, Georgy, Napoleon is made the type of Selfishness (an abstract vice somewhat different from his association with Titanic egoism among the Romantic poets). Georgy's school composition places him together with Achilles among its archetypes: "The selfishness of the late Napoleon Bonaparte occasioned innumerable wars in Europe, and caused him to perish, himself, in a miserable island—that of Saint Helena in the Atlantic Ocean. We see by these examples that we are not to consult our own interest and ambition, but that we are to consider the interests of others as well as our own" (lviii, 567). Thus Napoleon is taken out of history altogether and given a place in a school handbook of mythology and morality.

Although neither so widespread nor so potent, Becky Sharp's mythic aura functions similarly in her society, and in showing how we make myths even out of people we know—just as we do with historical figures—Thackeray undertakes another mode of social-symbolic analysis. The first encouragement Becky gets is under the aegis of the *carrière-ouverte-aux-talents* formula. Miss Crawley tells her: "What is birth, my dear? . . . Look at my brother Pitt; look at the Huddlestons, who have been here since Henry II., look at poor Bute at the parsonage;—are any one of them equal to you in intelligence or breeding? . . . if merit had its reward, you ought to be a Duchess—no, there ought to be no duchesses at all . . ." (xi, 105). It is then that Miss Crawley unconsciously encourages Becky to capture and elope with Rawdon: "I adore all imprudent matches.—What I like best, is for a nobleman to marry a miller's daughter as Lord Flowerdale did—it makes all the women so angry—I wish some great man would run away with *you*, my dear; I'm sure you're pretty enough." Miss Crawley's silliness is laden with social symbols of great efficacy; though she confuses Becky with the *schöne Müllerin* of ballads, she recognizes her as a competent adventuress and effectively points her in the direction of the vulnerable Rawdon (although later horrified by the results).

For her antagonists, on the other hand, Becky achieves something of the negative mana of myths. At the peak of her success, she acquires—largely through her own manipulation of classical images—the aspect of the *femme fatale*. The high point of her self-projection is her performance in the charades at Lord Steyne's: "A tremor ran through the room. 'Good God!' somebody said, 'it's Mrs. Rawdon Crawley.' Scornfully she snatches the dagger out of Ægisthus's hand, and advances to the bed. You see it shining over her head in the glimmer of the lamp, and—and the lamp goes out, with a groan, and all is dark" (li, 494). Little wonder, then, that "a great personage insisted upon being presented to the charming Clytemnestra" or that good people like Lady Jane and Major Dobbin shy away from her very touch. More remarkable still is the invasion of this mana into the space beyond the text itself; although no mention is made of the Clytemnestra image during the denouement, Thackeray's illustration of Jos Sedley's last stages of decline shows Becky as a hag lurking in the shadows and is captioned "Becky's second appearance in the character of Clytemnestra" (lxvii, 663).

It is by means of similar images that Becky projects her final role: "She has her enemies. Who has not? Her life is her answer to them. She busies herself in works of piety. She goes to church, and never without a footman. Her name is in all the Charity Lists. The Destitute Orange-girl, the Neglected Washerwoman, the Distressed Muffin-man, find in her a fast and generous friend. She is always having stalls at Fancy Fairs for the benefit of these hapless beings" (lxvii, 666). And so Becky creates her final self-myth, carefully placing it among the symbols generated by Evangelical and literary image makers like Hannah More and Wordsworth.

Thackeray shows himself in *Vanity Fair*, then, a master of the arts of myth making, of the social uses of self-imaging, which reach at times the status of collective illusions of the order of Napoleon. The novelist's ironic taste for snobs, poseurs, and fashionable stances of all kinds extended to the transmogrifications of Napoleon that filled his own Paris years—he would have relished the satirical thesis of Jean-Baptiste Pérès that the gross facts of Napoleon's career yield the conclusion that he was a solar deity and not a historical person at all.[6] Thackeray reacted in satires of his own to the successive stages of the Napoleonic myth, and three of his occasional pieces reveal his keen perception of the myth-making faculty at work in France generally and in the politics of Louis Napoleon in particular.

In *The Paris Sketch Book* of 1840, Thackeray's reflections on Louis Napoleon's recent attempted coup name the rhetoric of Napoleon's nephew simply claptrap and quackery: "If, in a country where so many quacks have had their day, Prince Louis Napoleon thought he might renew the Imperial quackery, why should he not? It has recollections with it that must always be dear to a gallant nation; it has certain claptraps in its vocabulary that can never fail to inflame a vain, restless, grasping, disappointed one."[7] But his perception goes beyond John Bull's easy explanation of French militarism and revanchism—"they hate us"—and takes in the susceptibilities of the English mind to the Napoleonic mystique:

> It is curious to think of the former difference of opinion concerning Napoleon; and in reading his nephew's rapturous encomiums of him one goes back to the days when we ourselves were as loud and mad in his dispraise. Who does not remember his own personal hatred and horror, twenty-five years ago, for the man whom we used to call the "bloody Corsican upstart and assassin?" What stories did we not be-

lieve of him?—what murders, rapes, robberies, not lay to his charge?
—we who were living within a few miles of his territory, and might,
by books and newspapers, be made as well acquainted with his merits
or demerits as any of his own countrymen. (V, 109–110)

Whatever the shortcomings of English insularity, it is presently the French
who show lack of imagination in their myths—the English image of Napoleon has changed but the French persist in theirs, based on their hatred of
perfide Albion and their hunger for glory.

Thackeray then submits Louis Napoleon's declaration to detailed semantic scrutiny and reduces it to its propositional core: "To keep the Republic
within bounds, a despotism is necessary; to rally round the despotism, an
aristocracy must be created; and for what have we been labouring all this
while? . . . O lame conclusion! Is the blessed Revolution which is prophe-
sied for us in England only to end in establishing a Price Fergus O'Con-
nor, or a Cardinal Wade, or a Duke Daniel Whittle Harvey? Great as those
patriots are, we love them better under their simple family names, and
scorn title and coronets" (V, 116). The sarcasm of the final sentences is
complicated by Thackeray's own ambivalent attitude toward social unrest
in England, his fear of violence, and his skepticism of radical leaders; but
this does not limit his indignation that the principle of revolutionary libertarianism has been desecrated by the imperial and aristocratic myths of its
inheritors. Thackeray shows himself at once touched by the myths of revolution, scornful of its manipulators and perverters, and aware of its power
to emerge in his own country, in local—and probably ludicrous—English
forms.

Thackeray's response to the new Napoleon is, then, as aware as Marx's
that history may indeed repeat itself, "the first time as tragedy, the second
as farce"; but it is only in his account of the re-interment of Napoleon's
remains at the Invalides that his taste for farce is allowed full scope. "The
Second Funeral of Napoleon" (1841) is a reportorial piece designed to please
(and twit) the English taste for French displays of panoply and, by reporting
through the persona of the tourist-artist Michael Angelo Titmarsh, Thackeray can indulge both his journalistic and his satirical commissions. After
a prologue on the unreliability of all historiography, he launches into a just-
so story on the origins of history writing in the fig leaves of our first ancestors:

> And such—(excuse my sermonising)—such is the constitution of
> mankind, that men have, as it were, entered into a compact among
> themselves to pursue the fig-leaf system *à outrance*, and to cry down
> all who oppose it. Humbug they will have. Humbugs themselves, they
> will respect humbugs. Their daily victuals of life must be seasoned
> with humbug. Certain things are there in the world that they will not

allow to be called by their right names, and will insist upon our admiring, whether we will or no. (IV, 675)

There follows a detailed description of the disinterment at St. Helena, the voyage to Paris, and the preparations for the funeral. The procession is then listed, in the manner of Eliot's "Coriolan":

Next comes—
His Royal Highness the Prince de Joinville.
The 500 sailors of the *Belle Poule* [which brought the body]
    marching in double file on each side of
                THE CAR.
Hush! the enormous crowd thrills as it passes, and only some
  few voices cry *Vive l'Empereur!* Shining golden in the frosty sun
—with hundreds of thousands of eyes upon it, . . . pushing, struggling,
heaving, panting, eager, the heads of an enormous multitude stretching
out to meet and follow it, amidst long avenues of columns and statues gleaming white, of standards rainbow-coloured, of golden
eagles, of pale funereal urns, of discharging odours amidst
      huge volumes of pitch-black smoke,
    THE GREAT IMPERIAL CHARIOT
    ROLLS MAJESTICALLY ON.   (IV, 700)

Not content with this mode of imitative gigantism, the persona provides an eyewitness version, laced with Thackeray's personal observations and ending with the alternative satiric mode, bathos:

[*Enter a fat Priest, who bustles up to the Drum-major.*]
Fat Priest.—Taisez-vous.
Little Drummer.—Rub-dub-dub—rub-dub-dub—rub-dub-dub, &c.
Drum-major.—Qu'est-ce donc?
Fat Priest.—Taisez-vous, vous dis-je, ce n'est pas le corps.
  Il n'arrivera pas—pour une heure. (IV, 710)

There is time and occasion, then, for more political sermonizing, and Titmarsh-Thackeray expands on the betrayal-of-the-revolution theme he had sounded in the *Sketch Book*:

But here, in the matter of Napoleon, is a simple fact: he founded a great, glorious, strong, potent republic, able to cope with the best aristocracies in the world, and perhaps to beat them all; he converts his republic into a monarchy, and surrounds his monarchy with what he calls aristocratic institutions; and you know what becomes of him. The people estranged, the aristocracy faithless (when did they ever pardon one who was not of themselves?)—the Imperial fabric tumbles to the ground. If it teaches nothing else, my dear, it teaches one a great point of policy—namely, to stick by one's party. (IV, 705–706)

The narrator seems to have been swayed by some of the myths of the day, but it is noteworthy that they are of the great republic and the faithless aristocracy, the would-be sun king and his true party—the people. That Thackeray is not proof against partisan myths shows less as a defect of his insight into political myth making than as an indication of its pervasiveness even among its keenest observers.[8]

The most elaborate expression of Thackeray's sense of political mythology is a satirical fantasy, "The History of the Next French Revolution [From a forthcoming History of Europe]" (1844), first published in *Punch*. Set in 1884, it tells of three contenders for the crown of Louis Philippe: "His Royal Highness Louis Anthony Frederick Samuel Anna-Maria, Duke of Brittany, and son of Louis XVI"; Henri of Bordeaux, modeled on the many Bourbon pretenders, who is locked in the famous insane asylum of Charenton; and "His Imperial Highness Prince John Thomas Napoleon—a fourteenth cousin of the late Emperor." Amid the good fun of depicting the mutual destruction of these competitors, Thackeray has room for an analysis of political rhetoric. He creates an appropriate proclamation for the latest Napoleon, which concludes: "Frenchmen, up and rally!—I have flung my banner to the breezes; 'tis surrounded by the faithful and the brave. Up, and let our motto be, LIBERTY, EQUALITY, WAR ALL OVER THE WORLD!" (VI, 240). The timing is important here: we are disarmed by the break in a familiar triad and by the utterance of an ordinarily suppressed truth; but a further doubt enters that perhaps the replacement of the goal of Fraternity by the war-of-each-against-all is by an easy transition. Yet more disturbing is the denouement in which the crown is seized by the mad pretender, freshly arrived from Charenton, who proclaims: "There shall be no more poverty; no more wars; no more avarice; no more passports; no more custom-houses; no more lying; no more physic" (VI, 262). The tendency of such perceptions of political behavior is toward cynicism, and the concluding paragraph flirts with it: "He is a poor reader, for whom his author is obliged to supply a moral application. . . . The drama of *Punch* himself is not moral: but that drama has had audiences all over the world. Happy he, who in our dark times can cause a smile! Let us laugh then, and gladden in the sunshine, though it be but as the ray upon the pool, that flickers only over the cold black depths below!" (VI, 263). The tone hints not only at cynicism but at a struggle with despair, at an effort to resist reducing all political rhetoric not to myth but to madness, and at a need to find more than comic relief in satirical writing.

Some such complex of feeling colors Thackeray's account of his visit to Waterloo in another *Punch* piece, collected in "Little Travels and Road-side Sketches by Titmarsh." He has first to explain why he had never before made the required pilgrimage: ". . . I am such a philosopher as not to care a fig about the battle—nay, to regret, rather, that when Napoleon came back, the British Government had not spared their men and left him alone" (VI, 295). It is by the loss of men that he is most affected in his account of the battlefields; the cemeteries contain memorials only to the officers, and the egalitarian in Thackeray is aroused: "But live or die, win or lose, what do *they* get? English glory is too genteel to meddle with those humble fellows" (VI, 298). Yet the Englishman's heart is warmed by the spectacle: "Let an Englishman go and see that field, and he *never forgets it*. . . . I will wager that there is not one of them but feels a glow as he looks at the place, and remembers that he, too, is an Englishman." Quickly recovering from this bout of mythologizing, Titmarsh-Thackerary concludes: "It is a wrong, egotistical, savage, unchristian feeling, and that's the truth of it. A man of peace has no right to be dazzled by that red-coated glory, and to intoxicate his vanity with those remembrances of carnage and triumph." The word and the ambivalent attitudes bring us squarely back to *Vanity Fair*.

This brief review of Thackeray's Napoleonic writings links that figure with some of the novelist's chief political interests: the high hopes and lost innocence of the French Revolution; Napoleon's displacement of—and then corruption by—the vanity of aristocracy; the anticipation, in fear and longing, of an English revolution—not so much an economic change as a biblical scourge of vanities. While clearly seeing the difference between Napoleon's historic role and the propagandistic uses made of his memory, Thackeray was repeatedly drawn to the myth when expressing his own ambivalent attitudes. This is what gives us assurance that it is myth with which the novelist was dealing: its structural openness to conflicting impulses, its ability—as in a Lévi-Strauss paradigm—to carry both libertarianism and authority, both social equality and individual preeminence, both moralistic denunciation and inventive self-projection. All these aspects of the Napoleonic myth were close to the novelist's own political imagination and were available to him when he drew the figure of Becky Sharp.

For Thackeray's attitude toward Becky, as the sharpest and the most manipulative of the puppeteers of *Vanity Fair*—after the Manager of the Performance himself—is an object lesson in ambivalence. The most seductive of *femmes fatales*, she is also the most memorable of fictional heroine-villainesses; the obvious dark side of a twin-heroine construction, she becomes the object of mixed attraction and revulsion throughout the narrative. Her famous economic-determinist justification of herself—"I think I could be a good woman if I had five thousand a year" (xli, 409)—receives the narrator's grudging agreement: "And who knows but Rebecca was right in her speculations—and that it was only a question of money and fortune which made the difference between her and an honest woman?" (xli, 410). Thackeray sets her up as a master of falsification in a world of phonies; he establishes her style as the perfect expression of the world which creates and succumbs to her. In all this she is both rebel against and master of the stratified English society, in the same dual way in which Napoleon both destroyed and reincarnated the system of European hierarchy. In the serio-comic adventures of Becky Sharp, Thackeray is enacting in synecdochic form a parable of European history.

Yet more: just as Becky and Napoleon represent the outsider taking over from a decadent social hierarchy and opening the nineteenth-century world to talent and intelligence, so they represent a particular skill of key importance in the new age. It is not simply that Napoleon has become a political, and Becky a literary, myth; they are both exemplars of the myth-making faculty in social action.

Their high facility in symbol manipulation leads to a final point of intersection between Becky Sharp and Napoleon Bonaparte. For the concomitant of their ability to regard images and words as artificial and functional, rather than as real and inherently valuable, is a corrosive skepticism of the validity of human symbol systems. For such men and women, society and politics, morality and history, are games which may be played better or worse according to one's recognition of their purely arbitrary character. And therein lies the fatal weakness of *femmes fatales* and men of destiny: their skepticism seems insufficient to sustain them in their imaginative enterprises, they become bored by their own artificiality (equal to that of the world which they exploit), and by a Hegel-like dialectic the masters of myth become its victims. Only in some such dialectic can one account for the vigorous self-destructive tendency that places Napoleon and Becky among the great losers of history and literature, respectively. For the gesture of throwing away the mastery of Europe for the conquest of Russia is equaled—given the difference of realm and scale—by Becky's overextended efforts to *play* her husband, Steyne, Briggs, Miss Crawley, and apparently even higher personages in the dizzying heights of her ascent. There is something unaccountable in her refusal to bail Rawdon out of debtors' prison, something lavishly gratuitous in her borrowing from Steyne to repay Briggs and then pocketing both proceeds. (As Steyne grimly acknowledges, "'What a splendid actress and manager! . . . She is unsurpassable in lies.' . . . Getting the money was nothing—but getting double the sum she wanted, and paying nobody—it was a magnificent stroke" [lii, 506].) But the other side of this high-spirited imagination is the sense of despair endemic to it: "She thought of her long past life, and all the dismal incidents of it. Ah, how dreary it seemed, how miserable, lonely and profitless! Should she take laudanum, and end it, too—have done with all hopes, schemes, debts, and triumphs?" (liii, 516).

This is very close to the vanity-of-human-wishes theme sounded by many a historian of Napoleon's career, e.g., Scott: ". . . he had not yet become aware that possession brings satiety, and that all earthly desires and wishes terminate, when fully attained, in vanity and vexation of spirit." It expresses more than Thackeray's affinity to a classical skepticism of human enterprises, whether personal or historical. Rather, it is a sudden, potentially tragic recognition of the illusion at the heart of social life itself, reduced to a system of artifices, symbols, and other arbitrary constructs. Yet this awe and anxiety of social myth fail to halt Becky for very long, any more than they did her creator or the archillusionist from whom he drew his prime example.

5. Master and Servant in *Little Dorrit*

In these people the social will, the will to status, is the ruling faculty.
To be recognized, deferred to, and served—this is their master passion.
—LIONEL TRILLING

THE human relationship most frequently found in the world of *Little Dorrit* is that of master and servant. Often these are the stated roles of the characters: Casby and Pancks, the Meagles and Tattycoram, Mrs. Clennam and the Flintwinches. The activities of several other important personages consist mainly in giving and receiving service. Rigaud/Blandois' bullying employment of Cavalletto is merely the extreme case of a relation that governs almost all life. It includes the central situation in the plot: the lifelong dedication of the heroine to her father's maintenance. Indeed, we can say that normal behavior in Dickens' image of society is governed by money and power—two words for the same force—and that these place people inevitably in positions of superiority and inferiority, dominance and obligation. *Little Dorrit* is our most telling study of a human condition so pervasive as to seem to us almost natural, until objectified and called into question by artistic portrayal. This is the condition described by the sociological term "class." It is Dickens' almost unique genius to tell us not only how it feels to be alive in a class society but also how people shape their own character under the spell of inequality.

The general form of the relations between masters and servants has been set out in a philosophical treatise which Dickens is not likely to have known, for it was little read outside philosophical circles in nineteenth-century England. To revert to Hegel's *Phenomenology of Mind*, moreover, for an explanation of events in a novel might appear to some to show undue deferrence to a self-contained and specialized system. Yet at least one of Hegel's chapters, entitled "Herr und Knecht," master and servant, is widely regarded by European intellectuals as a kind of master key to the pattern of modern history from the French Revolution down. It can provide us with suggestive terms in which to consider the generic similarities of widely different situations in the novel—to discover, if possible, the unifying theme of an otherwise diffuse plot.

Hegel begins his account of one stage of the development of the human spirit by defining master and servant in the most elementary terms: "The one is independent, and its essential nature is to be for itself; the other is dependent, and its essence is life or existence for another. The former is the Master, or Lord; the latter the Bondsman [or Servant]." All situations, then, in which one person labors for another's good come into this discussion: knight and vassal, conqueror and conquered, employer and worker, God and man, loved one and lover. Hegel's main effort is to trace the dialectic of independence and dependence in the minds of those involved in such relationships. His great discovery is to find in them an invariable process of displacement at work. Masters become dependent on servants for service and lose their own independence, while servants grow in strength through their activity itself and become masters of their own creative powers:

> Just where the master has effectively achieved lordship, he really finds that something has come about quite different from an independent consciousness. It is not an independent, but a dependent consciousness that he has achieved.

> . . . in fashioning the thing, [the servant's] self-existence comes to be felt explicitly as his own proper being, and he attains that consciousness that he himself exists in its own right and on its own account (an und für sich).[1]

When the difficulties of Hegel's special terminology are dissolved, his insight can be extended—as Marx extended it—to the rising of revolutionary movements in modern times, to the evolution of a secular culture replacing traditional religious authority, and to the development of personal freedom through an awareness of the inhibitions placed on or created by individuals in their psychological relations with others. It is my purpose to trace the latter process of personal liberation as it occurs in *Little Dorrit*, but this process has an inevitable bearing on social and religious questions as well.

The rise of freedom may take various forms, according to the kind of service rendered. In some cases liberation may be concurrent with the service itself and need not necessarily end it. The most outspoken of rebellions is, of course, Tattycoram's refusal to heed her master's urging that she "count five-and-twenty"—her usual means of self-suppression. It is noteworthy that this Dickensian orphan's rebellion does not take place because the Meagles treat her badly but precisely because they treat her so well. It is not ingratitude that Tattycoram expresses but the ignominy of inferiority, conveyed in the coyly deprecating nickname given her by her benefactors. "She would take no more benefits from us," says Meagles, evidently paraphrasing her own words. It is equally remarkable that her return to her masters is as abject a self-surrender as her declaration of independence had been imperious: "Dear Master, dear Mistress, take me back again, and give me back the dear old name!"[2] What she has discovered is that liberation can be as imprisoning as the servitude she has fled. Miss Wade, the instigator of her rebellion, proves a more domineering master than Meagles had ever been.

The perfect type of the unrebellious servant is, on the other hand, Cavalletto. Although he eventually defeats his master when he discovers him and brings him to Clennam in the Marshalsea, the little Italian is portrayed as a comic but pathetic innocent, unwilling to cooperate with evil but powerless to resist it (his only direct rebellion is to run away from the villain at a French inn). When the finally cornered Rigaud/Blandois turns on his pursuers and demands service from Cavalletto, the latter performs his habitual role with little hesitation but with his innocence preserved: "The blending, as he did so, of his old submission with a sense of something humorous; the striving of that with a certain smouldering ferocity, which might have flashed fire in an instant . . . and the easy yielding of all, to a good-natured, careless, predominant propensity to sit down on the ground again; formed a very remarkable combination of character" (II, xxviii, 746).

If Cavalletto is an abased form of humanity, he nevertheless knows how to keep his revolt smoldering and thereby preserve his moral integrity. The most dehumanized servant of the lot is not he but Affery, the housemaid of Mrs. Clennam taken to wife by Flintwinch in order to keep her bound to the house and its secrets. When she explains her marriage to Clennam, she offers the traditional excuse of the slave: "How could I help myself? . . . It was no doing o' mine. I'd never thought of it. I'd got something to do, without thinking, indeed!" (I, iii, 38). So completely does Affery renounce responsibility for her thoughts, deed, and will that she refuses even to acknowledge her own perceptions and stores them up in her memory as dreams, untrustworthy even to herself. It is true that she manifests a spate of rebellion when Rigaud/Blandois confronts her masters with his discovery of their wrongdoings, but she adds nothing material to the information the blackmailer extorts. The measure of her moral nature is to be taken from her refusal to help Clennam in his quest for the secrets of his birth: ". . . do you get the better of 'em afore my face; and then do you say to me, Affery tell your dreams! Maybe, then I'll tell 'em!" (II, xxiii, 690). She will follow power, whoever wields it—the fortune of the slave.

The most spectacular instance of rebellion in the novel is that of Pancks, a rebellion founded on a more acute awareness of his condition than that of any other servant in the novel. Pancks is a potentially tragic figure in his ironic denigration of Casby's rapacity, while remaining powerless to do anything other than his bidding. The poignancy of his assumption of his master's voice is as compelling as its irony: "You're not going to keep open house for all the poor of London," he tells the amiably agreeing Casby. "You're not going to lodge 'em for nothing. You're not going to open your gates wide and let 'em come free. Not if you know it, you ain't" (I, xiii, 156). The gusto with which Pancks eventually conducts a public humiliation of the landlord among the denizens of Bleeding Heart Yard is less a social revolution than an act of personal redemption, and we can say that it is not only from Casby that Pancks liberates himself but from the degradation he has imposed on himself.

The ultimate in rebelliousness is the lifelong war against society conducted by Miss Wade. The neurotic and homosexual elements in her personality should not lead us away from the more basic facts of her life: she is a bastard seeking to cancel her social inferiority by proclaiming, like Shakespeare's Edmund, her natural equality. The pattern of the experiences she relates in her "History of a Self Tormentor" (volume II, chapter xxi) is that of a consistent refusal of sympathy and help from others. Any acceptance of good from another is an admission that one lacks that good and is therefore inferior. But the more Miss Wade rebels and asserts her independence, the more she cuts herself off from others, deprives herself, and mismanages her life. To take the process a step further: the more she claims equality with the masters by spurning them, the more she proves her inferiority, her inability to live a normal life among them. Therein lies the defeat of the social inferior's—and of many a servant's—rebellion: hers is not a free choice of freedom but a compulsive drive to be free which only increases her bondage and her bitterness.

The most complicated case of servitude and revolt is that of William Dorrit. It can readily be seen that prison, especially the debtors' prison, is a form of servitude, in which not only the freedom but the dignity of the human person are surrendered, forfeit by law. Dorrit responds to this dehumanization by a self-delusion so absolute as to draw his entire community into a complicity of mystification. All agree that he is not only the Father of the Marshalsea but also a gentleman, irrespective of his temporary pecuniary embarrassment. Delusion turns into ironic inversion: not only is he a gentleman, a member of the master class, but they, his fellow prisoners, are servants, patronized and protected by their master, the lowliest debtor of them all. The web of illusion takes the form of a charade of feudal obligations: even when Dorrit is tipped by his more fortunate colleagues, the pretense of rendering him tributary dues is observed.

So much is clear from our initial meetings with the strange world of the Marshalsea. What emerges only gradually is the degree to which Dorrit employs both his servility and his pretended mastery as means of aggression, going well beyond his original motives of self-preservation in an alien environment. He not only uses his daughter as a servant, accepting her work and other sacrifices as his due, but also—without a thought of the self-contradictions involved—erects himself as a martyr of self-sacrifice, a servant to his family, by virtue of his imprisonment per se. When he notices Clennam's interest in Amy, he is not averse to playing the pander, demanding that she encourage Clennam in order to keep him as a soft touch for loans. When she shrinks from this ignominy, Dorrit pursues her with his aggressive servility: "What does it matter whether I eat or starve? What does it matter whether such a blighted life as mine comes to an end, now, next week, or next year? What am I worth to any one? A poor prisoner, fed on alms and broken victuals; a squalid, disgraced wretch!" (I, xix, 227). Dorrit shows himself a master of the fine art of creating guilt feelings in others and, with guilt, a sense of obligation. By turning himself at such times into a servant, he makes others his servants: ". . . whatever I have done for your sake, my dear child, I have done freely and without murmuring" (I, xix, 230). It is this false self-abnegation that is exposed in the novel by the creation of the image of a genuine servant, Little Dorrit.

The multifarious prison, which has been widely observed to be the central symbol of *Little Dorrit*, is to be seen in this context as the object which most firmly presents the condition of mastery and servitude. The debtor is the man who has committed the cardinal sin in a commercial society: he has used money—which is the instrument of social dominance—to be a master but has mastered others more than his money permits him legally to do. The appropriate penalty for such presumption is to make him the servant of his creditors, and this servitude is exacted from him in the form not of work but of literal bondage. For the prisoner is nothing but a slave without work: he has lost his power to do what he wills, to be a member of the free community. It is this or suchlike reasoning which prompts the heroine of the novel to make an otherwise incomprehensible departure from Victorian moral judgment. When Little Dorrit expresses the wish that her father not be obliged to pay his debts in money, after his accession to wealth, Clennam finds her mind "tainted" by the "prison atmosphere." But she understands that incarceration is not, as the law pretends, simply a restraint on the debtor from enjoying his creditors' money in freedom but a commensurate payment of the debt by the debtor's assuming the position of his creditors' servant. It is for this reason that she equates payment in money with payment in freedom: "It seems to me hard . . . that he should have lost so many years and suffered so much, and at last pay all the debts as well. It seems to me hard that he should pay in life and money both" (I, xxxv, 422).

Little Dorrit's penetrating view of her father's servitude is given her as a result of her own assumption of the servant's role. A large part of the novel is given over to an excruciating record of Dorrit's degradation of his daughter, his exploitation of her work and self-sacrifice with only sporadic recognition of her merits and of his own obligations to her. We are to find in this parabolic tale a modern instance of the Christian ideal of humility, expressed in dialectical terms. Little Dorrit is the servant of servants, the last and the least. In the words of the Gospel, "He who would be first among you, let him be the servant of all." By the spiritual inversion of worldly values, the lowest is most high, the servant is master. Her heroic strength

lies in her very weakness, and readers who are dissatisfied with her feeble-
ness have missed Dickens' ethical revaluations.

Little Dorrit is given her peculiar grace—the power known by the New
Testament word *agape*, the love Christ had for mankind—by virtue of being
placed at a limit of human experience. She is not of the children of this
world: she is the Child of the Marshalsea, the lowest of the low, and therefore of the blessed poor, of whom is the Kingdom of Heaven. Her name itself
is love—Amy, from the French *aimée*—and her power is to lead the wretch-
ed, the servants, the prisoners to bear their degradation with love. When
she offers herself to Clennam as a servant in his imprisonment, she pleads
to help not only him but herself: ". . . do not turn from your Little Dorrit,
now, in your affliction! Pray, pray, pray, I beg you and implore you with
all my grieving heart, my friend—my dear!—take all I have, and make it a
Blessing to me!" (II, xxix, 759). And when he asks that she not visit him in
his affliction, she pleads for herself alone: "O! you will never say to me . . .
that I am not to come back any more! You will surely not desert me so!" (II,
xxix, 761). We may interpret these exchanges in simple Christian terms—it
is more blessed to give than to receive—as Dickens himself would likely
have seen them. But we may also find in them the hallmark of the servant's
triumph: by becoming indispensable, service becomes power and conquers
the master. These scenes, where Clennam is conquered by Little Dorrit's
love, are among the most beautiful in the entire literature of love, for the
heroine wins her romantic suit for the hero by the force not of her attrac-
tiveness but of her submissiveness: *eros* triumphs by *agape*.[3]

Little Dorrit is the heroine of a novel of masters and servants because she
reaches an absolute of servitude itself: she is the perfect servant, who loves
those she serves, and indeed serves them only because she loves them.
When her "master" can learn to love her in return, as Clennam does, the
gulf between master and servant can be bridged, establishing a model for
similar social dichotomies to be resolved. There is little doubt that Dickens
intended this plot—the transcendence of master and servant relations by
the relationship of love—as his explicit moral in the tale. But its application need not be socially repressive. Meagles extracts from Little Dorrit's
servitude a lesson to instruct the penitent Tattycoram: Little Dorrit's
"young life has been one of active resignation, goodness, and noble service.
. . . Duty, Tattycoram. Begin it early, and do it well" (II, xxxiii, 812–813).
But Little Dorrit herself teaches that it is not to worldly masters that we
are to submit but to the only true one, the master servant, when she tells
Mrs. Clennam: "Be guided only by . . . the patient Master who shed tears of
compassion for our infirmities" (II, xxxi, 792).

The servant who learns to serve God and individual human beings with
love may be tempted to abandon the power to judge. The moral flaw in an
otherwise revelatory novel is that its heroine fails to condemn the injus-

tices which author and readers join in excoriating. We all feel the outrage of the Dorrits' treatment of Clennam, among others, after their accession to wealth. Yet, for Little Dorrit, her father's snobbery is to be pardoned because it can be understood: "She felt that, in what he had just now said to her [about conforming to Mrs. General's standards of gentility], and in his whole bearing towards her, there was the well-known shadow of the Marshalsea wall. . . . She had no blame to bestow upon him, therefore: nothing to reproach him with, no emotions in her faithful heart but great compassion and unbounded tenderness" (II, v, 478). It is an emotion which we are asked to admire but cannot share. Dickens' own feelings are most often with the rebels, furiously engaged against the exactions of the masters. Throughout his life, he—like many of his contemporaries—was attracted by Christian quietism, the patient acquiescence in evil as of the divine will, the forgiveness of enemies in the awareness of one's own sinfulness. These were the virtues which Nietzsche found the hallmark of the Christian slave psychology: unable to defeat the masters of the world, slaves make a virtue of their own powerlessness, their own servitude. It was this ideal that Dickens portrayed in the person of Little Dorrit, but his searing image of a class-subordinated society cannot be subsumed in the vision of grace, and the servant's revolt against unjust masters remains an imaginative option in the novel's denouement: Little Dorrit is to be complemented by Pancks.

At the exact center of *Little Dorrit*—between the indignant portrait of a commercial society and the transcendent loving-kindness of the heroine—stands the hero of the novel, Arthur Clennam. In his development lies a *modus vivendi* between the extremes of mastery and servitude, between domination and self-abnegation. Clennam has been slighted by most critics, and he is admittedly an unlikely prospect to play the heroic role in so grand an ethical drama as this novel presents. Much of the action is, however, narrated from his point of view, and his reflections on the world around him are closest to the informed observer's—that is to say, to Dickens' own. It is this very mediocrity that is his limitation and his strength as a hero: we have here to do with one of the finest exemplars of a character type that has come to dominate contemporary literature, the antihero. Clennam is, to be sure, a mixture of two earlier Dickensian protagonists, the innocent fronting a mysterious and hostile adult world and the good father figure or benefactor who can obviate the innocent's difficulties with his money. Although he combines elements of Dickens' stock-in-trade, Clennam nevertheless initiates a new type of Dickensian hero: the melancholy searcher after a meaning in life—to be followed by Sydney Carton of *A Tale of Two Cities*, Pip of *Great Expectations*, and John Harmon of *Our Mutual Friend*. In their status as seekers, they can be seen as modifications of the typical nineteenth-century hero, the young man from the provinces who comes to the metropolis to seek his fortune and is led through disillusioning experiences at all levels of society. Yet Dickens' disappointed middle-aged men represent a more advanced stage of the innocent youth's induction into the fallen world.

Their condition may best be described in terms provided by the French sociologist of literature, Lucien Goldmann: they are engaged in a "degraded research" (*une recherche dégradée*—the translation is best kept close to the original), a quest for authentic values in a degraded world, while themselves sharing in the degradation of that world. Such a hero—whether he be animated by abstract idealism like Don Quixote and his successors, by a labyrinthine psychology like Dostoyevsky's heroes, or by an educational curiosity about life like the heroes of Balzac and Stendhal—is always "a *problematic* personage whose degraded—and by the same token inauthentic—research of authentic values in a world of conformism and convention, constitutes the content of that new literary genre which writers have created in an individualist society, and which is called 'the novel.'"[4] Considered in this way, Dickens' erection of Clennam as a hero gives further ground for placing *Little Dorrit* in the great tradition not merely of English but of European fiction.

Clennam is introduced to us as a British colonial merchant, returning to England after twenty-five years in China (which seem to have passed without leaving any noticeable imprint on him), anxious to create a life for himself out of the scattered fragments of his past. On the one hand he is met by the coldest mother in the history of the novel (a mother surrogate who derives from fairy tale), and on the other by a gushing former love who pursues him relentlessly with the flow of her manic language. Depressed by the former and frightened—often absurdly embarrassed—by the latter, he sets out to solve the fundamental problems of life: the finding of a mate, the choice of a vocation, the problems of self-knowledge and social orientation. In every way he meets failure: the girl he first falls in love with marries a scoundrel, while patronizing Clennam tenderly but cruelly; he ruins his promising business enterprise with Doyce by investing all their funds in the Merdle house of cards; and he is frustrated in his attempts to wheedle information about his origins—and about the guilt he feels attaches to his family fortune—out of his implacable mother. His course lies, in sum, steadily downward, from his initial renunciation of his position in the family business, to his compromising of his business affairs by futile engagement in the toils of the Circumlocution Office, to the destruction of his fortunes by naïve speculation. In total defeat, he experiences the sickness unto death: his thoughts turn frequently to suicide as he watches the Thames flow to the sea, and his favorite characterization of himself is "nobody."

Yet Arthur Clennam is not merely the hapless nonentity he makes himself out to be. Dickens endows him with an elementary humanity rare in the world of the novel:

He was a dreamer in such wise, because he was a man who had, deep-rooted in his nature, a belief in all the gentle and good things his life had been without. Bred in meanness and hard dealing, this had rescued him to be a man of honourable mind and open hand. Bred in coldness and severity, this had rescued him to have a warm and sympathetic heart. Bred in a creed too darkly audacious to pursue, . . . this had rescued him to judge not, and in humility to be merciful, and have hope and charity. (I, xiii, 165)

The best thing to be said for Clennam is that Little Dorrit loves him from the first and that his worldly limitations and spiritual gifts make him an appropriate object of her love.

Why is it, then, that Clennam must go through a sort of purgatorial process which brings him as low as the Marshalsea before he can recognize Little Dorrit's and his own mutual attraction and finally join together with her? All sorts of explanations have been offered: the plotting of the novel in two volumes, entitled "Poverty" and "Riches," demands an ironic inversion which brings the gentleman hero to the bottom while the outcast heroine is thrust to the pinnacle of the social scale; the hero's adventures are like the trials of the heroes of medieval romance, and he must be rescued by the beneficence of his maiden fair; the repressed sexuality of their relationship must be led to a crisis in order to bring it to the surface; etc. These observations are all to the point—indeed, one of the guarantees of the novel's greatness is the accessibility of its plot to complementary symbolic interpretations—but the dialectics of mastery and subordination can help integrate them and show their realization in the denouement.

Little Dorrit comes to Clennam in her old, worn dress, comforts him in the room where her father lived, and calls herself, "Your own poor child come back!" (II, xxix, 756). It is to be seen not only that Clennam takes for her the place of her recently dead father but that she performs the role of a nurturing mother such as he has never known. The subsequent lines are quite explicit in their psychological sources: ". . . drawing an arm softly round his neck, [she] laid his head upon her bosom, put a hand upon his head, and resting her cheek upon that hand, nursed him as lovingly, and GOD knows as innocently, as she had nursed her father in that room when she had been but a baby, needing all the care from others that she took of them." The child becomes parent: the scene is fixed in the iconographic tradition of the *caritas Romana*—the daughter nourishing her father in prison (though not here at the breast).[5] This deeply rooted convention is made relevant to the transvaluation of values the novel effects. Just as her childlike innocence fits her for a higher realm, so Little Dorrit is able to bring up others, to educate and prepare them for a higher life.

Amy is both child and mother to her lover, as she has been to her father; but Clennam proves a better object of love than Dorrit, rejecting her attempts to abase herself by refusing to let her join him in prison. Clennam has been degraded to the same condition as Dorrit—even Rigaud/Blandois greets him as a "fellow jail-bird"—but he is given a chance to affirm his freedom from both mastery and servitude by refusing to become a new Dorrit for Amy. The train of subordinations must have an end; the pattern of competitive self-denial must cease. He refuses to allow her to sacrifice her fortunes for him: "'I am disgraced enough, my Little Dorrit. I must not descend so low as that, and carry you—so dear, so generous, so good—down with me. GOD bless you, GOD reward you! It is past.' He took her in his arms, as if she had been his daughter" (II, xxix, 760). When Clennam refuses to let Amy become merely a substitute mother to him, they are well on the way to a new relationship, that of equals in married love. When Clennam has reached this point, when he can refuse Amy's sacrifice, he has passed through the prison of the world to a higher freedom. The triumph of Clennam's degraded research is to be able, on the strength of his observation of Dorrit's and others' degradation, to refuse the servile system of the prison and to strip himself bare, neither having nor being a servant.

One further liberation is, however, necessary. Amy, in her turn, must dispense with her two fortunes, if the pattern of inequality and dependence is not to be revived. The Dorrit inheritance is, fortunately, lost in the Merdle crash, and she then voluntarily surrenders the Clennam bequest which would come to her on publication of the concealed codicil. Only when Little Dorrit announces the loss of her fortune can she and Arthur marry; for her it is a chance to divest herself of material superiority, while for him it represents the end of their initial disparity of class, which had colored their relations throughout their growing love. This marriage—along with Clennam's other equal partnership, with Doyce—is the only nonhierarchical relationship in the world of *Little Dorrit*. The closing image contrasts their equilibrium in equality with the world's instability in its competition for mastery: "They went quietly down into the roaring streets, inseparable and blessed; and as they passed along in sunshine and shade, the noisy and eager, and the arrogant and the froward and the vain, fretted, and chafed, and made their usual uproar" (II, xxxiv, 826).

6. The Wanderings of Melmotte

The poet does not "lend" any "new meaning" to the royal scapegoat;
he returns more closely to the universal source of meanings.

—RENE GIRARD

*T*HE *Way We Live Now* has been amply praised as Trollope's amplest imitation of English society in the heyday of finance capitalism. Its generalizing title has been taken to signal a comprehensive realism and has been readily applied to fictional accounts of social behavior in our own time.[1] When we find, however, that the most thorough study of the novel's historical references validates the account of a Jewish financier as faintly smelling because "Brehgert probably *does* smell,"[2] we can choose only between mimetic naïveté and racial prejudice to explain the assumption that *The Way We Live Now* is literal history. The pitfalls of taking fiction as a reliable record of social facts have been instructively marked out in a self-corrective article by the historian J. A. Banks[3] but, even without his witness to the evasive details of closely studied history, an adequate theory of literary realism would indicate that its truths are to be grasped only with the arts of symbolic interpretation.

Yet where are we to find symbolic depth in a work so close to the surface of contemporary manners and morals—and have not symbolmongers been sufficiently chastised by Ruth ap Roberts and other defenders of the surface?[4] Many readers recognize the central figure Melmotte's representative function in Trollope's version of a society organized and corroded by economic and other chicanery but are nonetheless reluctant to accord him a symbolic status. At least one character in the novel itself, however, has no such difficulty; Roger Carbury reads the significance of Melmotte's position as a "sign of the degeneracy of the age."[5] The concomitant dangers of this way of reading are suggested when Carbury continues: "It seems to me that the existence of a Melmotte is not compatible with a wholesome state of things in general" (II, lv, 45). The error of taking effects for causes and symbols for underlying realities is patent in the notion that one can check the degeneracy of an age by erasing its signs. Instead, *The Way We Live Now* offers opportunities to see the protagonist of a realist novel as exercising great imaginative authority, not simply by virtue of his typicality[6] or statistical representativeness but because he is invested with the complex evocations of a long-standing literary archetype.

If a novel composed under the conventions of realism is not literally realistic—as measured by strict correspondence with independently verifiable social facts—no warrant is thereby given for the pursuit of symbolic significances. Yet to be aware of realism as a set of conventions—changing steadily throughout its history—for producing the *effect* of verisimilitude will remind us of the strong marks on *The Way We Live Now* of Trollope's traditional materials. It has been observed that the primary plot, involving an impecunious young gentleman's suit for the hand of a wealthy Jew's daughter, is modeled on *The Merchant of Venice*; while Augustus Melmotte is no Shylock, he too derives from a long line of fictional conventions in the representation of Jews. It will also be found that many another element of the novel bears a marked relation to a fictional forebear: the grandiose dinner for a Chinese emperor, harking back to Goldsmith's and other satires of English culture seen from the perspective of a visiting Oriental; the staunch moral sentiments of the Tory squire, Roger Carbury, directly echoing those of *The Spectator*'s Sir Roger de Coverley; and the gambling fever at the Beargarden, broadly based on scenes of rakish life from Thackeray, Dickens (*Great Expectations*), and earlier novelists.[7] This is not to question Trollope's powers of literary invention, but it suggests that he is comprehensive not so much in gathering data on contemporary society as in assimilating his literary tradition. He was also self-consciously writing in the train of his recent predecessors in the portrayal of Jewish financiers: Bulwer-Lytton and Charles Reade. In his reworking of the Victorian Jew figure, Trollope is equally convention-minded but looks beyond the latest variants of the type to an older tradition, more closely linked with the Gothic novel.

The place of Trollope's novel within the tradition of fictional versions of the Jew has been well studied by others, and there is no need to rehearse the variations between Melmotte and Bulwer-Lytton's Baron Levy or Reade's Isaac Levi. There remains to be explored a literary relation who seems, at first blush, to be connected to Melmotte only by name: Melmoth the Wanderer. The title figure of Charles Robert Maturin's novel of 1820 has been much celebrated in recent studies of the Gothic but has yet to be appreciated as a seminal form—as Lewis' monk and Mary Shelley's monster have been. To connect the Jewish financier and the Mephistophelian tempter even by name may invite a quibble, since other Victorian characters—Bulwer-Lytton's Melnotte (*The Lady of Lyons*: 1838) or Kingsley's Mellot (*Two Years Ago*: 1857)—might have served as well in the quest for a nominal source. What singles out Trollope's and Maturin's complex characters from the others is their common relation to a literary archetype of abiding interest: the Wandering Jew. Since this figure permeates European literature in the nineteenth century, as an exhaustive study has shown,[8] Trollope might have found his inspiration in a number of places. But he does invent a name close to the eponym of Maturin's novel, one which was appropriated and modernized in Balzac's *Melmoth réconcilié* (1835), where the archaic damnée is placed in the role of a modern financier.

Before Melmotte can be shown to function as a Wandering Jew, Melmoth must be found to resemble one. Although Anderson indexes Maturin's novel with the typography reserved for signal instances of the tradition, his treatment of its chief character is as marked by reservations as is his subsequent discussion of Leopold Bloom. Clearly, Melmoth lacks the narrative motif of hurrying or rejecting the Savior, as well as the visible stigmata of the folkloric version which "Monk" Lewis was careful to write into his version of Ahasuerus. Nevertheless, Anderson broadens our concept of the type by noting that *Melmoth the Wanderer* "combines the legends of Faust and the Wandering Jew, for the Irishman Melmoth has sold his soul to the devil for prolonged life"—although the fusion of these legends is sternly rebuked in a parenthesis. From the superimposition of these damnées emerges a paradigm of inherent ambiguity: the protagonist is a man of power but also of pathetic weakness; he has enormous longevity but lives under the heavy threat of damnation; he acquires vast wisdom, whether by long experience or special manifestation, yet cannot discover the formula that will save his own soul; he is at times pathetic, at times grotesque—bearing the marks both of magus and *Schlemihl*, shaman and scapegoat.

It will be observed that these contradictory traits lose their oddness when related to the rubrics of a widespread religious institution: ritual sacrifice, whether of the priest-king or *pharmakos*, bears the mark of a similar duality.[9] That acquired wisdom demands a price—and that salvation exacts a blood price—these topoi are among the chief literary inheritances from elementary religious forms. It is no surprise, then, to find a comparable oxymoron at work in the displaced world of fiction, from the overt dualities of the Gothic[10] to the finer ironies of Joyce. In this tradition of manipulator as victim, con man as fall guy, Melmoth stands as the prototype, with Melmotte as his foremost Victorian avatar.

Melmotte is, however, a far cry from Melmoth in his line of work, and it requires a cultural transformation for the Wandering Jew to be imaginable in the trappings of a city gent. Yet, for all the premodern and un-English setting of Maturin's novel, Melmoth already emerges as a species of salesman in his efforts to trade his unhappy lot with a succession of mortals in the worst of circumstances. In the romantic world of Inquisition victims and Indian maidens, he is a consistent failure; no one will take Melmoth's fate upon himself, and he expires in agony, for all his efforts. It took the genius of Balzac to recognize that relief was at hand in the modern world: if a soul be required, a bit of sharp dealing on the Paris Bourse will quickly fetch the right person at the right price—and subsequent trading in a buyers' market may even drive the price down![11] When a similar vision of the modern world comes together with a similar con man, we find Trollope's London falling at Melmotte's feet in its haste to acquire some of his mana, if not his money. Although no pacts in blood are required, properly executed contracts will serve; although no sale of a soul is demanded, men of the highest class will compromise their names and titles for a place on Melmotte's board. Balzac supplies the commercialization of the Wandering Jew, transforming him from magus to mogul, while Trollope takes the short further step of removing supernatural elements entirely.

That Melmotte is both a wanderer and a Jew does not make him a Wandering Jew, and we must probe his literary tradition to recover the features which lend him power to become the symbolic focus of his society. We have seen that Melmoth and Melmotte manifest both the Wandering Jew's outcast status and his magian knowledge of the world. Such powers accord with the religious archetype of the *pharmakos*, whose exile from society generates a benefit to the community, whether by withdrawing an evil taint or by creating a specialized being who returns his gifts to the group. But Melmotte, like Melmoth, is a hindrance rather than a help to society, invading it with false words and vain schemes. This countertype of the Wandering Jew has its heyday at the very time that a more positive aspect of the Jew was becoming available: his potential for sympathetic rebellion and heroism. As Anderson sums up:

> Along with the rise of Zionism, near the close of the nineteenth century, one finds Ahasuerus identified with all Jews deprived of their homeland; on the reverse side of the coin, because of this identification, he becomes a target at which the anti-Semitic element of the world's Gentile population can aim its missiles. And so Ahasuerus becomes a source of inspiration to many as a symbol of either love or hate. He represents, as before, the eternal sinner or even, in a few instances, Antichrist or some other devilish creation; he may also be a vampire or a bringer of calamitous pestilence. On the other hand, he may represent the defiant rebel against convention and orthodoxy. . . . He can shine as a Prometheus, a helper of man in the individual or in the mass; he can be a grand manipulator when the occasion demands.[12]

The polarization of the Wandering Jew is only an instance of a more widespread pattern in the literary history of the Jews, as described in Edgar Rosenberg's *From Shylock to Svengali*.[13] It is Rosenberg's thesis that nineteenth-century characterizations of the Jew come down to two stock figures: the "Jew-villain" and the "Saintly Jew"–the latter by way of clumsy apology for the former, as in the case of Dickens' creation of Riah to compensate for the invention of Fagin, or Trollope's creation of Brehgert. What is missing from Rosenberg's indignant but witty analysis–including his discussion of *The Way We Live Now*–is an explicit awareness of the original homology of these two figures. For they are, despite their appearance as simplistic stereotypes, at bottom a single complex archetype. It is only when he turns to the Wandering Jew figure that Rosenberg acknowledges this inherent duality:

> Someone like Ahasuerus quite singularly incorporated the greatest possibilities at once for depravity and for sanctity. A figure who perpetrated a crime so foul that he heard his doom pronounced by the lips of Jesus himself and who, at the same time, lives the blameless life of an ascetic, dedicating his immortality to acts and gestures of penitence, invites every kind of interpretation. He is something of Christ and Anti-Christ both; his existence finally points at an insoluble paradox.

While Trollope's protagonist is neither Christ nor Antichrist, neither Prometheus nor vampire, the Jew figure's dual tendencies—toward subterfuge and exploitation, toward fertile invention and promised benefits—show up in equally high relief in Melmotte. Moreover, his melding of these traits does not reveal the sharp junctures found in other Jews of Victorian fiction like Reade's Levi, who moves, as Rosenberg puts it, from Philip Sober to Philip Drunk and back again in demonstration of the novel's title, *It Is Never Too Late to Mend*. Instead, Melmotte's career approximates the classic models in which the protagonist's promise of social benefits is annulled by his own character flaws—so as to invite comparison with the role of the tragic hero. That a predominantly comic novelist was able to create a villain and scapegoat with claims to tragic grandeur can be explained only by his dealings with literary conventions already heavily worked but supple enough for his genius to mold and transform.

Unlike the potentially tragic Shylock or Fagin, Melmotte is given no great speech of defiance or disturbing exit line, and his gropings toward tragic knowledge are reduced to silence at his demise: he rises to speak in Parliament on a country matter—game laws—and can find no words. Yet Melmotte has the power still of inducing words in others: "He might have wrapped his toga around him better perhaps had he remained at home, but if to have himself talked about was his only object, he could hardly have taken a surer course" (II, lxxxiii, 318). Throughout his career Melmotte maintains himself as a shadowy figure about whom little definite is known and thus as a focus of gossipy speculation whose influence depends on his notoriety. This peculiar combination of verbalization and inarticulateness is only the most prominent in a series of contradictions which also structures the Wandering Jew. It is Trollope's genius to have chosen this figure of oxymoron to stand at the center of the social structure which is the novel's panoramic subject. The title announces that it is "the way" of contemporary life that is in question, and it is the symbolic Jew who precisely exposes the *form* of this cultural mode in the contradictions which make and undo him.

"The way" is itself symbolic—or, more precisely, it is symbolism in action. In a society dominated by the "monied interest"–that is, by finance capitalism, rather than by agriculture or even industry–modes of behavior in all walks of life are modeled after those of the dominant institution, the stock market. Since this is a realm in which not things but tokens are exchanged–and in which not real values but constantly fluctuating estimates of generally believed values are the measures of price–it is to be expected that other social activities will also be governed by symbolism and subjectivity. This is the wider meaning of the infection of almost all the characters by confidence, the evil genius which Melmotte embodies; all play his game, which is to believe and induce belief, in the absence of genuine values. Trollope does not deal with the rise of market values as a Jewish intrusion but instead as the indexical symbol of the entire society's mode of operation.

The several plots of *The Way We Live Now* are each concerned with the symbol-oriented behavior which derives from the financial world. Lady Carbury's manufacture of shoddy literary products, mere tissues of clichés –books that imitate other books, with no claims of their own to history or art–this is only the most obvious case of market norms taking over a cultural sphere. Most noteworthy in this satire of nonbooks is the tendency to substitute for the usual relation of signs to things a structure of signs of signs: Lady Carbury imitates not historical events but the formulas for best sellers. A similar transformation occurs in other social activities touched by "the way": instead of gambling simply for money–where one symbolic system (cards) is employed for redistributing the tokens of another (specie) –the roués of the Beargarden take to exchanging IOUs, symbols of symbols. These develop their own rising and falling market values, based on subjective estimates of the financial and psychological state of the scrip writer. By the same token, in the marriage market–that long-standing institutional mixture of social, financial, and personal norms–mating activity is increasingly conducted by verbal significations of other code forms. The contrast between real love and symbolic transactions in marriage becomes prominent in three of the love plots as a question of potential legal suit for breach of promise, after the exchange of a word or substitutive contract of marriage. The genuine passion of Marie Melmotte, Mrs. Hurtle, and John Crumb is contrasted with the shifty verbalism of Felix Carbury, Paul Montague, and Ruby Ruggles–"the way" extending even to the lower classes and the distaff side. That way in marriage making is seen in its pristine form when we are given the correspondence of Georgiana Longestaffe and the banker Brehgert, where the consideration of marriage comes down to a set of offers and counteroffers for town houses and such–the couple's main relationship lying in written texts denoting money.

When the myriad social and cultural activities of *The Way We Live Now* are considered as a structure, they show uniform patterning by the prevailing ethos of finance capitalism. In almost every case, Melmotte is the touchstone of the phoniness of purely symbolic behavior, where the reference of signs to other social codes takes precedence over their representation of nonsymbolic realities. In religion, a priest who cites Melmotte's donation of a hundred guineas for the erection of an altar in a new church is challenged by Carbury ("That's another dodge, is it?") and replies: ". . . of course we are glad to welcome the wealthy and the great. . . . A man is great who has made for himself such a position as that of Mr. Melmotte. And when such a one leaves your Church and joins our own, it is a great sign to us that the Truth is prevailing" (II, lv, 49). The estimate of greatness by its benefits to religious institutions—that is bad enough; more insidious is the reading of religious signs by the testimony of worldly conversions. In the realm of politics, too, a merely verbal declaration of allegiance is magnified by party organs into a sign of principles which it by no means entails: "Any one reading the Conservative papers of the time, and hearing the Conservative speeches in the borough,—any one at least who lived so remote as not to have learned what these things really mean,—would have thought that England's welfare depended on Melmotte's return" (i.e., election) (II, liv, 32). (Note that, within the code system, insiders know what these propaganda gestures "really mean.") In the social world, as well, the traditions of the upper classes are replaced by new modes of operation and are codified into a new and equally formulaic system: "It had been an understood thing, since [Lord Nidderdale] had commenced life, that he was to marry an heiress. . . . It has become an institution, like primogeniture, and is almost as serviceable for maintaining the proper order of things. Rank squanders money; trade makes it;—and then trade purchases rank by regilding its splendour" (II, lvii, 59).

In a synecdoche of an entire society, this regilding of symbols is literally enacted with Melmotte's transformation of his Grosvenor Square house into a sham palace in order to entertain the emperor of China: "But in truth the house was in great confusion. The wreaths of flowers and green boughs were being suspended, last daubs of heavy gilding were being given to the wooden capitals of mock pilasters, incense was being burned to kill the smell of the paint, tables were being fixed and chairs were being moved. . . . The hall was chaos" (II, lvi, 54). Despite the prevalence of successive layers of deception in the domestic, cultural, and institutional realms, a considerable degree of conviction is generated, even among those most artfully engaged in playing the game: "The house had been so arranged that it was impossible to know where you were, when once in it. The hall was a paradise. The staircase was fairyland. The lobbies were grottoes rich with ferns. . . . the house seemed to be endless" (I, iv, 34). The social value of this grand deception is rendered in the stock responses of typical invited grandees: "Of course it's done for a purpose. It's all very well saying that it isn't right, but what are we to do about Alfred's children?" (I, iv, 35). A clear view of the utility of such illusions is present, to be sure, in the aristocrats' cynical use of Melmotte, but in other cases those caught up in the web of illusion lose contact with reality—thus the success of Melmotte's financial house of cards in generating public confidence, for a time.

"It seemed that there was but one virtue in the world, commercial enterprise,—and that Melmotte was its prophet" (I, xliv, 411). With this mock formula, Trollope establishes his protagonist in a central position in the structure of finance capitalism (irrespective of his actual economic power). That role is symbolic and the allusion parodic, for eventually stern realities tend to undo the myth of power that Melmotte fosters in support of his schemes. Beyond a passing financial bubble, he does little that can claim comparison with the Wandering Jew's prodigies, much less those of Mohammed. Yet, in his bumbling way, Melmotte knows how the system of illusion works; when Paul Montague questions it at a board meeting, he sputters: "Gentlemen who don't know the nature of credit, how strong it is,—as the air,—to buoy you up; how slight it is,—as a mere vapour,—when roughly touched, can do an amount of mischief of which they themselves don't in the least understand the extent! . . . do be unanimous. Unanimity is the very soul of these things;—the very soul, Mr. Montague" (I, xl, 379–381). By such emperor's clothes psychology does Melmotte manage to create "credit" in the absence of faith and unity in the absence of "soul." For a while he is able to palm everyone off with promises, and Trollope sums up: "As for many years past we have exchanged paper instead of actual money for our commodities, so now it seemed that, under the new Melmotte régime, an exchange of words was to suffice" (I, xlv, 423).

Melmotte runs his skein of substitutive symbols one turn too many, however, in his dealings with the elder Longestaffe, when he tries to place himself in a country gentleman's seat before having secured his position in the City. He never pays the purchase price, preferring to keep his capital liquid, and eventually a sharp lawyer—if not the fuming, anti-Semitic squire—brings him to ground. For this master of illusions and transposer of symbols has a flaw: he succumbs to his own deceptions, while aware that he is exchanging false coin for mere marks of social favor. Melmotte shows occasional signs of awareness that the values of high society are themselves shams, worth acquiring only as they bring with them more tangible assets of wealth and power. Yet his command of his own medium is uncertain, so that in the time of his troubles, when he stands increasingly alone, he is ready to play the game with willed self-deception:

And Melmotte himself had derived positive pleasure even from a simulated confidence in his [prospective] son-in-law. It had been pleasant to him to talk as though he were talking to a young friend whom he trusted. . . . Of course every word he had said to Nidderdale had been a lie, or intended to corroborate lies. But it had not been only on behalf of the lies that he had talked after this fashion. Even though

his friendship with the young man were but a mock friendship, . . .
still there was a pleasure in it. (II, lxxiv, 225)

It is the same thirst for supportive illusion that leads Melmotte, after the
banquet, to sit in the emperor's chair, thinking the hackneyed thoughts of
the self-made man who has risen from the gutter to his precarious emi-
nence. Whatever sympathy we might feel for the loser is quickly rebuked
by a truly Brechtian irony: what business does this fellow have to deceive
himself, when his existence depends on deceiving others? The rules of his
game do not allow for sharing in the Barmecide feasts he creates for others
and, when he indulges himself in the means as well as in the ends of his
scheming, he risks denunciation for unfair practices. As Trollope wittily
concludes: "Perhaps the most remarkable circumstance in the career of this
remarkable man was the fact that he came almost to believe in himself"
(II, lvi, 57).

To fully savor the symbolic character of Melmotte's self-indulgence, we
must have recourse to a social psychologist's explanation of the Jewish condition and its double-edged workings. Concerning "the Jew to whom geo-
graphic dispersion and cultural multiplicity have become 'second nature,'"
Erik Erikson writes: ". . . relativism becomes for him the absolute, exchange
value his tool. [Moreover,] exchange value may have become obsessive pre-
occupation with the comparative value—of values."[14] This acquired perspective on the relativity of values and of the symbols of value—whether
economic or more broadly cultural—in part accounts for the inventiveness
of certain revolutionary thinkers who were born Jews. Of such radical trans-
formers of scientific paradigms as Marx, Freud, and Einstein, Erikson continues: "Their strength in these fields lies in a responsible sense of relativity. But this defines Jewish weakness as well: for where the sense of
relativity loses its responsibility it can become cynical relativism." The
structural perspective of those who see cultural codes *as codes*—and who
can detach their thought from them sufficiently to propose alternative symbol systems—this very freedom makes both for social progress and for further alienation. The symbol manipulator not only runs the risk of "cynical
relativism" but is likely to be taken by those absorbed within the cultural
system to be an alien and corrosive questioner of its absolutes.

Melmotte is in the position of another inside-but-alienated Victorian
character, who has been used to exemplify the process of structural symbol
making known as *bricolage*:

> What, as a bricoleur, Mr. Wemmick of *Great Expectations* undertook
> and realized . . . was the establishment of paradigmatic relations be-
> tween the elements of these two [syntagmatic] chains: he can choose
> between villa and castle to signify his abode, between pond and moat
> to signify the piece of water, between flight of steps and drawbridge

to signify the entrance, between salad and food reserves to signify his lettuces. How has this come about?

It is clear that to begin with his castle is a small-scale model, not of a real castle but of a castle signified by camouflages and fittings which have the function of symbols. He has not indeed acquired a real castle through these transformations, but he has well and truly lost a real villa, since his fantasy binds him to a whole number of servitudes. Instead of living as a bourgeois, his domestic life becomes a succession of ritual actions. . . .

But the reverse is equally true. His old father's deafness lends to Mr. Wemmick's castle a real value: a stronghold is normally provided with cannons; and his father is so deaf that only the noise of a cannon can penetrate to him. . . . A practical problem is solved: that of communication between the inhabitants of the villa, but thanks to a total reorganization of the real and the imaginary, whereby metaphors take over the mission of metonyms, and vice versa.[15]

Unlike Wemmick's happy utilization of his double system of symbolic codes, Melmotte's proliferation of sign substitutes proves to be his undoing. As master of transformations, he can generate new fictions, like the "Great South Central Pacific and Mexican Railway Company," designed by Fisker, Montague, and Montague "not to make a railway to Vera Cruz, but to float a company" (I, ix, 77). But, as he depends on maintaining the fictions of infinite resources, he must submit to their internal dynamics: ". . . he must either domineer over dukes, or else go to the wall. It can hardly be said of him that he had intended to play so high a game, but the game that he had intended to play had become thus high of its own accord" (I, xxxv, 323). In the reciprocal action of his inventions, Melmotte is simultaneously glorified and derided by those whom he manipulates: "As the great man was praised, so also was he abused. As he was a demi-god to some, so was he a fiend to others" (I, xliv, 411). The significance of this paradox for the dialectic of the *pharmakos* figure is expressed in similarly mythological language on a more colloquial level. For the spongers of the Beargarden, the question becomes "who's to bell the cat?" when it comes to a loan; but that same animal, to be labeled and exploited, also serves as the totem for their tribe: "The cat in this matter I take to be our great master, Augustus Melmotte" (I, xxii, 209–210).

When Melmotte is placed in these dual functions, he may be seen to play an exemplary role, but there is no warrant to define that role as tragic without further evidence of traditional conventions. A preeminent quality of the tragic figure is eventual, if only partial, anagnorisis, so that he completes the circuit of his ironic fate with a recognition of its correspondence to the structure of reality. The preceding analysis has emphasized Melmotte's self-deluded entrapment in his own devisings, but there are moments of awareness to be found in the course of his undoing. At first, these are indistinguishable from clichés: "What's one man that another man should be afraid of him? We've got to die, and there'll be an end of it, I suppose," he says, to cheer himself up. But he quickly takes on a perspective that we associate with the tragic point of view:

> . . . he stood for a few moments looking up at the bright stars. If he could be there, in one of those unknown distant worlds, with all his present intellect and none of his present burdens, he would, he thought, do better than he had done here on earth. If he could even now put himself down nameless, fameless, and without possessions in some distant corner of the world, he could, he thought, do better. But he was Augustus Melmotte, and he must bear his burdens, whatever they were, to the end. He could reach no place so distant but that he would be known and traced. (II, lxii, 115–116)

This is both escapist and pragmatic, to be sure, but Melmotte's vision of the stars takes on a stern sense of reality as well, acknowledging not only the way things are but his own place among them: ". . . he must bear his burdens, whatever they were, to the end."

It is a like determination to be what he is that exposes an unexpected side of Melmotte, his manliness:

> But of what avail were such regrets as these? He must take things as they were now, and see that, in dealing with them, he allowed himself to be carried away neither by pride nor cowardice. And if the worst should come to the worst, then let him face it like a man! There was a certain manliness about him, which showed itself perhaps as strongly in his own self-condemnation as in any other part of his conduct at this time. Judging of himself, as though he were standing outside himself and looking on to another man's work, he pointed out to himself his own shortcomings. (II, lxxxi, 295)

If this be only the self-laceration of the loser, it still reveals the powers of the tragic figure who can stand outside and judge himself. Curiously, Melmotte's special adeptness at relative judgment comes to his aid in this moral realm; standing outside himself is no longer a gimmick of role playing but an accession to objectivity.

Given this power, Melmotte can take stock of his career and acknowledge his inveterate tendencies to hubris, excess, and fall:

> But why had he, so unrighteous himself, not made friends to himself of the Mammon of unrighteousness? Why had he not conciliated Lord Mayors? Why had he trod upon all the corns of all his neighbours? . . . Why had he not stuck to Abchurch Lane [in the City] instead of going into Parliament? Why had he called down unnecessary notice on his

head by entertaining the Emperor of China? It was too late now, and he must bear it; but these were the things that had ruined him. (II, lxxxi, 296)

And so Melmotte fades into silence, his moment of death marked only by a lacuna within the paragraph describing the last evidences of his existence but skirting his inner being at the point of suicide: "He was habitually left there at night, and the servant as usual went to his bed. But at nine o'clock on the following morning the maid-servant found him dead upon the floor" (II, lxxxiii, 319). When the uproar has subsided and the accounts are settled, it turns out that he is a solid citizen after all: "When Melmotte's affairs were ultimately wound up there was found to be nearly enough of property to satisfy all his proved liabilities" (II, xcii, 400). But this is not enough to satisfy the larger claims on his significance, for the enduring impression—erroneous, no doubt—is that this peopled townscape of a hundred chapters and a thousand pages is a novel about Melmotte. Modern readers can agree not only with Trollope himself that Melmotte is the best thing in the book but also with the view that "he is a symbol, something very rare in Trollope, of a way of life."[16] Yet this appreciation will not entirely account for the eerie authority which attaches to Melmotte. It can be found also emanating from the gnomic and faintly Semitic vendor of the Golden Bowl; in Max, the scapegoat tutor of Barth's goatboy Giles; and in Conrad's Stein (if his Jewishness is left in doubt, his exile and his shadowy wisdom fulfill the function). For all the contrary images of the Jew in Victorian and modern literature, the mana-laden, ambiguous, and disturbing appearances of these Wandering Jews continue to inspire moments of sublime creation —even among authors who might be otherwise inclined.

7. "Daniel Charisi"

He walked back along Dorset street, reading gravely. Agendath Netaim:
planter's company. To purchase vast sandy tracts from Turkish govern-
ment and plant with eucalyptus trees. . . . Can pay ten down and the bal-
ance in yearly instalments. Bleibtreustrasse 34, Berlin, W. 15.

Nothing doing. Still an idea behind it.

—"CALYPSO"

HE corpus of *Daniel Deronda* has not yet recovered from the
radical surgery performed on it by F. R. Leavis but, now that
his control over the reading of British fiction has weakened, it
becomes possible to return to the work anew. Yet so strong is the
memory of his proposal to pare the work to its "good" half, to be called
"Gwendolen Harleth," that some sort of shake must be given to the reader
in quest of the whole novel. I propose a new extraction—in view of an eventual reunification—to be called "Daniel Charisi" after its hero (the name
Deronda being a pseudonym applied to cover his obscure parentage). This
proposal is not, perhaps, entirely perverse, as the author's demonstrable intention was to shift attention from the English milieu in which Deronda is
exiled to the ideal community in which he will be called Charisi—a cut-off
member of an almost exterminated race who can yet return to a place of
refuge, as indicated by the Hebrew derivations of his name. In order to read
the novel, then, the English-language reader will have to join George Eliot
in picking up some Hebrew, in freeing the mind of local conventions—including some transient novel-reading conventions—and in acquiring a more
cosmopolitan perspective. It is the hope of this study to lead the willing
reader out of the land of bondage and closer to the inheritance of a sublime
work of art.

In taking this course with a novel that has appealed to many on far different grounds, it is regrettably necessary to question the sources of their
esthetic pleasure. One of the most vigorous of the Leavisite critics has
stated their underlying assumptions:

> George Eliot somehow failed to realize the ideology in the novel.
> (Whether this was the fault of the novelist, or of the ideology itself,
> must remain a matter of opinion.) Daniel fails to rise to the demands
> of his role, while Gwendolen escapes from the confines of George Eli-

ot's moral scheme and surprises the novelist into a magnificent impartiality. In her veracity, Gwendolen transcends the category in which George Eliot proposed to contain her. Perhaps she comes to embody not "egotism," but the stubborn sense of self, the personal *élan*, which we acknowledge as a form of experience more primary than that which Daniel is meant to represent. . . . it is to Gwendolen that the true vitality, and thus the literary immortality, belong.[1]

Despite the parenthetical disclaimer, it will be shown that the main issue for such critics is not Deronda's validity as an embodiment of ideology but that ideology itself. Further, their distaste for Eliot's ideology is not casual but crucial, for she challenges the value of what "we acknowledge as a form of experience more primary than that which Daniel is meant to represent." That "form of experience" takes in the modern ego, individualism, subjectivity, and self-consciousness—"the stubborn sense of self, the personal *élan*, . . . the true vitality." It is good to have this extreme and honest statement of a widespread position, for it leads not only to critical self-awareness but to a closer grasp of Eliot's subversive operations.

Eliot wrote to a number of early admirers of the novel that she was surprised by the favorable responses and not at all surprised by the unfavorable ones. Since her statements to Harriet Beecher Stowe and to her publisher John Blackwood are frequently quoted, I here cite her letter to Abraham Benisch, the editor of the *Jewish Chronicle*:

> You are probably better aware than I am that the elements in "Daniel Deronda" which have called forth your generously appreciative words have met in the ordinary public chiefly with an ignorant surprize and lack of sympathy. This was what I expected. But I did not expect the cordial encouragement [by] which you and other instructed men have given me to believe that my anxious effort at a true presentation is not a failure, and may even touch the feeling of your people to welcome issues.[2]

While to Stowe and to Blackwood she expressed her expectation that the widespread and fashionable anti-Semitism of the English would work against the novel, Eliot here suggests that this was only one of the shortcomings she had anticipated from English readers. While hinting at a special sort of inspiration that Benisch's "people" might derive from the novel, she suggests that a wider group of "instructed men" might be able to avoid "ignorant surprize and lack of sympathy." Although instructed preparation and capacity for sympathy are at a high premium in the reading of any Eliot novel, a special kind of awareness and imagination is called for here.

In another letter of the period, Eliot suggests these desiderata: ". . . I confess that I had an unsatisfied hunger for certain signs of sympathetic discernment, which you only have given. I may mention as one instance your clear perception of the relation between the presentation of the Jewish element and those of English Social life." This is to David Kaufmann, professor at the Jewish Theological Seminary of Budapest and rather an unlikely perceiver of the relation between the "Jewish element" and "English Social life." But that this was the focus of Eliot's concern is shown in her preceding praise of Kaufmann's "George Eliot und das Judenthum," "an article which must be written by a Jew who showed not merely sympathy with the best aspirations of his race, but a remarkable insight into the nature of art and the processes of the artistic mind." That Kaufmann was capable of this intuition is, therefore, an indication that neither sympathy with the Jews nor acquaintance with English society is by itself—or even taken together—sufficient.

While it is no more necessary to subscribe to a particular social philosophy than it is to be a philo-Semite in reading this novel, it is at least desirable that one be capable of yielding to the view of English social values that Eliot creates and of imagining the alternative society that she envisions. For "Daniel Charisi"—and, ultimately, *Daniel Deronda*—is a work of systematic social criticism and at the same time a visionary, even "utopian," novel, acidly etching what is real and, in close juxtaposition, imagining what is possible.

It is this mixture of "realistic" social depiction and the prophetic (if not the fantastic) that has given grounds for the soundest negative criticism of the novel. For those who reject such a mixture of modes, a criterion of generic purity is the esthetic norm, not an ideological disagreement with the author. Yet, when we look closely at the "realistic" part, it is no such thing, if measured by the canons of verisimilitude. One of the novel's earliest defenders was quick to seize on this astonishing lapse in the "Gwendolen" camp's notion of realism: "A Grandcourt[,] whose nature is one main trunk of barren egoism from which all the branches of fresh desire have withered off, is recognized forthwith to be human. But Deronda, sensitive at every point with life . . . Deronda is a pallid shadow rather than a man!"[3] The perception contained in these canny lines is that of Grandcourt's utterly unrealistic mode of existence. Dukes of Ferrara have come and gone in literature, and cool, blond sadists have tortured many a soul in marriage, but repeated reptilian allusions and vigorous anathemas against the unredeemable villain do not conduce to a satisfying psychological study according to realistic conventions. Grandcourt is far inferior as a creation to Tito Melema of *Romola* and belongs in the contemporary mode of American romance, if not in the Gothic novel. Gwendolen is better as a sustained psychological study, but not much is gained by it to mark an advance beyond Rosamond Vincy of *Middlemarch*; both are figures of the low mimetic mode, rendered incapable by their egoism of grasping the busy world of action and idea around them. In short, the "Gwendolen" story works well as an exhibition of the world that Daniel rejects, but that exhibition is not free of the charge of satiric reduction, if not of virulent distortion. For the Grandcourts and Gascoignes and Arrowpoints make so shabby a showing that even a non-Victorian is led to resent the abuse hurled at genteel English society.

What redeems the unremitting dissection of the dominant culture in *Daniel Deronda* is its progressive revelation of a philosophic stance on which that severe judgment is formed. A crescendo—both of denunciation and of theoretical implication—is reached in the grand scene at Monk's Topping—or the Abbey, as the Mallinger estate is called—which marks the beginning of book five: "Mordecai." In this, the thirty-fifth of seventy chapters, a turning point is reached that both completes the initial account of a moribund society and opens the way for prophecy of the society to come. An extended quotation is required:

> They walked on the gravel across a green court, where the snow still lay in islets on the grass, and in masses on the boughs of the great cedar and the crenelated coping of the stone walls, and then into a larger court, where there was another cedar, to find the beautiful choir long ago turned into stables, in the first instance perhaps after an impromptu fashion by troopers, who had a pious satisfaction in insulting the priests of Baal and the images of Ashtoreth, the queen of heaven. . . . it had still a scarcely disturbed aspect of antique solemnity, which gave the scene in the interior rather a startling effect; though, ecclesiastical or reverential indignation apart, the eyes could hardly help dwelling with pleasure on its piquant picturesqueness. Each finely-arched chapel was turned into a stall, where in the dusty glazing of the windows there still gleamed patches of crimson, orange, blue, and palest violet; for the rest, the choir had been gutted, the floor levelled, paved, and drained according to the most approved fashion, and a line of loose-boxes erected in the middle: a soft light fell from the upper windows on sleek brown or grey flanks and haunches; on mild equine faces looking out with active nostrils over the varnished brown boarding; on the hay hanging from racks where the saints once looked down from the altar-pieces, . . . and on four ancient angels, still showing signs of devotion like mutilated martyrs—while over all, the grand pointed roof, untouched by reforming wash, showed its lines and colours mysteriously through veiling shadow and cobweb, and a hoof now and then striking against the boards seemed to fill the vault with thunder, while outside there was the answering bay of the bloodhounds.
> "Oh, this is glorious!" Gwendolen burst forth. . . . "This *is* glorious! Only I wish there were a horse in every one of the boxes. I would ten times rather have these stables than those at Diplow."[4]

At such a pass, we might be prepared to say farewell, tender little parasite —grow green in your pursuit of power, prestige, and possession—but we would not have named the glories that Gwendolen has missed. These are not primarily or inherently religious, any more than they are simply esthetic. Although the scene speaks for itself in deploring the crass appropriation of the national heritage in behalf of the frivolous and sadistic pursuits of the aristocracy—the "time-honoured British resource of 'killing something'" (x, 134)—its precise effect is delivered by a symbolic drama. The "gutted" choir, the "mild equine faces," and the "four ancient angels, . . . mutilated martyrs" are set against the bloodhounds, carriers of the rapacity that characterizes their masters. There is even a sort of dialogue or antiphony between the two animate clusters: the hoofs "seemed to fill the vault with thunder, while outside there was the answering bay of the bloodhounds." What are these symbolic agents saying? One cannot be categorical about this, but the horses' thunder speaks of lofty discontent with a nation given to false gods and impious pursuits, while the baying answers with the voice of Grandcourt, the Mallingers (pregnant name!), and, alas, Gwendolen Harleth. When Daniel bares his head in reverence of the scene, Grandcourt sneers, "Do you take off your hat to the horses?" and he answers, "Why not?"

Small wonder that modern critics, lovers of "the stubborn sense of self, the personal *élan*," have found "Daniel Charisi" uncomfortable reading. For this is a profoundly partisan and at times declamatory work, an indictment not merely of the manners of the Victorian upper classes but of the spiritual poverty of modern Western culture. It remains, however, to identify that party to which George Eliot belongs—whether or not we enjoy its program or her provocations.

Matthew Arnold's term, "Philistinism," has been observed at work in this novel—in the epigraphs, narrative idiom, and closing chorus—but the fitness of his terminology and of the culture criticism it conveys has yet to be savored. As Barbara Hardy notes in her edition, the term covers a major subject in the "English" half of the text: "The novel is very much concerned with the question of true and false culture and the relation of culture to social and individual morality" (page 886). Hardy all but touches the related point that a novel poised on an opposition between a debased English culture and the vision of a revived Jewish one will readily derive its metaphors—perhaps even its narrative structure—from the biblical topos of Philistines and Israelites. She does, however, invoke the "long-standing nonconformist equation of [the Philistines] with false values and false gods, particularly relevant in a novel where the associations can be remade in allusion to actual Jews." If we make explicit the implied equations, we shall find the Jews of the novel the descendants of the Israelites, standing in opposition to the English equivalents of their ancestral enemies, the Philistines.

It becomes possible to read "Daniel Charisi" as a fictional enactment of some of the oppositions set out in *Culture and Anarchy* seven years before its publication. Less known than Arnold's famous opposition between Hebraism and Hellenism (which terms are not in question here) is his classification of the British by sociocultural types: Barbarians, Philistines, and Populace. Of these, the middle classes or Philistines are characterized by their resistance to the humanizing influences of culture or, as Arnold's phrase making puts it, they are "the enemy of the children of light or servants of the idea"[5]—who might be called Israelites if the biblical metaphor were pursued. Although Arnold accounts for this resistance to culture as the residue of Puritan antiintellectualism in the nonconformist bourgeoisie, he reserves his greatest scorn for the aristocracy or Barbarians, who have never risen to a principled antiintellectualism and who are characterized by "the passion for field-sports." Overriding his distinction between Barbarians and Philistines, Arnold emphasizes their common pursuit of the principle of individualism, which he labels "doing as one likes." After two chapters devoted to tracing the origins of this principle in the nonconformist tradition—whose slogan is "The Dissidence of Dissent and the Protestantism of the Protestant religion"—Arnold traces the principle even further back, to the roots of aristocracy: "The Barbarians brought with them that staunch individualism, as the modern phrase is, and that passion for doing as one likes, for the assertion of personal liberty, which appears to Mr. Bright the central idea of English life, and of which we have, at any rate, a very rich supply" (iii, 102).

It is to this proudly English individualism, bourgeois and aristocratic together, that Arnold opposes the values of culture, not as an esthetic withdrawal from the crude world but as a civilizing force that has not yet completed its work. In a summary passage, he juxtaposes culture with Philistinism/Barbarism in a way that returns us to "Daniel Charisi":

> But in each class there are born a certain number of natures with a curiosity about their best self, with a bent for seeing things as they are, for disentangling themselves from machinery, for simply concerning themselves with reason and the will of God, and doing their best to make these prevail;—for the pursuit, in a word, of perfection. . . . culture being the true nurse of the pursuing love, and sweetness and light the true character of the pursued perfection. Natures with this bent emerge in all classes,—among the Barbarians, among the Philistines, among the Populace. And this bent always tends to take them out of their class, and to make their distinguishing characteristic not their Barbarianism or their Philistinism, but their *humanity*. They have, in general, a rough time of it in their lives. (iii, 108)

And, we may add, in their fictional lives, too, for "Daniel Charisi" is nothing other than the story of such a—to give it Arnold's name—genius: "To certain manifestations of this love for perfection mankind have accustomed themselves to give the name of genius; implying, by this name, something original and heaven-bestowed in the passion" (iii, 108).

The universal resistance to geniuses in fiction would be enough to account for the nervous remarks that have been made about Daniel ever since Henry James'—Henry James'!—subtle sneers at his manhood. But James' corresponding pleasure in Gwendolen and the Philistine part of the novel —with "its deep, rich English tone"—derives from a more interesting and more historically determinate cause. For Gwendolen, too, is a historical study, as much a demonstration of what happens to people under the impress of a cultural ideology as Daniel and Mordecai are exponents of a counterculture. Her ideology is simply that of "doing as one likes," which Arnold had balefully denominated the "central idea of English life." Eliot sees to it that Gwendolen is quite explicit in her pronouncements of this ideology; when under assault by Grandcourt's propositions of marriage, she reacts against the inevitable subjugation to his matrimonial dominance: "This subjection to a possible self, a self not to be absolutely predicted about, caused her some astonishment and terror: her favorite key of life—doing as she liked—seemed to fail her, and she could not foresee what at a given moment she might like to do. . . . was she going to fulfill her deliberate intention? She began to be afraid of herself, and to find out a certain difficulty in doing as she liked" (xiii, 173–174). The entire Gwendolen plot —her predominant motivations, the conflict of wills in her marriage, and the questions about unconscious wish-fulfillment in her failure to save Grandcourt from drowning—both the psychic and the overt action hinge on a critique of the ideology of doing as one likes.

Gwendolen's career may be read as a systematic study of the difficulty of knowing what one likes, of doing it when associated with others who do only what they like, and of the ironic and belated discovery that best rewards are obtained from doing what others like (or, at least, what may be good for others). While she may be an interesting dramatic enactment of the Philistine impulse and its breakdown in practice, Grandcourt may serve as an allegory (or gargoyle) of the liberal ideology erected into a way of life. His tawdry sadism is creditable only as a reduction to the absurd of the individualist ethos: the pleasure not simply in doing as one likes but in doing it at the cost of others' *not* doing as they like. It would be too much to claim that Eliot indicts in the person of Grandcourt the competitive and utilitarian strain dominant in Victorian society, but he does suggest the perfect adjustment of the aristocratic or Barbarian class to the prevailing ideology of the time.

Another watchword of Grandcourt's requires attention in an assessment of Eliot's ideological critique. For him, marriage is a contract, and the use of this word by a man given neither to the sanctity of marriage (or of anything else) nor to excessive legalism supports a variant reading of the term's connotations. Here is the *locus classicus* of his doctrine:

> And Grandcourt might have pleaded that he was perfectly justified in taking care that his wife should fulfill the obligations she had accepted. Her marriage was a contract where all the ostensible advantages were on her side. . . . he had won her by the rank and luxuries he had to give her, and these she had got: he had fulfilled his side of the contract.
>
> And Gwendolen, we know, was thoroughly aware of the situation. She could not excuse herself by saying that there had been a tacit part of the contract on her side—namely, that she meant to rule and have her own way. (liv, 732)

What is at stake here, although not directly invoked, is the contract theory of the state that accompanies the ideology of individualism, laissez-faire, and utilitarianism (in some of its aspects). This philosophy of government is ornamented by the greatest names in British thought from Hobbes and Locke to the pundits of the present Labour party (although there was some debate on whether its recent, lamented "social contract" with the trade unions was really a "social compact"). It is also the prime target of the countermovement that descends from Burke and takes in some of the greatest British novelists on its way, including Scott, Eliot, and Conrad.[6] The tenets of the contract theory, aside from debating points made in connection with the claims for popular sovereignty in the civil wars and later political crises, come down to these: what really exists are individuals and, concomitantly, the state is only a fiction or an instrument created by those individuals; the initial act (either temporally or logically) in establishing the state is the contractual surrender of part of the individual's otherwise absolute rights to the state, for purposes of maintaining the peace and for the common benefits that flow from it; the tenuous balance of society rests on this legal fiction that individuals are artificially associated by a contract which keeps them from perpetual war on each other, as their original rights would allow. Small wonder, then, that Grandcourt, like other great individuals, becomes especially incensed by his wife's failure to keep up her part of the marriage contract—the social contract *in nuce*—for he has made the disagreeable surrender of his rightful wish to be her absolute master in mind and body and contents himself with exerting only the mastery which the contractual system allows him. This is the "deep, rich English tone" that prevails in the "Gwendolen Harleth" part of the novel, and readers who share the assumptions of a contract theory of society, of individualism, and of "doing as one likes" have a particular satisfaction in it.

George Eliot joins Matthew Arnold among the embattled Victorian proponents of the contrary view of the state as a collective entity, with the individual relegated to a derivative status in metaphysical and social reality –an aberrant status unless connected to the nurturant organs of the collective body.[7] There are differences, of course: Arnold's organicism derives from Burke and Coleridge, while Eliot draws from Continental (mainly Comtean) sources. The most significant difference between them is the vigor of Eliot's nationalism for, though Arnold responded to Celtic and other regional strains in poetry, he was antagonistic to the least jingoistic stirring in British public life. Eliot, while sharing his ear for cant and his cosmopolitan perspective in art and scholarship, was sympathetic with national causes. She finds her place in the tradition of Romantics from Wordsworth to Conrad who approve of nationalism as a repository of organic values–although they remain sensitive to some of its depredations in war and empire.

Where Eliot is closest to Arnold is in her sense of the collective body as an improvement–and as an improving influence–on the lone individual. Compare Arnold, in a chapter entitled "Doing as One Likes": "By our every day selves, however, we are separate, personal, at war. . . . But by our *best self* we are united, impersonal, at harmony. We are in no peril from giving authority to this, because it is the truest friend we all of us can have. . . . We want an authority, and we find nothing but jealous classes, checks, and a deadlock; culture suggests the idea of *the State*. . . . *the State*, or organ of our collective best self, of our national right reason" (ii, 95–97). And Eliot: "What has grown up historically can only die out historically, by the gradual operation of necessary laws. The external conditions which society has inherited from the past are but the manifestation of inherited internal conditions in the human beings who compose it; the internal conditions and the external are related to each other as the organism and its medium, and development can take place only by the gradual consentaneous development of both."[8] While the relation of individual to group is of a moral and intellectual kind in Arnold and of a historical and quasi-biological kind in Eliot (following Riehl), the hierarchy of value and social power is the same for both: the ego opposes but the collectivity disposes.

One could not find a body of ideas better calculated to put off modern readers when used as the ethical burden and esthetic program of a work of art. Whether George Eliot succeeds in embodying her ideas has been much debated (although the ideas themselves have not, to my knowledge, been accurately described). It would seem unlikely that *any* manifestation of such ideas could win the imaginative sympathy of James, Leavis, and others focused on the personal life. Attempts to cover Eliot's impertinence with an aura of sanctity–like U. C. Knoepflmacher's suggestion that she was turning toward religion in her declining years and that her last novel was pervaded by religious yearnings[9]–can only muddy the waters. George Eliot projects an extension of organicist thought into which many readers, weary of the horrors of nationalism, will be unwilling to follow her. In place of

Arnold's *state* as an instrument of social harmony and culture—in place of *religion* as a collective idealism, ultimately worshiping the idea of the human community itself (the idea of religion which Eliot derived from Feuerbach and never entirely abandoned)—our novelist substitutes the *nation* as the ideal object of loyalty and the guarantor of whatever salvation human beings can hope for.

A common response to Eliot's national ideal is that of a critic who finds the novel's denouement wanting because it anticipates hopeful results from Daniel's emigration and from the Zionist movement: "The treatment of Mordecai and the Jews, of course, is hopelessly superficial, and no attempt is made to deal with the very confusing political implications of Jewish nationalism. . . . one wonders what Deronda would have made of the illiberal fanaticism which often becomes a part of such campaigns."[10] This suspicion of nationalism's "illiberal fanaticism" is given a special piquancy by the tone of an English critic undoubtedly alive to the "confusing political implications" which Zionism exhibited during the British mandate in Palestine and under attack by neighboring Arab states. Eliot's treatment of the Jews, given her scholarly preparation and her imaginative sympathy, will be shown to be as profound and detailed as her treatment of other social groups; at the present juncture it need only be said that she knew very well the "confusing political implications" of nationalism and strongly supported the national ideal without undue fear of its becoming "illiberal fanaticism."

It is well known that Eliot wrote an essay, roughly contemporary with *Daniel Deronda*, in behalf of the Jews, or more precisely against anti-Semitism and for a Zionist-type solution to the Jewish problem. Bernard Paris has seen beyond these allegiances and shown that the argument of the essay—"The Modern Hep! Hep! Hep!" (an anti-Semitic slur roughly equivalent to "here comes a kike")—takes the Jews as an illustration of the larger theme of nationalism.[11] Paris' exposition of the value of nationalism in Eliot's scheme of things is wanting in only one respect: it should be noted that her organicist version of the concept of nationhood was a critique of the prevailing liberal/individualist orthodoxy. The targets of her attack are evident in the essay itself, albeit on its last page:

> A modern book on Liberty has maintained that from the freedom of individual men to persist in idiosyncrasies the world may be enriched. Why should we not apply this argument to the idiosyncrasy of a nation, and pause in our haste to hoot it down? There is still a great function for the steadfastness of the Jew: not that he should shut out the utmost illumination which knowledge can throw on his national history, but that he should cherish the store of inheritance which that history has left him.

... the effective bound of human action is feeling, and the worthy child of a people owning the triple name of Hebrew, Israelite, and Jew, feels his kinship with the glories and the sorrows, the degradation and the possible renovation of his national family.

Will any one teach the nullification of this feeling and call his doctrine a philosophy? He will teach a blinding superstition—the superstition that a theory of human well-being can be constructed in disregard of the influences which have made us human.[12]

The "modern book on Liberty" is of course John Stuart Mill's, and the "theory of human well-being" that disregards feeling, tradition, and the other "influences which have made us human" is utilitarianism. Eliot's critique is hardly to be distinguished from that of Dickens, Ruskin, and other late Romantic prophets of sentiment, local custom, and the wisdom of the heart—who are wrongly considered conservatives and may better be referred to as *populists* in political expression. The marked extension of Eliot's version of the antiutilitarian theme lies not in her instancing the Jews as late Wordsworthian creatures of suffering and endurance but in her conception of entire nations under rubrics ordinarily reserved for peasant communities (like Cumberland crofters) or tribes apart (like Sleary's circus).

Eliot extends the idea of Romantic organicism in one other way, and this fillip may lead us to a sphere in which the central issues in the novel are played out. The relation of individuals to society is, in Mill, treated negatively: individual deviation from the norm may be a social benefit; therefore diversity is to be encouraged through removal of conformist restraints on free expression. But Eliot sees the relation, in the Riehl essay, as a more complex one which is best expressed by organic metaphors. Taking up Mill's idea of the utilitarian value of individual idiosyncrasy in the national sphere, Eliot syllogistically amplifies it into an analogous argument for the value of national idiosyncrasy in the total human community. When she argues that the Jews can make a contribution to humanity if they are different from other nations, and that therefore their distinctness ought to be encouraged, she is not taking a *parti pris* for Zionism any more than she is enchanting us with the prospect of unique tourist opportunities in a folkloric Israel. She suggests that the human community is an organic unity of its separate members, just as the nation is the organic union of its constituent individuals. Further, the "members" of the human race are its nations, and the benefits of their "development can take place only by the gradual consentaneous development of both" (as in "The Natural History of German Life"). These are the ideas which Mordecai espouses in "Daniel Charisi" (especially at xlii, 585 and 595) and when they are found unconvincing it is not the excesses of a fanatic that are uncomfortably exposed but the central thought of the author herself. Whether the presence of such ideas in fiction can be justified, or whether this particular evocation of ideas is esthetically successful, can be left to the judgment of novel readers conditioned by Dostoyevsky, Mann, and Proust—to cite only three novelists given to lengthy exposition of questionable philosophical ideas.

While the provenance of a character's ideas in his creator's thought is no more—and no less—significant an esthetic fact than that character's origin in the imagination, the close association of so repellent a character with his creator is one to conjure with. Little approbation can be expected to be gained by showing that Mordecai speaks for Eliot and that she designed him as an estimable literary invention—the manifestation of a biblical prophet on the streets of modern London. For Mordecai is repellent, there can be no doubt; he is febrile for one thing, and has an idée fixe, and is close to despair but keeps alive an unreasonable hope, and makes no effort to adjust to his surroundings—indeed, to act like an ordinary creature of fiction, let alone of society.

The deficiencies will not be redeemed by knowledge of Eliot's model for Mordecai, the German-Jewish émigré Emanuel Deutsch, who taught her Hebrew and much else from his enormous store of theological and philological learning.[13] Yet there is something to be learned from her letter to Deutsch, during the time of his declining health and before his final voyage to the East:

> My dear Rabbi [i.e., teacher, not necessarily religious]
> I have heard from others that you are "better" and "very well," but I want to have an account of you from yourself. Since I wrote to you last I have been ailing and in the Slough of Despond too, and am only just emerging. . . . Hopelessness has been to me, all through my life, but especially in painful years of my youth, the chief source of wasted energy with all the consequent bitterness of regret. Remember, it has happened to many to be glad they did not commit suicide, though they once ran for the final leap, or as Mary Wolstonecraft did, wetted their garments well in the rain hoping to sink the better when they plunged. . . . She lived to know some real joys, and death came in time to hinder the joys from being spoiled.
> Which things are a parable.[14]

What is perhaps most remarkable about Eliot's frank personal identification with Deutsch's despair—and her evocation of Mirah's suicidal actions in chapter xvii—is the beautiful tone of equality in this letter. Although mingling notes of respectful attention to her "Rabbi" and of gentle concern, as for an ailing child, Eliot writes as woman of the world to man of the world, as troubled intellectual to troubled intellectual, as resigned sufferer to not-yet-resigned sufferer. Although Deutsch had lived in England some sixteen years, had acquired a reputation for specialized scholarship after his *Quarterly Review* article on the Talmud, and was received in both fashionable and academic circles, his was not a striking instance of rapid assimilation. Yet Eliot expects that he will understand when she closes her letter, "We had thought of going to Scotland next month, but we shall not do so, my health not being strong enough for me to incur the fatigues of the journey and the literary mob." Which things are a parable. For Eliot ranges herself with the Mary Wollstonecrafts and Emanuel Deutsches of the world, not with the "literary mob," and her affinity is not simply with the Jews but with the alienated intellectuals and artists, the perennial outsiders in the dominant culture of her time.

Mordecai's idea of the organic relation of the smaller to the greater social unit may only partially be accounted to Eliot's usual intellectual resources. Feuerbach suggested a concept (derived from Hegel) of humanity as a philosophic whole and laid the religions of the world under individual contribution to its developing self-consciousness. Yet here Judaism is assigned a lower role by its worship of nature, of the separate tribe, and of "Utilism" —as Eliot translates.[15] Comte's positivism elaborated a coherent idea of humanity and employed organicist terminology (without disturbing its essentially rationalistic and even mechanistic form of thought). But Comte laid little stress on the diversified workings of the nations, envisaging instead a uniform development independent of their unique traits. It becomes necessary to seek beyond Eliot's normal intellectual affinities to find an idea of the potential Jewish contribution to humanity cognate with that espoused by Mordecai and Theophrastus Such.

Such an idea was elaborated in a book published in 1862 by Moses Hess, one of the forerunners of the Zionist movement. In *Rome and Jerusalem: The Last Nationality Question*, Hess described his growing awareness of anti-Semitism, his withdrawal from an assimilated (and early socialist) career, and his discovery of meanings in Jewish history of potential value to humanity at large:

> Our people not only created the noblest religion of the ancient world, a religion for civilized people, but have continued to develop this religion, keeping pace with the progress of the human spirit. . . . And this mission will remain with the Jews until the end of days, that is until the time when, according to the promise of our prophets, the world will be filled with the knowledge of God. . . . The "end of days" is not to be interpreted as the end of the world but as a period when the development and the education of humanity will reach their highest point. . . . we can say that Judaism is not a passive religion but an active life factor. Its history coincides with the development of humanity, and the Jews are a nation which is destined to be resurrected with the rest of the civilized nations.
>
> . . . True, the "end of days," when the knowledge of God will fill the earth, is still far off; yet we firmly believe that the time will come when

the holy spirit of our nation will become the property of humanity, and the earth will be a grand temple where the spirit of God will dwell.

. . . Signs of such readiness are appearing even now. To one who lacks the historic sense, the existence of a nation is not important to the historical development of humanity. But the organic creation of the Jewish literature of the past three thousand years grew out of the essence of Judaism. In order to create new values in Judaism we must utilize our creation of all ages.[16]

A number of points must quickly be made: (a) Hess' concepts of humanity, progress of the human spirit, and organic relation of culture to national "essence" derive from the same place—Hegel—as do those of the more sustained source for Eliot, Feuerbach; (b) Hess' version differs from Feuerbach's not only in his higher estimation of the Jewish contribution but in his sense of the continued distinctness of the nations that will join in the "end of days," the age of humanity's self-consciousness; (c) the historical process sketched by Hess is not reducible to a series of Hegelian or Feuerbachian stages through which humanity passes in its growth but is closer to a biblical view of history, seizing not only on "the promise of our prophets" but on the synthetic growth of Jewish culture with that of other nations ("I believe that the divine teaching of the Jewish genius was never completed, but is undergoing an organic development which is based on the process of 'harmonizing of the Jewish genius with that of life and humanity'"); (d) along with his prophetic ecumenicalism,[17] Hess takes from the Bible a catastrophic view of history, with its associated themes of winnowing and return of the remnant: the assimilated Jew "will be shattered by a blow from without by world events which are already being prepared and will fall upon him in the near future. . . . After this catastrophe Israel will find its legitimate place in universal history"; (e) Hess is closest to Eliot in his condemnation not of assimilationist Jews or of slavish Hegelians but of those described above as utilitarian-individualist-liberal: "The modern idea of anti-national humanitarianism asserts only a uniform inorganic mechanism and is against real humanitarianism as it does not foster co-operativeness but rather destruction of organs or nations, which otherwise could be unified in a brotherhood. It is against these destructive forces that I appeal to the original national power of Judaism, which expresses the living creative force in universal history." If we take these vaunts of Judaism's spiritual power at face value, a certain megalomania shows up in Hess, as it does in Mordecai; but if we acknowledge the immediate context of these claims —the prevailing ideologies, whether Hegelian or utilitarian, which denigrate nationalism in their search for human uniformity—then their stridency carries an urgent appeal for national survival.

While Eliot's organic conception of the nation has its roots in a broad intellectual tradition, her application of this doctrine to the Jewish nation derives from a Hegelian strain that reaches articulation most vividly in Hess. There were, however, in the same period, a number of non-Hegelian, non-Jewish racial theorists who posit a similar relation between the Semites and the rest of humanity. Eliot is known to have read Ernest Renan and Adolphe Pictet in preparation for the novel,[18] and both exhibit a philological and historical approach strongly marked by late nineteenth-century racialist thinking. In Renan's 1864 inaugural address on assuming the chair of Semitic languages at the Collège de France, he credits the Semites with a prime and almost unique contribution to humanity: "Nous leur devons la religion. Le monde entier, si l'on excepte l'Inde, la Chine, le Japon et les peuples tout à fait sauvages, a adopté les religions sémitiques. Le monde civilisé ne compte que des juifs, des chrétiens, ou des musulmans." To Christianity, considered as a self-adaptation of Judaism to develop qualities opposite to its defects, Renan accords a special role, in language strikingly like Eliot's: ". . . Jésus fonda la religion éternelle de l'humanité. . . . Le centre féconde où l'humanité devait pendant des siècles rapporter ses joies, ses espérances, ses consolations, ses motifs de bien faire, était constitué."

Pictet's view of the Semitic role in humanity's future is different, while his assumptions about racial contributions are similar to Renan's: "Sans doute, les Hébreux, ces fidèles gardiens du pur monothéisme, ont eu dans le plan providentiel une parte magnifique, mais qu'on se demande où en serait le monde s'ils étaient restés seuls à la tête de l'humanité. . . . la Providence réservait déjà à une autre race d'hommes le rôle de continuateurs du progrès. Or, cette race était celles des Aryas, douée dès le début des qualités mêmes qui manquaient aux Hébreux pour devenir les civilisateurs du monde."[19] Pictet then proceeds to sum up the divergent racial qualities with which his ostensibly philological study of Aryan civilization is filled; they need not detain us, being the stock-in-trade of racialist mythology before and after him. What is perhaps most striking about such theorists is their agreement on the supersession of the Semites by the Aryans (or Indo-Europeans, in Renan's terms); they agree that the future belongs to those who can advance scientific technology and hold sway over empires, and these roles the Aryans are selected to perform. While there is no evidence that Eliot reacted directly against these conclusions, her vision of the future of the Jews presents a marked contrast with these important expositors of the future of the human race, or races.

Another late nineteenth-century stream of thought is echoed in Mordecai's discourse: a variant of the great-man theories that descend from German Romantic philosophy, although best known in England in their formulation by Carlyle. In an invaluable article on Eliot's sources among eight historians of the Jews, William Baker has emphasized this aspect of her dependence on Heinrich Graetz, the most important of these historians and still a major guide in Jewish studies. Although loosely characterizing Graetz'—and Mordecai's—ideas as Hegelian,[20] Baker goes on to single out what is most striking in them: "Graetz tends to look at Jewish history as consisting of powerful personalities who have been keeping Jewish history alive. . . . Spiritual forces are dominant structures in Graetz' work. He concentrates on charismatic leaders who are important carriers of these forces." And Baker nails the point home by citing Eliot's marginal note in her copy of Graetz: "Beside Graetz' explanation of these methods of preservation, George Eliot wrote in the margin, 'Transmitters' (*Geschichte der Juden*, IV, 17)." This is the ideational bridge to Mordecai's encomium of "the great Transmitters, who laboured with their hands for scant bread, but preserved and enlarged for us the heritage of memory, and saved the soul of Israel alive as a seed among the tombs" (xlii, 580).[21]

Although Mordecai's concept at this point is a historical one, singling out the poets and religious leaders who have maintained a central vision of national integrity and reconstitution, his mind is quick to turn to another kind of leader, and it is the latter which has caused most discomfort among modern readers. For Mordecai's vision is a frankly messianic one and, more embarrassing still, he locates such a figure among the men of his own generation—indeed, despite all appearances, among one of the high and mighty of the Gentiles. Annoyance often shifts to Eliot for taking such visions, credible though they may be when ascribed to a religious fanatic, as the paradigm of her novel, twisting the plot so as to allow Mordecai to fulfill his mad hopes of a redeemer—at least a potential one. Though readers may be disappointed to find a charismatic hero in the dress of an English gentleman, Mordecai himself is, surprisingly, not, and this lack of astonishment on the part of her character may yield a clue to the author's conception.

For Mordecai is actually pleased that his great man has appeared clean-shaven and cosmopolitan: "Rather, it is a precious thought to me that he has a preparation which I lacked, and is an accomplished Egyptian" (lii, 721). The unspoken comparison here is to Moses, if not to Joseph; the biblical archetype of the disguised hero ascendant in the alien kingdom, who ultimately returns to lead his own people, is here given a new imaginative life. Skeptics like Freud will ask, "Was Moses an Egyptian?" and skeptical readers will question the verisimilitude of the revelation of Deronda's Jewish birth; but practiced mythologues will see nothing unduly remarkable in a late literary displacement of a widespread archetype.[22] Moreover, the language of the revelation scene clearly indicates that Eliot was consciously working in a mythological mode, mixing figures of folklore, literary prototypes, and religious symbols in her portrayal of Daniel's mother[23] so as to create the appropriate esthetic medium for the emergence of a hero in our times.

If we take the short step that opens Mordecai's vision and Daniel's character to mythological interpretation, we may be willing to go the extra mile toward a biblical context for these unlikely protagonists. For what other novel presents us with a title figure whose name is Daniel, accompanied by a herald or forerunner whose name is "really" Ezra? The biblical overtones of these names are not absent from the text; when Daniel thinks his quest for Mirah's brother ends with the pawnbroker, Ezra Cohen, he is "half inclined to decide that he would not increase his knowledge about that modern Ezra, who was certainly not a leader among his people" (xxxiii, 435). In the course of Daniel's discovery that Mordecai is Mirah's brother, the prophetic name attaches itself to the latter with accelerating force as he reveals in passing that his name is Ezra:

> "Ezra!" exclaimed Deronda, unable to contain himself.
> "Ezra," repeated Mordecai, affirmatively. . . . "I opened the letter [from mother] and the name came again as a cry that would have disturbed me in the bosom of heaven, and made me yearn to reach where that sorrow was.—'Ezra, my son!'" (xliii, 601)

The highlighting of the name is invested with a significance beyond plot revelation, but that significance can be specified only in relation to Daniel and his eponyms.

Ezra, the founder of historical Judaism, as he has been called, was scribe and priest in the Palestinian community restored after the defeat of Babylon by Cyrus of Persia. Although dating is still a matter at issue (ranging from 458 to 397 B.C.), authorities are more certain of his influence: "He is also thought to have been the first to introduce into Palestine the synagogue—and with it the public reading and explanation of the Law—the institution which has been the heart of the religious life of the Jewish people to the present time."[24] Daniel, on the other hand, remains a name surrounded by mysteries, not the least of which derives from its appearance in a text and in a context far removed from the book of the Old Testament which it heads. The book of Daniel "purports to be an autobiography of a person living in Babylon from 605 B.C.," but "for various reasons this long-puzzling book is . . . ascribed by modern liberal scholars to the years 167–165 B.C., when the Syrian king, Antiochus IV . . . attempted with fiendish severity to Hellenize the Jews and thus gave occasion for such cryptic writing." The cryptic key to Daniel's miracles in the courts of Nebuchadnezzar and his successors is thus their reflection on the resistance of the Jews to Hellenization at a later time. His interpretation of the king's dream, the fiery furnace, the handwriting on the wall, and the lion's den are all exploits of a leader capable of rallying his people not merely with signs of God's favor but with his own intellectual resourcefulness and absolute faith. Finally, in Daniel's dream of the four beasts, we find a messianic prophecy that directly feeds the hopes not only of Jews but of Christians—through its salient use of the term "Son of man" and its unique Old Testament instances of the term "Messiah."

But in a book of the Apocrypha, written only slightly later than the book of Daniel, another figure of that name becomes a hero of what we may call personal integrity and the protection of innocence. For, when Susanna is accused by the elders in such a way as to preclude any fate but stoning for alleged adultery, she is able to raise a personal redeemer by her call: "And the Lord heard her voice. Therefore when she was led to be put to death, the Lord raised up the holy spirit of a young youth, whose name was Daniel: Who cried with a loud voice, I am clear from the blood of this woman"– that is, denying complicity in the public sanction against her. Then, using the time-honored resources of the folk hero in exposing the bearers of false witness, he elicits the truth and saves the justified wife. This Daniel exemplifies faith in the word of the pure in heart as he demands investigation of the heart's inner reaches in order to find the truth: "Are ye such fools, ye sons of Israel, that without examination or knowledge of the truth ye have condemned a daughter of Israel?"

It is easy to see how these two knights of faith would recommend themselves to Eliot in naming her contemporary heroes–although there is room for debate on the application of any specific aspect of their careers to the circumstances of the plot (the correlation of Susanna and Gwendolen seems the closest approximation). More exacting, but nonetheless requisite, is the interpretation of Daniel's surname. Deronda, being merely a reference to the Spanish town where his Jewish forebears may have located in their exile, is quickly cast off as an accouterment of the Diaspora. Charisi is the family name–as much in the maternal as in the paternal line, his parents being cousins. A hint of the Christian virtue of charity attaches to the transliteration, but the Hebrew word has other burdens. The noun כָּרֵת means "extermination" or "destruction" and refers in the Bible to the separation from God inflicted on those who sin against divine law; in its more general application it takes in the state of being cut off, divided, or buried, implying the separation of the individual from his community. Although this meaning of Charisi (the -i ending being the first-person singular possessive form, i.e., "my alienation") is a fair description of the negative state in which Daniel finds himself in his separation from his nation, another possible root of the name suggests its positive locus.

For an additional biblical term enters Daniel's iconography: "And the word of the Lord came unto [Elijah], saying, Get thee hence, and turn thee eastward, and hide thyself by the brook Cherith, that is before Jordan. And it shall be, that thou shalt drink of the brook; and I have commanded the ravens to feed thee there" (1 Kings 17:2–4). This powerful injunction is full of promise for the poetic imagination: Milton recalls it to Christ's mind during his dream in *Paradise Regained*, as a place in which God feeds his prophet:

Him thought, he by the Brook of *Cherith* stood
And saw the ravens with their horny beaks
Food to *Elijah* bringing Even and Morn,

. . . .

Sometimes that with *Elijah* he partook,
Or as a guest with *Daniel* at his pulse.[25]

Ruskin, on the other hand, finds the setting itself full of interest; in the chapter on medieval landscape in *Modern Painters*, he discusses the "idea of sanctity attached to rocky wilderness," with Cherith as a prime example: "Men acquainted with the history of Moses, alone at Horeb, or with Israel at Sinai,—or Elijah by the brook Cherith, . . . were not likely to look with irreverent or unloving eyes upon the blue hills that girded their golden horizon." In these versions, the *place* of divine sustenance tends to be detached from the activity and becomes a generalized term—a metonym rather than a metaphor—for the promised land. In Jewish tradition, the name acquired the general connotation of a place of refuge and, when attached to a person, suggested one who hides in such a place by divine command—e.g., the medieval Spanish poet, Judah Charizi, whose name probably suggested Eliot's nomenclature.[26] Unmistakable in these variant readings is the power of the name to suggest a promised redemption, whether the sustenance be Elijah's manna or Daniel's winy "pulse" (Daniel 1:12).

The inevitable result of such applications of biblical types and Semitic philology to a well-known English novel is to make it seem foreign. Foreign to whom? The "English" part of the novel is impervious to such alienation and is approved by Anglo-Saxon readers of whatever critical persuasion. The "Jewish" part was lauded by Jewish scholars and Eliot was gratified by their approbation. Who can be in possession of the whole novel, see the relation between "the Jewish element" and "English Social life," and confirm the novel's much argued unity? It is my contention that the novel is indeed unified, but not as a harmony—rather as a conflict of antagonistic forces between which we are asked to choose. Its drama is describable in the terms Eliot used to characterize Harriet Beecher Stowe's novel of slavery, *Dred*: ". . . that *conflict of races* which Augustin Thierry has pointed out as the great source of romantic interest—witness 'Ivanhoe.'"[27] In its English side, the novel comes down squarely against one of the contending parties: the English are the equivalents of the Normans of Scott and the slavers of Stowe. This is unfortunate; while its broad description of upper-class manners may be accountable to the facts, its satire of English Philistinism is as tendentious as its grotesque portrait of Grandcourt. But Eliot was not in a mood to be fair; the darkening vision which some readers have found in her later work here rises to a prophetic pitch in excoriating English society. In antithesis, Eliot erects an alternative cultural ideal and, unable to magnify it in the person of the artist Klesmer alone, she envisions an entire race as the potential carriers of that culture. The final question one may ask of "Daniel Charisi" is whether it can sustain the burden of Eliot's utopian vision of a nation, the Jews, as embodying her cultural ideals.

The ending of the novel has been much derided; the comment perhaps freest of personal distaste is Graham Martin's:

> Where does the world of Deronda's extensive aspirations offer a strong, imaginative challenge to the one he has to leave? The answer surely is that it never does. Underlying all the links and parallels which draw the two stories into significant relationship there is a more powerful imaginative logic drawing them apart. There are a number of reasons for this. The outsider-critics (Deronda, Mordecai) are not only Jews, but European Jews, who look elsewhere than England for their origins. . . . Withdrawn, meditative, without any of the settled purposes or desires which make the basis of predominantly "social" characterization, Deronda is a wanderer, a man in the making, whose energies only crystallize at the very end of the novel. . . . The choice of Zionism has the effect of removing the ideal aspirations associated with Deronda from any effective engagement with the English scene.[28]

In response to such incisive negative criticism as this, one is tempted to reply, exactly! and that is the point of the novel. After her shadowy disengagement from provincial society at the end of *Middlemarch*—which Martin also holds up to mild rebuke—Eliot comes in this work to disengage from England. It is not simply that the English have been found unforgivable when measured against, e.g., the artist Klesmer: "His foibles of arrogance and vanity did not exceed such as may be found in the best English families" (xxii, 282). It is rather that, as he acknowledges, English Philistinism offers no scope for a revival of true culture, given the prevailing ideology of liberal individualism. Little wonder that a Mr. Bult, "an esteemed party man who . . . had the general solidity and suffusive pinkness of a healthy Briton on the central table-land of life," is "a little amazed at an after-dinner outburst of Klesmer's on the lack of idealism in English politics, which left all mutuality between distant races to be determined simply by the need of a market" (xxii, 283). Mr. Bult's response—grasping at the notion that Klesmer's is a purely political view—is to call him a Panslavist; the musician (that is what his name means in Yiddish) delivers as rejoinder, "No; my name is Elijah. I am the Wandering Jew" (xxii, 284). We cannot take this as an expression of racial identification with the Jews, any more than we can take his fiancée's apologetic "He looks forward to a fusion of races" as a full statement of his views. For Klesmer seizes as his symbol a traditional figure of alienation, of eternal quest, and of exclusion from the social life of Western nations.

If so much is true, that the artist finds an adequate symbol of his alienation from the dominant culture in the figure of the Wandering Jew, it is not
far to a complementary hypothesis: the figure of the Jew in the novel is a
symbol of the artist's condition in Western society. By this interpretation,
one would not wish to diminish the immediate weight of the symbol, its
concrete particularity, and its striking insight into both the actual condition of the Jews and their possibilities of national revival. But, if this were
simply "George Eliot's Zionist novel," it would remain an excrescence at
the end of her career instead of being the fulfillment of the line of idealistic
aspiration from *The Mill on the Floss* to *Middlemarch*. The view I wish to
take—without stinting the novel's special tone or subject matter—is that
Zionism is a metaphor for the pursuit of a higher culture and that by this
ideal the culture of England is judged and found wanting. From this it becomes inevitable that "there is a more powerful imaginative logic drawing
[the two stories] apart," that the "outsider-critics . . . look elsewhere than
England for their origins," and that "the choice of Zionism has the effect
of removing the ideal aspirations associated with Deronda from any effective engagement with the English scene."

Part of the resistance to the novel's conclusion in emigration derives
from an understandable distaste for the sweeping rebuke of England and its
culture that is delivered by the same stroke. A share in the critical dises-
teem is, however, reserved for the lack of realism involved in the gesture;
Deronda is seen not as going to another place on earth but as taking straight
off for the clouds. The view is a sophisticated one, basing itself on the belief that so little was known of Palestine at the time of the novel that a
character's self-exile there was roughly the equivalent of Lawrence's Arabi-
an or Rimbaud's African adventures and, thus, out of place at the end of
a realist fiction. Unfortunately, this view is mistaken, given the evidence
not only of Eliot's own learning but of the general audience's grasp of
Palestine's contemporary condition. For many Victorians, Palestine was
not merely a biblical abstraction but a living survival of their religious history. It was not only the Jews who longed to visit there but the most important figures in the English church, leading statesmen (not only Disraeli
but Gladstone), and the more advanced minds among the wealthy and
noble. Eliot's knowledge of Palestinian geography and the current conditions of life in that country derived not only from the Jewish historian
Salomon Munk but also from the dean of Westminster, A. P. Stanley; her
sense of Jewish history and the nation's present state of affairs came to her
not only from the eight historians described by Baker but from the former
dean of St. Paul's, H. H. Milman.[29] Moreover, the notion of Daniel's going
off to Palestine to "do something for the Jews" was not quite so vague; land
in Palestine was already being acquired by Sir Moses Montefiore, proto-
Zionist groups were already in the field, and the first agricultural settlement was founded shortly after, in 1878.

It would seem that a measure of resistance to the conclusion must inevitably derive from its storybook atmosphere. But which storybook? It is true, as the astuter critics have observed, that Daniel is lucky; a later avatar of the seekers in all the Eliot novels, he chances on what they fail to find —a spiritual community, a vocation, an ideal cause amid the constricted opportunities for heroism in the modern world. Eliot does not stint the marks of fairy-tale romance in the denouement; Daniel's visit to Joseph Kalonymos, the guardian of his grandfather's chest, is executed with full application of its obvious parallels in myth and legend. Nevertheless, Daniel's subsequent description of the hidden treasure brings it out of its allegorical mode into a historical concreteness we can take seriously:

> . . . I come of a strain that has ardently maintained the fellowship
> of our race—a line of Spanish Jews that has borne many students and
> men of practical power. And I possess what will give us a sort of com-
> munion with them. My grandfather, Daniel Charisi, preserved manu-
> scripts, family records stretching far back, in the hope that they would
> pass into the hands of his grandson. . . . Some of them I can read easily
> enough—those in Spanish and Italian. Others are in Hebrew, and, I
> think, Arabic; but there seem to be Latin translations. . . . We will
> study them together. (lxiii, 817)

Daniel's hope of Mordecai's help is thwarted by the latter's death, but one can feel sure at least of this hero's ample intellectual activity after his story closes. Though his vocation seems to lead to political-Zionist channels, his avocation will surely be to further "communion" with his ancestors by tracing the ramified branches of their nation's experience in history.

Such a journey out of England—and such an intellectual pursuit—will seem arcane only to those who disapprove of the ending of *Women in Love* as a flight from England and its debased culture, or who resist any fiction that ends in a "happy valley" (even when the land remains to be acquired). For there is no doubt that "Daniel Charisi" is a utopian novel—or at least a sweeping rejection of this world and an indicated quest for another and better. The tendency to opt out of bourgeois society was of long standing in Eliot, and her heroines' flights—to death in *The Mill on the Floss*, to a plague-stricken village in *Romola*—have not been without their detractors. In her final fiction, Eliot does not allow her protagonist to act out his flight and his mission on the narrative stage. Instead, she has recourse to what may seem an evasion but may also be read as a genuinely original imaginative device. In place of the well-established Romantic topos of the westward journey of discovery, Eliot has her hero *change direction*.

The West had remained a potent symbol of escape from the economic constriction and personal disappointments of a tight little island. When Rex Gascoigne is brutally repulsed by Gwendolen, his first thought is of America, and his younger sister paints a picture of their proposed life there with suggestive exaggeration: "I would sooner go there than stay here in England. I could make the fires, and mend the clothes, and cook the food; and I could learn how to make the bread before we went. It would be nicer than anything—like playing at life over again . . ." (viii, 118). This is touching and amusing, but the Romantic values of return to nature, independence, and divestment of the past in an opening to the future are all implicit in even this childish speech. In contrast, Eliot envisions a return not to nature but to genuine culture, an opening not to the future so much as a recovery of the best values of the past, and an assertion of community in place of the American pioneer's symbolic individualism.

This transvaluation of utopian values must be accompanied by an imaginative shifting of symbols, and a dramatic stage for such a shift is given in the notorious bridge scene. The language of this chapter no doubt departs from the fustian of ordinary realism, and even from the normal tenor of Eliot's somber prose, for it is put at the service of a vision not restricted to Mordecai's hallucinations. To set the scene: Mordecai waits on Blackfriars Bridge while Daniel rows down the river from Chelsea—the familiar London names work against any imaginative flights. As Mordecai looks westward for Daniel, his face is illuminated by the setting sun, but the movement is all *eastward*. From Daniel's perspective, Mordecai's face is turned to the west in expectation: ". . . his eyes caught a well-remembered face looking towards him over the parapet of the bridge—brought out by the western light into startling distinctness and brilliancy—an illuminated type of bodily emaciation and spiritual eagerness" (xl, 549). But, from Mordecai's standpoint, the hope is fulfilled from out of the west by one who moves toward the east: "The prefigured friend had come from the golden background, and had signalled to him: this actually was: the rest was to be" (xl, 550). Here, at about the midpoint of the novel, we are asked to change direction, not only in our sympathies but in our outlook; to see—if not with the spiritual eye, at least with an eastward-oriented one. It is not required that we see Daniel arriving at his goal; it is enough that we follow him imaginatively in his quest of organic community and ideal culture.

Thus, were it not for the possible improprieties involved, one could assent to the general criticism that *Daniel Deronda* is too much like church —so long as it is acknowledged that it is not quite like *shul*. It tells us perhaps too insistently of our modern worship of individualism and of Western culture's limitations, and it also specifies—subtly, by comparison with Lawrence—what to think, if not what to do. Yet along with its appeals for our conversion—in the literal sense of changing direction—it provides what might be called an imaginative bridge of sympathy for our limitations, along which we may return to the ordinary world:

Extension, we know, is a very imperfect measure of things. . . .
A man may go south, and, stumbling over a bone, may meditate upon

it till he has found a new starting-point for anatomy; or eastward, and discover a new key to language telling a new story of races; or he may head an expedition that opens new continental pathways, get himself maimed in body, and go through a whole heroic poem of resolve and endurance; and at the end of a few months he may come back to find his neighbours grumbling at the same parish grievance as before. . . . Such differences are manifest in the variable intensity which we call human experience, from the revolutionary rush of change which makes a new inner and outer life, to that quiet recurrence of the familiar, which has no other epochs than those of hunger and the heavens. (lviii, 771)

8. The Buried Giant of Egdon Heath

I tell of Giants from times forgotten,
Those who fed me in former days. . . .

—VÖLUSPA SAGA

Agog and magog and the round of them agrog. To the continuation
of that celebration until Hanandhunigan's extermination!

—FINNEGANS WAKE

ONE would search long for a commentator on *The Return of the Native* who has failed to locate the story of Clym Yeobright and Eustacia Vye in the elaborated space of its landscape. Still it may be said that Egdon Heath has not been recognized as a figure in its own right—in both narrative senses of "figure," as person and as trope. One of the closest observers of the novel, John Paterson, has listed some of the heath's associations: ". . . it is a stage grand enough to bear the weight of gods and heroes; more specifically still, it is the prison-house of Prometheus, the fire-bearing benefactor of mankind."[1] Paterson and others have supported such identifications by quoting the novel's repeated attribution of Promethean characteristics to the major characters. Hardy is never one to make his classical allusions evasively; the demonic rebelliousness of Eustacia and the bonded martyrdom of Clym are steadily projected upon the heath in the mode of scenic amplification. Yet the felt connection between the human actors and their inanimate setting exceeds the scope of metonymic associations like the scene-act ratio of Kenneth Burke. The ruling passions of the protagonists in *The Return* and the awesome powers of the heath need to be treated as forces of a like nature—the heath manifesting the same impulses as do the fictional characters.

To return to the setting of Hardy's first major novel is to seize his imagination at an originative position, where his sense of the past and his complex feelings about modern life intersected at a place with which he identified himself. Throughout his career, Hardy was inclined to express his strong response to the history-laden landscape of his shire in images of a special kind—special, that is, when compared with those of other Victorian novelists but commonplace in the tradition of local observers with a bent for narrative explanation. He was born, it will be recalled, in a cottage on the edge of the fourteen miles or so of high ground that has come to be identified with Egdon Heath, and he built his home, Max Gate, near its southwest flank five years after writing *The Return*.² In 1878, the year the novel was published, the Folk-Lore Society was founded in London, and at about this date Hardy joined the Dorset Natural History and Antiquarian Field Club. To the latter he also delivered a paper on "Some Romano-British Relics Found at Max Gate, Dorchester"³—found, that is, during the digging of foundations for his house. These delvings in the earth encouraged Hardy in a long series of reflections on the presence underfoot of a many-layered past: beginning as early as the passage in *The Return* on Clym's attendance at the opening of a barrow (book III, chapter iii); continuing with the account of unearthed Roman skeletons in *The Mayor of Casterbridge* (chapter xi); and developing a fine blend of fascination and detachment in poems like "The Roman Gravemounds" and "The Clasped Skeletons."

The sense of the past, it has been abundantly demonstrated, touches Hardy's work at innumerable points, but one may be isolated for the present discussion: his adumbration of an animate (or once-animate) being dormant in the earth, whether in the form of a buried skeleton incarnating the ghosts of the past, or of a quasi-human figure underlying or constituting certain topographical features (usually hills), or of a *genius loci* residing not in an aerial or other evanescent medium but in the soil of the place itself. It will be seen that some such preternatural beliefs are at work amid the rationalist skepticism which Hardy tried to maintain and that, while his own beliefs are not to be equated with those of the peasants in his tales, his absorption in them resembles the intellectual sympathy which modern anthropologists and folklorists have been recommending.

The prime instances of buried figures in the Hardy country are, quite naturally, those associated with a number of massive formations which surpass anything comparable in the southwest—the region of England perhaps most densely populated by ancient remains. Foremost is Maiden Castle, a Celtic hillfort a few miles south of Dorchester, which Hardy described as "an enormous many-limbed organism of an antediluvian time . . . lying lifeless, and covered with a thin green cloth, which hides its substance, while revealing its contour."⁴ Comparable in fame and grandeur is the Cerne Abbas giant, with his club and explicit phallus, on a hill seven miles north of Dorchester in a region Hardy favored for his rambles; it is mentioned in *Tess of the d'Urbervilles* and other writings, most saliently when described by the local peasantry in *The Dynasts* as a malevolent ogre, comparable to Napoleon.⁵

Besides those and other gigantic erections in the vicinity, like Stonehenge, additional outcroppings of the land contour Hardy's writings. In a poem titled "The Moth-Signal," specifically set on Egdon Heath and reminiscent of an incident in *The Return*, the waywardness of modern domestic life is seen from the perspective of a dweller in the earth:

> Then grinned the Ancient Briton
>   From the tumulus treed with pine:
> "So, hearts are thwartly smitten
>   In these days as in mine!"[6]

Hardy takes up the point of view of an inhabitant of the heath in a more personal way in another poem, "A Meeting with Despair" (noted in the manuscript as set on Egdon Heath):

> As evening shaped I found me on a moor
>   Sight shunned to entertain:
> The black lean land, of featureless contour,
>   Was like a tract in pain.
>
> "This scene, like my own life," I said, "is one
>   Where many glooms abide;
> Toned by its fortune to a deadly dun—
>   Lightless on every side."
>
> .   .   .   .
>
> Against the horizon's dim-discernèd wheel
>   A form rose, strange of mould:
> That he was hideous, hopeless, I could feel
>   Rather than could behold.

Although Hardy metaphorically identifies the pattern and tone of his life with the heath's, he resists the insinuations of the apparition—named "Despair" in the title but referred to only as "the Thing" in the poem itself—so as to argue that the glowing sunset portends better prospects for the future. In a voice we recognize as that of the stupid giant of fairy tales, his interlocutor replies, "Yea—but await awhile! . . . Ho-ho!— / Now look aloft and see!" More striking, perhaps, than either the poem's finale (with the loss of light and portent of defeat) or the similarities between its treatment of Egdon Heath and the novel's is the encounter with an abiding presence there—the black lean land, featureless, in pain, from which a hideous, hopeless form arises.

These poems call to mind others in which one of the most familiar features of Hardy's style, personification, is employed in its mode of gigantism. The best-known instance of this trope is found in "The Darkling Thrush": "The land's sharp features seemed to be / The Century's corpse outleant. . . ." In the periodical publication of the poem, its original title emphasized this figure rather than the thrush: "By the Century's Deathbed" enforces the idea not simply of a localized spirit but of the entire earth as a body suffering a secular decline. A more sharply focused version of this image occurs in the poem "By the Earth's Corpse" (from the same volume as "The Darkling Thrush"), in which Time and "the Lord" conduct a dialogue on the themes of guilt and repetition, while placed like mourners near "this globe, now cold / As lunar land and sea," at some future time "when flesh / And herb but fossils be, / And, all extinct, their piteous dust / Revolves obliviously. . . ."

The most highly developed vision of the earth as an organic, vaguely human being is, however, that of *The Dynasts*. A stage direction of the "Fore Scene" is justly famous for its panoramic sweep, anticipating (but still surpassing) the movement of the camera eye in epically scaled movies:

> The nether sky opens, and Europe is disclosed as a prone and emaciated figure, the Alps shaping like a backbone, and the branching mountain-chains like ribs, the peninsular plateau of Spain forming a head. . . . The point of view then sinks downwards through space, and draws near to the surface of the perturbed countries, where the peoples, distressed by events which they did not cause, are seen writhing, crawling, heaving, and vibrating in their various cities and nationalities.

With the return to this vision in the "After Scene," Europe is "beheld again as a prone and emaciated figure. . . . The lowlands look like a grey-green garment half-thrown off, and the sea around like a disturbed bed on which the figure lies." In this instance, human forms in the mass join with geographical features to create the image of a total organism: the earth itself (or its European portion) as a giant, going through the stages of awakening, struggle, and exhaustion—a composite being living out the disturbances and sufferings of humankind.

Is it this (or a related) giant who confronts the reader from the title of the opening chaper of *The Return*: "A Face on which Time makes but Little Impression"? The rhetoric of the so-called pathetic fallacy suggests that it is a creature on the scale of the earth: it "wore the appearance of an instalment of night" and, reciprocally, "the face of the heath by its mere complexion added half an hour to evening."[7] Not only are vital reflexes, human apparel, and personal physiognomy suggested, but the sustained comparison of Egdon Heath and mankind is raised from mere analogy to essential identity:

> It was at present a place perfectly accordant with man's nature —neither ghastly, hateful, nor ugly: neither commonplace, unmeaning, nor tame; but, like man, slighted and enduring; and withal singularly colossal and mysterious in its swarthy monotony. As with some persons who have long lived apart, solitude seemed to look out of its countenance. It had a lonely face, suggesting tragical possibilities.
> (I, i, 35)

It is on the basis of this profound identity that the epithets used for the heath come to resonate like personal designations: "Haggard Egdon," "the untameable, Ishmaelitish thing that Egdon now was," "the people changed, yet Egdon remained." In the most pathetic of these characterizations, the place is defined in relation to other natural forces in a style usually reserved for romantic fiction: "Then Egdon was aroused to reciprocity; for the storm was its lover, and the wind its friend." But the role hardly suits a figure that has emerged as not merely humanized but on a larger-than-individual scale: "singularly colossal and mysterious in its swarthy monotony." Such a colossus can be a hero only of a special sort.

In inventing the name itself, Hardy seems to have had in mind not a place-name but a personal one. Its closest analogue is a forename: *Egbert*, from Old English *ecg* ("sword") and *bryght* ("bright")—the latter term also appearing in the chief surname used in the novel. *Egdon* would be its derivable opposite: the second syllable is equivalent to *dun*, the word used since Anglo-Saxon times to describe the natural shades of landscape, animals, and atmosphere in a dull, brown grey range. (But compare the Celtic name of Maiden Castle: *mai dun* ["strong hill"].) Etymology resolves nothing, but this name goes beyond the expansive suggestiveness of well-wrought place-names in fiction, encouraging instead the identification of a personal presence by a favored technique of characterization.

If these two processes are indeed comparable—if a somewhat amorphous terrain is presented here in the manner in which fictional characters are conventionally introduced—we shall have to revise our expectations of the role of landscape in this novel more radically than we may be prepared to do. Landscape is not satisfied to act in *The Return of the Native* as a background, with human subjects in the foreground (although some positioning of people against a background of natural elements is at work, e.g., in the chapter entitled "The Figure against the Sky"). Instead, Egdon Heath becomes one of the principal agents of the action, a protagonist in the classical sense of the dramatic actor, and probably the most memorable figure to emerge from the events. The title of the novel has been given some new turns in recent criticism, so as to widen its reference beyond the donnée of Clym's return to Wessex.[8] If its individual implications are taken seriously, the title refers somewhat sardonically to Clym's return to the native state in the course of the action; it also suggests more broadly the heath's renewed prominence in the life of the characters and of the modern age generally. "The Return of the Native" would name, then, a story about Egdon Heath.

The operation of these narrative traits makes the term "personification" no longer adequate to describe the process by which Egdon Heath is generated by the text. When natural categories are fixed, one may speak about the ascription of human characteristics to inanimate beings or about the representation of an abstract or other impersonal entity in human terms. But Egdon is not so clear-cut: it is never given as entirely on one side of the animate/inanimate polarity before being assimilated to the other. Even in the opening chapter, the metaphoric expressions by which it is rendered human are immediately posited as literal (or as leading to literal statements about the heath's role in human psychology): "Then [in storms, etc.] it became the home of strange phantoms; and it was found to be the hitherto unrecognized original of those wild regions of obscurity which are vaguely felt to be compassing us about in midnight dreams of flight and disaster, and are never thought of after the dream till revived by scenes like this" (I, i, 35). Without drawing conclusions about Hardy's version of the unconscious, we find his prose moving from the metaphoric level (movement of storms ‖ movement of phantoms), to statements that posit the heath as the original model of dream landscapes, to a final suggestion of its function as a permanent index of the unconscious "regions" of the mind itself. So steadily cumulative is this assimilation of the heath to the animate level that toward the close of the novel, as intensity of style mounts in tempo with intensity of action, we are prepared to take in stride such passages as this: "Skirting the pool [Eustacia] followed the path towards Rainbarrow, occasionally stumbling over twisted furze-roots, tufts of rushes, or oozing lumps of fleshy fungi, which at this season lay scattered about the heath like the rotten liver and lungs of some colossal animal" (V, vii, 370). While it is Eustacia who is stumbling toward her death, it is the heath that is seen here as a dismembered giant—neither clearly human nor, as Lawrence thought, merely bestial but a "colossal animal" who is martyred and distributed in a spectacular way.

While the interconnections of the animate and the inanimate must be deduced from the rhetorical modes of the opening chapter, later passages state their inherent identity in the heath with some urgency. The chief of these occurs in the first description of Eustacia Vye:

> There the form stood, motionless as the hill beneath. Above the plain rose the hill, above the hill rose the barrow, and above the barrow rose the figure. Above the figure was nothing that could be mapped elsewhere than on a celestial globe.
>
> Such a perfect, delicate, and necessary finish did the figure give to the dark pile of hills that it seemed to be the only obvious justification of their outline. Without it, there was the dome without the lantern; with it the architectural demands of the mass were satisfied. The scene was stangely homogeneous, in that the vale, the upland, the barrow, and the figure above it amounted only to unity. Looking at this or that member of the group was not observing a complete thing, but a fraction of a thing. (I, ii, 41)

Hardy employs the term "organic" in the next sentence to describe the internal relations of the "entire motionless structure"; we may apply it equally to the tenor of his thinking in this passage. Although the human figure is to be regarded esthetically as a "necessary finish" and a satisfaction of an "architectural" demand, it is more fundamentally a "fraction" of a larger "unity." Nor is the heath complete without the person: it needs it as its "obvious justification," to become a "homogeneous" being in its own right. The text speaks of this organic unity of the human and the non-human "members" of Egdon Heath as "a thing" and elsewhere adds, "a thing majestic without severity, impressive without showiness, emphatic in its admonitions, grand in its simplicity" (I, i, 34).

Although Eustacia is most striking in her unwilling assimilation into Egdon Heath, other characters exhibit a spectrum of possible relations to it, ranging from identification to detachment. Although the gigantic "thing" takes in both human beings and the heath, there are a number of possible modes of integration, which various characters explore. The peasants live in wary observance of the land and its seasons, but their limited mentalities are none too gently satirized in Hardy's folkish chapters. The reddleman, Diggory Venn, shows himself adroit not only in the world of commercial and (eventually) erotic competition but is especially competent among the highways and byways of the heath. (It is noteworthy that he gets no particular credit for this intimacy with the heath, as measured by the conventions of heroic stature; given Hardy's view of him as an "isolated and weird character"–in the "Author's Note" of 1912–he is scarcely ennobled by his numerous displays of omnicompetence.) It is Clym who displays the most complex relation to the heath, being the one who exercises a series of considered choices in the matter. In his first characterization, his constitution or generation by the place is stressed: "If any one knew the heath well it was Clym. He was permeated with its scenes, with its substance, and with its odours. He might be said to be its product" (III, ii, 197). At the end of his series of ideological shifts and personal misfortunes, he stands before the heath in an alien position, as of one face impervious to another: ". . . there was only the imperturbable countenance of the heath, which, having defied the cataclysmal onsets of centuries, reduced to insignificance by its seamed and antique features the wildest turmoil of a single man" (V, ii, 342). But the most extreme separation from the heath–indistinguishable from a kind of rationalistic stupidity–is represented by the pragmatic objectivity of Thomasin Yeobright: ". . . Egdon in the mass was no monster whatever, but impersonal open ground. Her fears of the place were rational, her dislikes of its worst moods reasonable" (V, viii, 380).

Despite their differences, the characters have a common connection with the heath, a unity of fate that is consistently figured in allusions to Prometheus: "Every night [the heath's] Titanic form seemed to await something; but it had waited thus, unmoved, during so many centuries, through the crises of so many things, that it could only be imagined to await one last crisis–the final overthrow" (I, i, 34). The iconography of Prometheus chained to a mountain in the Caucasus is strikingly transmuted in this and similar passages: the *scene* of suffering becomes the sufferer (Egdon is not Caucasian but Titanic), while at least part of the demigod's character is ascribed to the land itself in its "unmoved" martyrdom. Yet the myth's primary orientation toward apocalypse (the final overthrow of Zeus) is, as we shall see, fully employed in *The Return.*

The heath's Promethean, long-suffering form of resistance is picked up in the characterization of the human actors but is resourcefully applied as a differentiating factor. The peasants' lighting of fires to celebrate Guy Fawkes Day, although localized as a modern British survival of the ritual death and rebirth of the year, is seen as the expression of a universal need: "Moreover to light a fire is the instinctive and resistant act of man when, at the winter ingress, the curfew is sounded throughout Nature. It indicates a spontaneous, Promethean rebelliousness against the fiat that this recurrent season shall bring foul times, cold darkness, misery and death. Black chaos comes, and the fettered gods of the earth say, Let there be light" (I, iii, 45). Here humans, heath, and Titans are seen on the same side, resisting—or at least protesting—an imposition from without, the fiat of a being or realm representing black chaos, winter, and death. Humanity joins with the land itself in "Promethean rebelliousness," and it is with one voice that they register their counterfiat; theirs is the voice of the "fettered gods" or Titans, which proclaims light—a biblical equivalent for the Promethean fire that is the subject of this passage.

The chief characters are, however, subtly distinguished in their articulations of this rebellion and thus in their associations with the band of "fettered gods." Eustacia is described from the first in terms derived from the preceding passage: "Egdon was her Hades, and since coming there she had imbibed much of what was dark in its tone, though inwardly and eternally unreconciled thereto. Her appearance accorded well with this smouldering rebelliousness. . . . A true Tartarean dignity sat upon her brow . . ." (I, vii, 94). The term found in both passages, "rebelliousness," is linked to its consequences of banishment or living burial, whether of humans in Hades or of Titans in Tartarus (the variability of mythological traditions is exploited here to make these roughly equivalent terms for confinement in the earth). It is notable that this passage begins by emphasizing Eustacia's unwilling bondage in Egdon, the setting of her unsatisfactory station in life, but it gradually identifies her with the heath insofar as the latter, too, is unreconciled to its bound condition under the fiat of the ruling gods.[9]

Precisely the opposite shift occurs in the course of Clym's characterization: beginning as one fully at home on the heath—"its product"—he becomes so thoroughly acclimated in his return to the soil that he renounces rebelliousness: "Now, don't you suppose, my inexperienced girl, that I cannot rebel, in high Promethean fashion, against the gods and fate as well as you. I have felt more steam and smoke of that sort than you have ever heard of. But the more I see of life the more do I perceive that there is nothing particularly great in its greatest walks, and therefore nothing particularly small in mine of furze-cutting" (IV, ii, 276–277). Clym's liberal renunciation of the Promethean stance is part of an explicit cultural theme in the novel, concerned with the vulnerability of the modern mind by virtue of its skeptical intelligence, its loss of traditional, organizing mythologies (a loss and a vulnerability in which Hardy felt himself implicated). But Clym's career also involves a break with the creaturely tendency to rebellion against earthbound suffering, a separation from the Titanic "fettered gods" with whom Eustacia, involuntarily, associates herself. And it is this loss of Promethean vision that is his true undoing, for he sees "nothing particularly great in [life's] greatest walks" or, by the same token, in the heath's.

Having detected the signs of a giant figure buried in the verbal integument of *The Return*, noted its provenance in Hardy's imaginings of his native place, and considered its shadowy relations with the characters of the drama, what can we say of the wider significance of this massive presence? The range of relevant contexts extends to the margins of the human imagination, for giants have populated not only folk and fairy tales, cosmogonies and epics, but also topographical prominences the world over. It is evident that Hardy would have known the Greek versions of this mythology, as well as its variants among the English Romantic poets; it is perhaps less known that he was attentive to local legends accounting for curious outcroppings by tales of giants buried or sleeping in the land. Hardy recorded one such topographical fable in his notebook:

> The Legend of the Cerne Giant. He threatened to descend upon Cerne and to ravish all the young maidens on a particular night and to kill the young men next day. Goaded to desperate courage they waylaid and killed him, afterwards cutting his effigy on the hill. He lived somewhere up in the hills, was waited on by wild animals and used to steal the farmers' sheep, eating one a day. The *Giant's Head Inn* nearby evidently related to the tradition.[10]

This explanatory tale registers what may be called the subdued-ogre variant of topographical gigantism but, as this is only one in a range of possibilities, a brief review of the alternatives will suggest a need for closer inspection if we are to single out the special face of Egdon Heath.

In contrast to the subdued ogre, the Titan lore with which Egdon Heath is associated stands in a tradition of proto- or prohuman giants reaching back to classical myth and descending to Hardy by way of Aeschylus and Shelley. Unlike the dead and buried giant whose form is left in the shape of hills or in markings upon them, the bound and tortured colossus of the Promethean strain is often placed within caves or in the rock face—the better to express his continued protests in the form of rumblings, quakes, and other seismic phenomena. While the subdued ogre testifies to past victories by humanity, or at least by the local inhabitants, the bound Titan testifies to the present dominance of inimical powers and encourages continued but passive resistance to them. Hardy stands with his poetic master Shelley in removing the Titanic will from Aeschylus' mythic drama—making outspoken resistance like Eustacia's futile while establishing Egdon Heath as a figure of patient though brooding endurance.

A further extension of this long-suffering martyr to earthbound existence lies in a train of apocalyptic heroes of folk tales and legendary history around the earth. This figure is known to the Aarne-Thompson motif index under the rubrics "Culture hero still lives," "Culture hero asleep in moutain," and "Culture hero's expected return."[11] Examples may be drawn from history (Charlemagne asleep within the Unterberg), religion (Balder and a host of other deities), or a mixture of history and myth (Arthur being the foremost example, one who is at home in the west of England). Neither dead and buried nor bound and rumbling, the culture hero looks to the promised future, and his legends partake of a popular apocalyptic impulse independent of religious eschatology. Common to these figures is their human scale; although invested with supernatural graces, they avoid the grotesquerie of gigantic expansion. Yet they are akin to the buried giants in their generalized potentiality: it is man himself who lies sleeping but latently liberated in these tales. Moreover, in some of his most spectacular variants, this sleeping savior is localized not merely under a hill or at a place but within an entire landscape: as Blake's Albion is the incarnation not merely of a national leader but of the land itself and the race's destiny.

Beyond Hardy's interest in topographical legends and primordial rituals, he was inevitably exposed to giant figures in the course of his lifelong absorption in the Romantic poets. It is well known that he considered Shelley "our most marvellous lyrist"[12] and quoted or alluded to his work perhaps more often than to any other, barring the Bible and Shakespeare. Although he devoted lavish encomiums to several favorite lyrics, Hardy clearly found *Prometheus Unbound* more to his fictional purpose. While it is relatively unrewarding to retrace the specific transactions with that epic-drama in *The Return*'s Promethean imagery, there are important elements of Shelley's poetic mythology in Hardy's world view. Most striking in the action of both poem and novel is the appearance of the earth itself as a force in human destiny: for Shelley, this force is associated with the mysterious role of the earth-dwelling giant, Demogorgon, while for Hardy it is localized in Egdon Heath. The two are not the same, nor do they entail fully commensurate ideas of fate or necessity, but they are individualized figures of natural power abiding in the earth, with enormous regenerative potential. Indeed, the ambivalent reactions of awe and fascination generated by Demogorgon's gross majesty are akin to those inspired by Egdon's characterization.

Even more may be suggested, if without perfect assurance: the prescientific geological theories which have been shown to be at work behind Shelley's phrase "the breathing earth,"[13] as well as other references to animate underground expressions of the human condition, may have a place in the substructure of Hardy's setting. Earl Wasserman's studies of the poem's complex imagery of volcanism, earthquakes, and other geological processes reveal an ambiguity in Shelley's use of the figure which is matched in Hardy: ". . . the single dominant image of the breathing earth symbolizes such opposite values as the volcanic disordering of the earth by Prometheus' curse and enchainment and also the revolutionary eruption that removes Jupiter. . . . volcanoes are catastrophic, but they also can stir the lethargic earth to action and to new forms." This mixture of rocklike, impervious, but restive power, subdued to long endurance yet rancorous in its arrested potentiality—along with quirky manifestations of smoldering hostility and a threat of direr disturbances—makes up the heroic stature of Shelley's earth demon and Hardy's heath. In both writers, the pathetic and the promising elements of the human condition are attached to the figures of giants; for Shelley, Prometheus and Demogorgon convey humanity's spiritual bondage and potential liberation; for Hardy, Egdon Heath combines the exhalations of age-old suffering and the expectancy of long-looked-for awakening: "The sombre stretch of rounds and hollows seemed to rise and meet the evening gloom in pure sympathy, the heath exhaling darkness as rapidly as the heavens precipitated it. . . . The place became full of a watchful intentness now; for when other things sank brooding to sleep the heath appeared slowly to awake and listen" (I, i, 33–34).

The common fund of traditional lore for both conceptions lies in the classical mythology and localized legends of the Titans. Whether associated with Prometheus or Demogorgon,[14] whether connected with volcanoes and earthquakes or the formation of islands and mountain ranges, the Titans play a vigorous role both in Romantic poetry and in Hardy's latter-day version of its themes. The long theomachy of the Olympians and the Titans is a malleable political paradigm and has been adapted to national interests far beyond its Greek source; most germane for English myth makers is the exiling of the defeated deities not to subterranean Tartarus but to an Atlantic island. The inevitable association of one of their number, Atlas, not only with the lost island of Atlantis but also with the British Isles[15] provides abundant opportunities for the poets to connect the origins of Britain with a primal act of cultural rebellion, an exiled condition, and a foretold apocalypse.

Blake was well informed of such imaginative possibilities and, while Hardy's involvement with Blake has yet to be adequately assessed, it is clear that his sense of Titanic powers at work and at rest beneath the soil of England is matched only by Blake's among the English poets. While Hardy carefully selects the Titanic features of his landscape—seeing, e.g., Rainbarrow as a "wart on an Atlantean brow" (I, ii, 41)—Blake works out the features of his Albion in spectacular detail:

> London is between his knees, its basements fourfold;
> His right foot stretches to the sea on Dover cliffs, his heel
> On Canterbury's ruins; his right hand covers lofty Wales,
> His left Scotland; . . .
>
> .   .   .   .
>
> He views Jerusalem & Babylon, his tears flow down.
> He mov'd his right foot to Cornwall, his left to the Rocks of Bognor.
> He strove to rise to walk into the Deep, but strength failing
> Forbad, & down with dreadful groans he sunk upon his Couch
> In moony Beulah. . . .[16]

Lest there be any doubt about Blake's identification of Albion with a Titanic source, he makes this point explicit in the "Descriptive Catalogue" to his paintings, with regard to the lost "Ancient Britons": "The giant Albion, was Patriarch of the Atlantic; he is the Atlas of the Greeks, one of those the Greeks called Titans." And again in "A Vision of the Last Judgment": "He is Albion, our Ancestor, patriarch of the Atlantic Continent, whose History Preceded that of the Hebrews & in whose Sleep, or Chaos, Creation began. . . ." The generation of Blake's ideas from among the syncretic mythographers and their complex developments in the fabric of his poetry are matters to be followed up in other commentaries.[17] But we can see in his poetic mythology and Hardy's a common concern to identify the sources not only of the present nation but of the land itself with a Titanic giant whose traces still lie open to inspection in the formations of the soil of England.

What emerges from these poetic and fictional versions of Britain's antediluvian history is a pattern of original settlement by gigantic creatures, following defeat and exile; their withdrawal, whether from renewed defeat or other calamity, into the earth (a significant variation on most myths of chthonic ancestors, who emerge *from* the native soil); and their dormant persistence under the feet of the present inhabitants, while awaiting a threatened cataclysm and possible restoration. Although human fate is inextricably bound up with the primal structures of the land and its speculative inhabitants, their restoration has no simple issue; the rising of the sleeping giants by no means guarantees a permanent liberation from their common oppression—and may portend the opposite. Thus Blake names one of the sons of Albion as Hylé (Greek for primal matter) and identifies him with Gog, taken in the biblical sense of the baser form of man.[18]

Though *Jerusalem*'s climactic awakening of the sleeping giant, Albion, redeems all his sons in a general easement, the term Gog is again used to suggest that the terrible aspect of humanity's gigantism can never finally be put down. As Frye explains, "if behind the Bible there is the memory of an age of murderous ogres who perished in a stench of burning flesh, then in front of it there is an apprehension of a returning power of gigantic self-destruction. The former survives in the Bible as the Covering Cherub; the latter is portrayed as the giants Gog and Magog who return with the full power of darkness after the millennium."[19]

Sifting through his web of folklore—both popular and poetic, markedly British and within Hardy's favorite range of reading—which of the strains of gigantism can be found uppermost in *The Return*? It is clear that the first type, the subdued ogre, is furthest from prominence, although Egdon has its baleful features; Hardy is least interested in celebrating humanity's past triumphs over chthonic powers in nature, for his view of both emphasizes their unity. The bound Titan, on the other hand, is the figure most obvious in the language of the text, and it seems evident that Hardy establishes in the Titanic heath the burden of a mankind forced to submit to an order of things that can only be explained (if it can be explained at all) as deriving from an arbitrary, if not a malevolent, authority. Yet space should be made for the third type of giant, not so much rebellious as long-suffering, dormant but expectant, who is implicated in the common fate of man and nature yet looks forward to an ultimate liberation.

In transforming *The Return* from the "ballad and pastoral romance" elements of its "Ur-novel,"[20] Hardy was applying to a more profound level of folklore, where reside the popular imaginings of origin, authority, and apocalypse which are given scope in giant lore. And, in effecting a "classical transvaluation" into the tragic mode, Hardy was drawing on a potentiality in Aeschylus which inspired Shelley, perhaps too avidly, in his *Prometheus*: the opening to the future which inspires hope. Egdon Heath carries, among its many resonances of power and endurance, a vibration not so much stoical as regenerative and creative—whatever the failures of its denizens to make much of their connections with it. This potentiality need not be—indeed resists being—specifically tied to historical events, either past revolutions or future ones.[21] In underscoring the action of *The Return* with traces of apocalyptic promise, Hardy adds to a long tradition of English poetic figures—from Blake's, to Yeats' Rocky Face and Thomas' White Giant,[22] who mark the intimations of aeonian change in the contours of the land.[23]

9. Speech and Writing in *Under Western Eyes*

AARON: *Ich, dein Mund, bewahre deinen Gedanken,*
      wie immer ich ihn ausspreche.
MOSES: *Durch Bilder! . . .*
      O Wort, du Wort, das mir fehlt!
                —SCHÖNBERG

A long line of theoreticians of language, from Rousseau to Saussure and on into our time, have maintained that writing is a cursed labor inherited from the Fall, while speech, despite Babel, remains a vital and creative activity. For the living flow of spoken words and the organic changes of popular language, writing substitutes the sterile forms of imposed conventions and fixes the dynamic immediacy of individual speech in an embalmed and lifeless hulk, the text. More skeptical writers on language have called into question this preference for speech over writing, holding that spoken words cannot escape the taints of their origin in previously written words. Recent discussions of these and related matters by linguistics-oriented critics have renewed our questioning of the special nature of literary texts; they also show that literature itself regularly questions its privileged status as writing. We shall examine such self-scrutiny in a Conrad novel to see how the options of speech and writing present themselves dramatically to a fictional protagonist—and, by implication, to his author.

The discussion of the priority of speech and writing goes back to the ancient world but receives a definitive form in Rousseau's *Essay on the Origin of Languages*. Positing the origin of languages in the vocalic gestures of primitive expression, Rousseau finds that the codification of languages as relatively stable systems comes in only later, with writing. But this succession represents a hierarchy, for the later development is made to seem a distortion or a loss of the original immediacy, emotion, and personal presence carried in speech. Writing is, moreover, at a greater distance from truth because it is a second-level representation:

> Languages are made to be spoken, writing serves only as a supplement to speech. . . . Speech represents thought by conventional [phonetic] signs, and writing represents the same with regard to speech.

Thus the art of writing is nothing but a mediated representation of thought.[1]

This view of language has been subjected to a painstaking analysis in Jacques Derrida's *Of Grammatology*, where its critique becomes the seed-bed for Derrida's own philosophy of representation in general. At the core of his characterization of Rousseau is Derrida's perception of the ironies at work in the concept of writing as a "supplement to speech." Derrida accepts and generalizes this substitution: "The sign is always the supplement of the thing itself." From this inherited concept, he shows that speech is in the same position as writing with regard to its object, that there is no privileged original language, and that all representation involves a loss of presence. Giving this shake to our primitivistic assumptions about the primacy of speech, Derrida is able to shift the focus to the study of writing, to language as studied by grammatology.

Derrida makes a more specific analysis of the powers and limitations of speech in another philosophical critique, this time of the phenomenology of Husserl. *Speech and Phenomena* takes up Husserl's version of the common assumption that speech is a better carrier of the living presence of its originator than is writing. This view Derrida discovers to rest on the Husserlian claim that "every non-phonic signifier [e.g., writing] involves a spatial reference . . . The sense of being 'outside,' 'in the world,' is an essential component of its phenomenon. Apparently there is nothing like this in the phenomenon of speech."[2] What makes the phoneme the most "ideal" of signs is not only its satisfaction of a long-standing philosophical prejudice in favor of the less bodily, the lighter among material impingements on the senses, but also the peculiar relation of speakers to the signs they produce:

> When I speak, it belongs to the phenomenological essence of this operation that *I hear myself* [je m'entende] *at the same time* that I speak. The signifier, animated by my breath and by the meaning-intention. . . , is in absolute proximity to me. The living act, the life-giving act, the *Lebendigkeit*, which animates the body of the signifier and transforms it into a meaningful expression, the soul of language, seems not to separate itself from itself, from its own self-presence. It does not risk death in the body of a signifier [i.e., writing] that is given over to the world and the visibility of space.

Subjecting Husserl's view to a phenomenological analysis, Derrida is by a technical demonstration able to resist the parceling out of time and presence to speech, of space and externality to writing. But he has brought forward one of the more plausible explanations of the prevalent impression that speech is a more intimate, more "existential" act than is writing.

Instead of remaining bound by a sentimental attachment to the myth of presence and its vocalic medium, instead of falling into an equally mythic primordial nonpresence and its negative emanation of written traces, it is possible to follow a philosopher who moves between Husserl and Derrida and arrive at a closer grasp of the human speech situation. In Maurice Merleau-Ponty's *Phenomenology of Perception*, we are given a sense of speech as a pragmatic function in the life process, an activity by which human beings orientate themselves in the world or even create a world for themselves.

Merleau-Ponty, too, is skeptical of the traditional view of speech as a mere sign of a prior mental state, whether it be sensation or thought:

> What I communicate with primarily is not "representations" of thought, but a speaking subject, with a certain style of being and with the "world" at which he directs his aim. Just as the sense-giving intention which has set in motion the other person's speech is not an explicit thought, but a certain lack which is asking to be made good, so my taking up of this intention is not a process of thinking on my part, but a synchronizing change of my own existence, a transformation of my being.[3]

This existential transformation need not be so dramatic a stance as Merleau-Ponty's somewhat feverish style seems to imply; as he elsewhere puts the case: "What then does language express, if it does not express thoughts? It presents or rather it *is* the subject's taking up of a position in the world of his meanings." This leads to the summative formulation: "The spoken word is a gesture, and its meaning, a world." One may discover fictional enactments of such decisive gestures in many works of literature, but I shall choose one Conradian work to exemplify the process.

Although Merleau-Ponty's elaboration of the social/personal dynamics of speech is uppermost in his thought, he makes a place for writing which also opens vistas on literary language. While he usually restricts himself to speech as representative of language behavior (with an occasional striking sally into the phenomenology of reading), Merleau-Ponty posits two kinds of speech: ". . . we have been led to distinguish between a secondary speech which renders a thought already acquired, and an originating speech which brings it into existence, in the first place for ourselves, and then for others." This secondary speech would seem to be the codified language that formalizes our inventive responses to life situations, i.e., it is roughly equivalent to Rousseau's writing. The originating speech is, however, not simply the primitive gestures of the archaic speakers of our language but the correlative of other creative activities. Merleau-Ponty describes this kind of language making in the context of the creative arts, and it is clear that he has literature in mind as the field of linguistic invention.

Thus literary writing becomes a cardinal instance of creative language making or "originating speech" (while "secondary speech" has been found equivalent to writing in the formal sense). What accounts partially for these vagaries is the existential picture of the writer's silent sense of himself and of language, prior to both speech and writing:

> Thus language presupposes nothing less than a consciousness of language, a silence of consciousness embracing the world of speech in which words first receive a form and meaning. . . . Behind the spoken *cogito*, the one which is converted into discourse and into essential truth, there lies a tacit *cogito*, myself experienced by myself. . . . The tacit *cogito*, the presence of oneself to oneself, being no less than existence, is anterior to any philosophy, and knows itself only in those extreme situations in which it is under threat: for example, in the dread of death or of another's gaze upon me.

Many of these elements of the writer's situation—the anxiety of death and alienation under which he labors, his silent consciousness of language as his very self-consciousness, his movement toward writing as an embrace (in both senses) of the world of speech—are to be found in certain literary accounts of men in the act of writing, but in none more vividly than in *Under Western Eyes*.[4]

What does it mean to say that the object one holds in one's hand is a literary text? It would seem, quite apart from the contextual signals provided by publishers, merchandisers, and reviewers, that there are linguistic indicators in the text itself that mark it as writing of a certain kind. But, if the signal is made, it is never made unambiguously; there is a standing opportunity for writers to express their anxieties about the nature of their act of writing. A prime virtue of the linguistic critics is their discovery that self-referentiality is not confined to the more modish contemporary novels but is apparently inherent in literary texts. From the Greeks on down, writers attest to the problematic assumptions in positing a fictional world—whether they do so in the form of authorial intrusions about the difficulties of executing the task in hand, or by the self-conscious use of certain conventions of narrative that always startle us when their peculiar locutions are singled out for attention.

Among these expressions, one of the strangest—and among the rarest, although presenting itself as perfectly conventional—is the epigraph of *Under Western Eyes*:[5]

> '*I would take liberty from any hand as a hungry man would snatch a piece of bread.*'
>
> —MISS HALDIN

Quite apart from the striking metaphor by which the revolutionary impulse is here expressed, the quotation might trouble an orderly mind. Assuming what may be called the *linearity* of a literary text—that is, that its elements exist in the order in which they are presented—the epigraph comes before the novel proper and thus before the later statement that a Miss Haldin said, "I would take liberty from any hand as a hungry man would snatch at a piece of bread" (II, iii, 135). Epigraphs conventionally quote statements made in historical time before the appearance of the text they decorate; what can we say of an inscription that adds a piece of the writing to itself—and not after but before that writing is presented? And what uneasiness must we feel when we observe that the epigraph, in common with so many literary and scholarly citations, is a *misquotation*, the word "at" being omitted?

Some of our disturbance at a work that quotes itself, and does not even quote itself correctly, may be relieved when it is remembered that *Under Western Eyes* is one of those novels that presents itself as a text written by one of its characters. If we call the fiction written by Joseph Conrad the A text and the document prepared by the narrator the B text, we can associate the epigraph with the A text as a quotation from the B text. If it be objected that the two texts are identical, a short search will suffice to assemble the elements of the A text that distinguish it from the B text; in addition to the epigraph, there are the title, the author's name, the dedication, and the "Author's Note." (The latter, added after the original publication, is admittedly of another order of existence in the A text, and I would surrender it if pressed.) Here may lie a justification for that curious misquote: the A and B texts are accepted as not identical, for in the transition from one citation of Miss Haldin's statement to the other a change of assumptions occurs, such that the reader accepts the disparity as an instance of the rule that misquotations *will* occur when one text quotes another.

The peculiar epigraph, then, must be counted among those linguistic devices by which the author of the novel establishes (or gives the appearance of establishing) that he is not an inventor but only the conveyer of an authoritative document written down by another, the narrator. Conrad's apology for the narrator, in the "Author's Note," is well known: "He was useful to me and therefore I think that he must be useful to the reader both in the way of comment and by the part he plays in the development of the story. In my desire to produce the effect of actuality it seemed to me indispensable to have an eye-witness of the transactions in Geneva" (pp. viii-ix). These are the standard arguments of verisimilitude, which link Conrad's experimental technique to the esthetics of realism; yet, even while we register the "effect of actuality" produced by the "eye-witness," we also register the effects of the multiple narrative structure. Quite apart from the objections that have been raised about the characterization, the usefulness, and the consistency of the narrator, a number of statements ascribed to him call into question the authority claimed by his act of writing and help define Conrad's highly inventive role.

At two points in his narrative, the English émigré language teacher pauses to deliver an apparently heartfelt expression of sincerity. On both occasions he puts forward as a reason for believing his narrative its "artlessness," both in the literal sense (without the traits pertaining to a work of art) and in the figurative sense (ingenuous, unfabricated, straightforward). Both statements reek of dissimulation on someone's part: "In the conduct of an invented story there are, no doubt, certain proprieties to be observed for the sake of clearness and effect. . . . But this is not a work of imagination; I have no talent; my excuse for this undertaking lies not in its art, but in its artlessness" (II, i, 100). And: "A novelist says this and that of his personages, and if only he knows how to say it earnestly enough he may not be questioned upon the inventions of his brain in which his own belief is made sufficiently manifest by a telling phrase, a poetic image, the accent of emotion. Art is great! But I have no art . . ." (II, iv, 162). Now there is nothing here to shock the initiated; novelists, like rhetoricians, have always protested that they are to be believed because they are plain speakers, not artful deceivers—that they speak truth without adornment, although their conventional disclaimers are themselves striking instances of adornment. But the effect of these protestations in *Under Western Eyes* is very like that produced by Cervantes' elaborate explanation that the text of *Don Quixote* is not his own work but came into his hands in a Toledo marketplace. Both make the disclaimer in so playful a way that the artfulness of the authorial hand is thereby underscored. To put the matter in my somewhat awkward code, the language teacher's insistence that his writing, the B text, is not a work of fiction like the A text has the contrary effect of reminding us that it, too, is a fictional construct (B text within A text), a "useful" arrangement in an artist's effort to create an illusion—the illusion that his invention is true because reported by an eyewitness.

If so much artfulness can be ascribed to the devices of the B text, even more may be discerned in the elaboration of the narrative structure by the positing, if not the complete presentation, of a *C text*. For the scheme requires that the language teacher's report be based on written documents, as well as on his direct observation of the action. Among these documents —which include the newspaper report of Haldin's arrest, Peter Ivanovitch's autobiography, and sources relating to Mr. de P— which provide a background sufficient to place if not to understand events in Russia—there is a primary source, Razumov's notebook. Assigning this writing to a precise genre gives the language teacher some difficulty: "The document, of course, is something in the nature of a journal, a diary, yet not exactly that in its actual form. For instance, most of it was not written up from day to day, though all the entries are dated. Some of these entries cover months of time and extend over dozens of pages. All the earlier part is a retrospect, in a narrative form, relating to an event which took place about a year before" (I, 4). The language teacher's awareness of esthetic form is obviously sufficient to make him sensitive to the difference between a diary, written more or less daily, a journal, written more randomly but keeping some chronological order, and something else, which he calls a retrospect, characterized by its narrative form and covering events in the life of its author at some remove from the time of writing. The usual term for a self-narrative of one's life is *autobiography*, and we are given to understand that Razumov's text contains not only fragmentary memoranda of events as they occur but also large autobiographical reflections on the shape of his career and the tragic ironies of his destiny.

There is at least one other kind of writing included in the C text: Razumov's letter to Nathalie Haldin, which is quoted in the B text and constitutes four weighty pages (IV, iv, 358–362). The language teacher's artless method of presentation is inevitably disturbed by his elegant use of the words of his primary source, at the precise moment when the protagonist rises to a height of fervor and decision. The B text introduces the quotation in this way: there comes "a page and a half of incoherent writing where his expression is baffled by the novelty and the mysteriousness of that side of our emotional life to which his solitary existence had been a stranger. Then only he begins to address directly the reader he had in his mind, trying to express in broken sentences, full of wonder and awe, the sovereign (he uses the very word) power of her person over his imagination, in which lay the dormant seed of her brother's words" (IV, iv, 357–358). At such moments, not only is the seminal power of speech (Haldin's) attested to but the fusion of subjects in writing (Razumov's letter entering the narrator's text and conveying the current of feeling both are incapable of separately).[6]

Despite the greater drama of Razumov's previous confession to Nathalie and of his subsequent self-exposure to the revolutionists, this written declaration is the climactic moment in the novel, bringing to a crescendo the tragic theme of the hero's loneliness. Moreover, as an expression of Razumov's love for Nathalie, the letter reveals a new dimension of the novel: it is, besides being a political novel, a love story, complicated by subtle but unmistakable hints of the narrator's competing love for the heroine and his suppressed jealousy of Razumov. If a quotation from the primary source, the C text, has the power to endow the B text with a tragic dimension, and further to elaborate the formal order of the A text, it is because a "sovereign power" *is* at work in all three texts. That this power is a linguistic one is made clear when the hero acknowledges that Nathalie's sway over him takes its potency from "the dormant seed of her brother's words." (We may even find here the shadowy apparition of a fourth level of discourse, or D text, composed of Haldin's written letters to Nathalie [not quoted] and his spoken words to Razumov, some of which the latter quotes in the C text.)

It would be too much to claim that Razumov falls in love because Nathalie embodies Haldin's revolutionary spirit, as carried by his words. But it is evident that language exhibits here its character of *resonance*, flowing from Haldin into Razumov and Razumov's writing, on into the observer's record of their relationship, and finally into the language of art, becoming part of the fabric of Conrad's creation. Language has this peculiar ability to allow itself to be seen on one level of discourse or another, for a series of words can exist at one and the same time within a novel, within a quasi-historical report, within a personal notebook, and within a letter or a direct address. Although as sensible people we know that there is only the one set of words, all of them written by Conrad and to be found only in the pages of a book called *Under Western Eyes*, as sympathetic readers we also assent to the varied modes of discourse in which those words are engaged.

Given the multiple resonances of language, it is not surprising that we discover that writing which we think we compose on one level of discourse exists simultaneously—sometimes primarily—on another. An absurd limit of such linguistic malleability is proposed in *Under Western Eyes* by the radical journalist, Laspara, who urges Razumov to "write something for us": "He could not understand how any one could refrain from writing on anything, social, economic, historical—anything. Any subject could be treated in the right spirit, and for the ends of social revolution" (III, iv, 287). A more profound linguistic transformation occurs in the narrator's discovery that he is writing not simply a personal but a social history: "The task is not in truth the writing in the narrative form a *precisé* of a strange human document, but the rendering—I perceive it now clearly—of the moral conditions ruling over a large portion of this earth's surface . . ." (I, iii, 67). But the most important shift in the nature of a writing occurs at the peak of Razumov's career as a writer. Beginning as the inscriber of school exercises, bursting out as the composer of his gnomic set of theses ("History not Theory," etc.), Razumov moves at last from merely instrumental writing, designed for attack or defense, to what we may consider the esthetic manner, creating a verbal image of his own identity. As this process is essential to the dramatic action, yet complicated in its stages, it is worth tracing in some detail.

What Razumov writes, in response to Laspara's invitation, is his first spy report: "Write. Must write! He! Write! A sudden light flashed upon him. To write was the very thing he had made up his mind to do that day" (III, iv, 288). The decision to write, however, even when the content is clear and the motive strong, presents problems both spiritual and practical: "But the idea of writing evoked the thought of a place to write in, of shelter, of privacy, and naturally of his lodgings, mingled . . . with a mistrust as of some hostile influence awaiting him within those odious four walls" (III, iv, 289). The practical problem of writing without fear of interruption, as well as the spiritual one of writing without the ghostly presence of Haldin in his room, are both solved when Razumov discovers a sheltered spot on an islet in the mouth of the Rhone. The Ile Rousseau provides not only security from sudden interruption but a symbolic aegis to take the place of Haldin's baleful influence: ". . . the exiled effigy of the author of the *Social Contract* sat enthroned above the bowed head of Razumov in the sombre immobility of bronze" (III, iv, 291). The irony of the position is not simply that this commitment to writing takes place under the sign, as it were, of the arch-exponent of speech but also that Razumov is here associated with the *confessional* writer par excellence–the autobiographer whom Conrad somewhat scornfully singled out in *A Personal Record* for "the extreme thoroughness he brought to the work of justifying his own existence" (p. 95). In keeping with the literary imperatives represented by Rousseau, the hero finds that writing a spy report is not enough and that he must go on to confessional writing; Razumov returns to his room and regains "a certain measure of composure by writing in his secret diary."

The one kind of writing leads into the other, it seems, and the kinetic effects which the writer hopes to accomplish with the report give way to the esthetic effects of the notebook. For it is an esthetic evaluation of the notebook that emerges: "Mr. Razumov looked at it, I suppose, as a man looks at himself in a mirror, with wonder, perhaps with anguish, with anger or despair" (III, i, 214). The traditional metaphor of the mirror of art is deceptive, suggesting an already prepared reflecting surface to which the Narcissus-like figure approaches, whereas language-become-art is something not found but made. Razumov sees himself in his own language, not as something given but as a composition created by his acts of writing. Insofar as the notebook provides the materials out of which the B text and ultimately the A text are composed, we can say that the writing of the notebook establishes the linguistic equivalent of Razumov's identity.

The hero, moreover, affirms his own creation by bequeathing it to his beloved. The power of writing to preserve the vital being of the writer is attested to when Nathalie turns the notebook over to the language teacher (by virtue of which action we are allowed to have the text): "She walked to the writing-table, . . . a mere piece of dead furniture; but it contained something living, still, since she took from a recess a flat parcel which she brought to me. 'It's a book,' she said rather abruptly. 'It was sent to me wrapped up in my veil'" (IV, v, 375). Thanks to the gift of this writing, we are enabled to project the living Razumov, for in it he achieves the esthetic self-realization at which autobiographical writers aim. How does the notebook fulfill so august a role? There is no hint here of the traditional motif of immortality through art–"So long as . . . eyes can see, / So long lives this"–even though the notebook is considered "something living" while wrapped in a veil within a piece of "dead furniture." To grasp the dynamics of self-embodiment in language may help us fathom the complex structure of writings that is *Under Western Eyes*.

At first, the process seems simple: "I want to be understood," says Razumov (I, ii, 39). If one can convey one's inner life to another there may be said to exist a image of the self outside one's own skin. But the narrator, in tune with Conrad's skepticism, immediately describes Razumov's wish as "the universal aspiration with all its profound and melancholy meaning." The language teacher has already given us his views on the limits of communication by language: "Words, as is well known, are the great foes of reality. . . . To a teacher of languages there comes a time when the world is but a place of many words and man appears a mere talking animal not much more wonderful than a parrot" (I, 3). Not only language teachers may find it so; many a creative and critical writer shares the view. If one and all wish only to be understood, it would seem that language, as here described, would be a last resort. Yet we are all more or less Russians, to judge by the succeeding account of "the Russians' extraordinary love of words": "There must be a wonderful soothing power in mere words since so many men have used them for self-communion. Being myself a quiet individual I take it that what all men are really after is some form or perhaps only some formula of peace" (I, 5).

This last may appear to be another sign of the narrator's immersion in language, like his continuation of the trope: "What sort of peace Kirylo Sidorovitch Razumov expected to find in the writing up of his record it passeth my understanding to guess." But the nice distinction he draws between a "form" (or kind) and a "formula" (or verbal equivalent) provides a clue to the function of language envisaged here. If one can formulate a verbal equivalent of one's sense of self, or of life, or the ideal, one has done something to fend off silence, which in *Under Western Eyes* is repeatedly seen as a kind of death. (Merleau-Ponty might claim that what language does is to propitiate the silence by building it into the fabric of the text.)

Although words grope for an understanding that is never reached, and for a peace not to be found in this world, the alternatives to language are disturbingly meager. Silence may be golden but, as with other precious metals in Conrad's world, the possession of such a treasure may prove one's undoing. Indeed, the entire tale is generated by Razumov's taciturnity, for he is misjudged as a sympathizer with revolutionary action because of his very detachment and restraint: "Amongst a lot of exuberant talkers, in the habit of exhausting themselves daily by ardent discussion, a comparatively taciturn personality is naturally credited with reserve power" (I, 6). After Haldin acts on this assumption and involves him, Razumov's reliance on silence produces only undesirable effects; when he forbids another conspirator to address a "single word" to him, the schoolfellow replies: "You don't wish[,] for secret reasons . . . perfectly . . . I understand" (I, iii, 75). Silence can also prove an effective weapon against a man determined to keep silent, as Razumov finds at Councilor Mikulin's: ". . . the silence during which they sat gazing at each other . . . lasted some little time, and was characterized (for silences have their character) by a sort of sadness imparted to it perhaps by the mild and thoughtful manner of the bearded official. . . . [Razumov] could bear the silence no longer, and cursing himself for his weakness spoke first, though he had promised himself not to do so on any account" (I, iii, 86–87). Moreover, when in the subsequent discussion the hero tries to absolve himself of complicity with Haldin on the grounds that he had not encouraged him, the virtue of silence fails to be acknowledged: "He talked and I listened. That is not a conversation," Razumov says. "'Listening is a great art,' observed Mikulin parenthetically" (I, iii, 92).

Other situations in the plot indicate that silence, far from implying innocence or even detachment, actually tarnishes what it touches. When Haldin keeps silent under the tortures of the czarist police, he seems heroic; but, when he "preserves the same stubborn silence" (I, iii, 93) as Razumov is revealed to him as his betrayer, does he nobly refrain from revenge or only more deeply implicate the hero? (Speech might either exaggerate or minimize Razumov's involvement, but silence seems only to underwrite the presumption of the hero's complicity.) By the same token, when the Russian government remains silent about its success in capturing and executing this assassin of a high official, is it a sign of grandiose self-assurance or a subtle form of torturing the survivors? Certainly the latter is the effect; as Nathalie puts it, "For us–for my mother specially, what I am afraid of is incertitude. People do disappear. . . . Yes, I am afraid of silence . . ." (II, i, 109). Eventually, the news of Haldin's death brings no relief but only silence in its turn: the narrator envisages "the motionless dumb figure of the mother in her chair. . . . The silence in there seemed to call aloud for vengeance against an historical fact and the modern instances of its working" (IV, ii, 324). Here silence becomes a form of speech, perhaps the most precise articulation of the unspeakable. But it is that same still voice of anguish which drives Razumov away from his interview with Mrs. Haldin and which is one of the proximate causes of his confession: "The silence which had fallen on his last words [to Mrs. Haldin] had lasted for five minutes or more. What did it mean? Before its incomprehensible character he became conscious of anger in his stern mood, the old anger against Haldin reawakened by the contemplation of Haldin's mother" (IV, iii, 340–341). While so disturbing to Razumov, silence is equally potent in bringing Mrs. Haldin closer to her death; her failure to express her grief seems to be one of the contributory factors in her rapid decline: ". . . she seemed to die from the shock of an ultimate disappointment borne in silence" (IV, v, 372).

After such a display of the dangers of keeping silent, we come back to language with renewed faith–or is it only with more urgent needs? Words may be impotent, but silence is empty; though language may fail in all its declared aims, at least it is not nothing, and it helps fill the vast empty spaces in existence. As the language teacher has suggested, if we can't have peace, at least we can content ourselves with a "formula of peace." Yet such faint praise may seem to damn language too thoroughly. I have been speaking as though language were all of a piece, but it may be possible to distinguish between relative and utter vanity in its operations. One conclusion that might be drawn from Razumov's career is that writing is in vain but that speech may not be so ineffectual after all. On completing his letters to Nathalie and, with the same stroke, bringing his notebook to an end, Razumov "stopped writing, shut the book . . . and then flung the pen away from him into a distant corner" (IV, iv, 362). At this point, the hero turns to oral language, most dramatically in his declaration to the revolutionaries, but also in his subsequent role: "Some of *us* always go to see him when passing through," Sophia Antonovna relates. "He is intelligent. He has ideas. . . . He talks well, too" (IV, v, 379). How does it come about that this, the most literate of Conrad's heroes (barring Heyst, perhaps), a man of books who spends much of his time making a book, turns at the end, without being able to hear them, to spoken words?

Let us consider Razumov's sequence of confessions as a means of interpreting his passage from the written to the spoken word. For the hero, we recall, makes three distinct confessions in the denouement. The first is a spoken one, made privately to Nathalie (with the narrator present when he shouldn't be); in it, Razumov exposes only his guilt, naming—or, rather, pointing to—himself as Haldin's betrayer: "There is no more to tell! . . . [The story] ends here—on this very spot" (IV, iii, 354). The second confession is also person to person, but written, amending the spoken revelation: "Listen—now comes the true confession. The other was nothing. . . . do you know what I said to myself? I shall steal his sister's soul from her. . . . [but] I felt that I must tell you that I had ended by loving you" (IV, iv, 359, 361). This is a confession not of guilt but of love and hate, not of the overt deed but of the inner life. Just as it looks back to the earlier confession, it anticipates the later one: "And to tell you that [I love you] I must first confess. Confess, go out—and perish" (IV, iv, 361). (Here Razumov makes the avowal of love conditional on his avowal of guilt—in effect, makes the second confession [the emotional climax] follow from the third [the dramatic climax] by arranging that the delivery of the letter and the notebook occur after he has spoken out.) The third confession is, unlike both the first and the second, public: "Haven't you all understood that I am that man?" (IV, iv, 366). The sequence, then, moves from impulsive speech through written preparations to dramatic oratory, and Razumov's subsequent discourses to the faithful suggest that he has taken on the role of a populist sage.

If we find this transformation from author to oracle a falling-off, we must nevertheless admit that writing has failed the hero. The pathos of his letter writing is all too clear: "In this queer pedantism of a man who had read, thought, lived, pen in hand, there is the sincerity of the attempt to grapple by the same means with another profounder knowledge" (IV, iv, 357). Having tested, not to say exhausted, the potentialities of writing—having achieved whatever self-definition and personal revelation are available to the writer—Razumov can never hope to bridge the gap between him and his beloved with words. He is still very much alone—has named his tragic loneliness but not overcome it. By public speech, however much hostility it rouses, he remarkably accomplishes something which all his writing cannot: his rhetoric puts the speaker into a collective relationship with his audience. The alienated hero is suddenly transformed into a communal oracle, though this may be only a new form of alienation; and Russians will continue to listen to him, as he indulges in the national trait of speech for its own sake. For better or worse, he is deafened and doesn't have to listen to his own words; speech may not be the occasion of presence and communion, but it effects the taking up of a viable stance in the world.

It would be too much to claim, from this evidence alone, that Conrad's final twist of the denouement is a declaration of ultimate despair of written language and of the art of fiction along with it. Yet the elaborate structure of writings which constitutes *Under Western Eyes* perhaps expresses no more than the anxiety of every conscientious writer about the efficacy of writing. Certainly there must be some sympathy with the man who, when invited to contribute a paper, can say, "I have written already all I shall ever write" (IV, iv, 364).

10. Science in "Ithaca"

It is curious that, for nearly another four centuries after the acceptance of the Copernican theory, the Sun and the Solar System were believed to be at the center of the stellar universe. The decade following 1918 was the critical epoch during which astronomical measurements finally eroded man's fundamental egocentric concept of his place in the universe.

—SIR BERNARD LOVELL

> I am writing *Ithaca* in the form of a mathematical catechism. All events are resolved into their cosmic physical, psychical, etc. equivalents, e.g., Bloom jumping down the area, drawing water from the tap, the micturition in the garden, the cone of incense, lighted candle and statue so that not only will the reader know everything and know it in the baldest coldest way but Bloom and Stephen thereby become heavenly bodies, wanderers like the stars at which they gaze.[1]

Joyce's statement on the seventeenth section of *Ulysses* is, like most of his other explanations of that novel, notable both for what it conceals and what it reveals. We are told the narrative mode: catechism, not in the context of Catholicism but in that of scientific inquiry. Four sciences are mentioned: mathematics, astronomy ("cosmic"), physics, and psychology. And Joyce reveals the main symbolic transformation: the change of Stephen and Bloom into heavenly bodies. These facts have their place in Joyce's well-known tale of the elements of *Ulysses*: the "Technic" is "catechism (impersonal)," the "Art" is "science," and the "Symbol" is "comets." We sense something of Joyce's esthetic intention in his desire to communicate a vision of experience "in the baldest coldest way," something of his larger significances in the equation of the heroes with eternally recurrent astral wanderers. But no one could justify the second-longest section of *Ulysses* as anything but a stylistic tour de force if these elements did not tell us something about the character and mental life of Bloom and Stephen, something about the world in which they live.

With the publication of a thorough study of the astronomical references in "Ithaca,"[2] the section has begun to receive the kind of sustained attention it deserves. As the authors point out, few prior commentators have discussed, even briefly, the astronomical aspect—a striking omission in view of its importance and of the attention given to much less obvious veins of Joyce's scholarship. Harry Levin emphasizes the impersonality of the catechism and the emptiness of the heavenly spaces on which the characters gaze: ". . . Joyce contemplates his characters *sub specie aeternitatis*, from the scope of planetary distances."[3] Richard Kain employs but does not elaborate on the terms "perspective" and "relativity."[4] James Atherton has enlarged the problem of Joyce's interest in modern science by associating the four old men of *Finnegans Wake* with four-dimensional space-time.[5] But the pursuit of these wisps of meaning has been discouraged by Joyce's own passing barbs at science and scientists,[6] by his apparent adherence to the antiscientific maxims of Tolstoy and other antirationalists,[7] and by the scanty evidence of his studies of the subject after his early distaste for the classical "natural philosophy" offered by his Jesuit schoolmasters.[8]

We are nevertheless confronted by the striking historical coincidence that *Ulysses* was written (1914–1921) in the same years in which the general theory of relativity (1915–1917) and the conception of an expanding universe (1917 ff.) were being published in a series of papers by Einstein and others, while the original impetus to the new vision of the cosmos was given in the special theory of relativity (1905) at just about the time in which the novel is set. Although temporal coincidence does not establish causal relation, we should find it odd if the novel's view of the modern world were to overlook the epochal revolution in man's conception of his place in the universe that marked these years. By placing Bloomsday in the year prior to the first widely noted (though not the first) of Einstein's relativity papers, Joyce did, of course, avoid the burden of direct reference to the new science. But, in choosing the four above-mentioned sciences as his symbolic and thematic matter in "Ithaca," Joyce could not avoid expressing the educated layman's response to the liberating implications of relativity theory in the physical, psychological, and moral spheres.

As will be seen in the following analysis, Joyce's scientific vocabulary and the theory underlying even the most bizarre suggestions of his prose are drawn from long-established classical mechanics and astronomy. But the traditionalism of his information does not diminish the originality of his literary use of science—no more than their firm links to the Newtonian system diminish the originality of the Einsteinian theories. As Bertrand Russell puts it:

> Most of what we have said hitherto was already recognized by physicists before Einstein invented the theory of relativity. "Force" was known to be merely a mathematical fiction, and it was generally held that motion is a merely relative phenomenon—that is to say, when two bodies are changing their relative position, we cannot say that one is moving while the other is at rest, since the occurrence is merely a change in their relation to each other. But a great labor was required

in order to bring the actual procedure of physics into harmony with these new convictions.[9]

We may take Russell's statement to apply to the literary imagination as well as to the scientific. The relativity of personal, social, and historical perspectives had been a truism at least since the Romantic era, while the social and psychological processes regulating moral and esthetic values had come to the fore with the Naturalists, but it required a Joyce to establish these notions as elements of modern fiction by making them the narrative principles of his great novel. The double status of modern physics as both the inheritance of the old and the inauguration of the new is appropriately paralleled by the intimate relations of the traditional novel and the modern temper in *Ulysses*.

The old and the new appear together in typical fashion in one of the strands of *Ulysses'* scientific reference that is not confined to "Ithaca": parallax. This astronomical term, which occurs to Bloom periodically throughout his day and reaches a crescendo in his vision of his grandfather during the "Nighttown" scene, has remained obscure despite the widespread recognition that it has something to do with the novel's basic meanings. Littmann and Schweighauser offer a broad summary of the matter:

> But great as this universe is, it too is subject to metamorphosis, to change, to motion: the world on which we stand is in motion, giving rise to the precession of the equinoxes. . . . And the "fixed" stars around us are themselves in motion, as measured in terms of parallactic drift. Thus we human beings are an infinitesimal model of the ever-changing world. We exhibit parallax in our relations with other human beings, as *Ulysses* demonstrates.[10]

What is suggested by such accounts is the more general observational principle of aberration, the apparent change in the position of a body due to the motion of the observer—the necessary correction that must be made for physical "subjectivity." From this standpoint, Joyce seems to be courting an analogy between the relative positions of astronomical bodies and those of human beings, subtly urging as much self-consciousness in our observations of others as astronomers exercise in astral sightings. But further attention to the history of the concept of parallax suggests further relations to the scientific theme of "Ithaca."

Parallax, simply put, is the degree to which a star's position varies in relation to other stars as our point of observation changes with the rotation of the earth. Two bodies seen from one position will be in a different spatial relation from the same two bodies seen from another position and, when the angles of these observations are measured, the distances between these bodies can be calculated by trigonometry.

Much of the principle of stellar parallax was worked out by the Royal

Astronomer Bradley as early as 1728 (although it was first measured in 1838), but the more delicate problem of solar parallax was a nineteenth-century discovery of considerable notoriety. The distance of the sun from the earth can be calculated in the same manner as stellar distances if it can be seen in close relation to another body, i.e., by measuring the positions of the sun and a planet as seen from various places on the earth. The most opportune conditions for such measurement occurred twice in the nineteenth century during Venus' rare transits of the sun—its passage between the earth and the sun. These took place in 1874 and 1882 and aroused not only worldwide interest but international rivalry; expeditions went out to remote corners of the earth, with uniformly disappointing results.[11] No turn-of-the-century amateur astronomer—neither Bloom nor Joyce—could have failed to be aware of the fierce debate surrounding this scientific undertaking—events of the order of the space launchings of our day. (The measurement was finally accomplished by employing the minor planets.)

More germane to "Ithaca," however, is the peculiar nature of solar parallax. Unlike the measurements of stellar parallax, involving the relative positions of one observer on two occasions, the sighting of the sun and another body must be undertaken by at least two observers at precisely the same moment. This conforms much more closely to the situation in "Ithaca," where Bloom and Stephen are traced in successive instances of coincidental and divergent perception and response to experience. To anticipate somewhat, the twin observations of Venus in relation to the sun are embodied in the two protagonists' attitudes toward Molly, the love goddess of the novel. At this point, be it maintained only that an attentive reading of "Ithaca" in line with detailed physical and astronomical information can yield not only a view of Joyce's absorption of classical and modern science but also an approach to some of his central symbolic themes.

Another element of "Ithaca" that calls for scientific explanation is its form, the catechism. No doubt the coldness and baldness of the abrupt questions and technical responses ring in echoes of a Catholic education like Joyce's at Clongowes, but these effects are directed here toward an end different from that of A Portrait of the Artist as a Young Man. In literary terms, catechism is a close approach to the point of view of an omniscient narrator: the respondent gives the impression of being a memory bank from which can be drawn complete information on any subject. The amplitude and assurance of his answers suggest a parody of the complacent scientist who thinks any question can be resolved by reducing it to its material components. There is no more need to think that Joyce identifies himself with this point of view than there is to think he is any one of his personae.

A further characteristic of the catechism form has a more precise relevance to scientific activity. The form by its very nature is a discontinuous one: the questions divide up reality into segments and the responses give only the requisite data. There is no criterion of esthetic taste or human relevance to direct the responses. Thus, instead of considering the micturating in the garden as a splendidly comic, all-too-human act of friendship, the response describes the parallelism and divergence of the urine streams. There are symbolic suggestions in the physical facts that allow us to feel the moral import of the action, but the respondent seems unaware of or above them. This point of view accords with that of self-conscious scientific research, which limits its interest to the observable phenomena, designs its investigation for a controlled approach to certain elements of the field, and presents its data in their narrowest, verifiable form, leaving inference and implication to the reader.

Despite this carefully self-limiting approach, the respondent's self-assured tone may suggest an absolute certainty that would seem to accord poorly with a relativistic theory of nature. The difficulty lies in some mis-apprehensions about relativity theory that appear to be widely current among humanistic scholars. Relativity is not relativism, as the latter term has evolved in the psychological and anthropological disciplines. Einsteinian physics does not leave knowledge in doubt, subject to the vagaries of personal perspective or social conditioning. While it builds the observer into its observations, it provides stable formulas for "transforming" measurements from any one frame of reference into any other. In fact, the Einsteinian enterprise may be considered a search for invariants—like the relation of mass and energy, or the speed of light—which do not change their values with their frame of reference. To put it into Einstein's terms: "It should be possible to formulate the laws of the physical universe in such a fashion that they should hold in all possible frames of reference."[12] Like Einstein, Joyce was dedicated to a quest for the constants in human experience, and his invocation of Viconian cycles and Jungian archetypes was designed to portray the genus *homo* in all its climes and ages. Human subjectivity is, then, not the method but the subject matter of his investigation. In "Ithaca" we observe the divergent perspectives of Bloom and Stephen, but the narrator's perspective on them is a firmly objective one.

It is not, however, the whole of "Ithaca," for the totality of life includes not only the scientific observer's objectivity but the participants' subjectivities—and the symbolic associations these evoke in the reader's mind. To see the interplay of narration, characterization, and symbolism in Joyce's use of scientific materials, we must follow the text in sequence —although an exhaustive commentary is not possible here.

"What parallel courses did Bloom and Stephen follow returning?" (p. 666)[13]

"Ithaca" begins with a Euclidean universe, in which parallel lines do not intersect (they *do* in some branches of non-Euclidean geometry). In tracing the heroes' course home from the cabmen's shelter, Joyce begins to sound one of the notes of his thematic burden: two human beings can come together only to the extent of approximating each other's courses, but they can never be united—because they are two! Relationships are at best the maintenance of a constant distance, as in parallel tracks; any change is either a collision or a cumulatively greater divergence. This theme is taken up in Bloom's reflections on the transitoriness and limitations of his "interindividual relations": "From inexistence to existence he came to many and was as one received: existence with existence he was with any as any with any: from existence to nonexistence gone he would be by all as none perceived" (pp. 667–668). The absolute that emerges at the outset, then, is the isolation—the noncombining nature—of the individual human being.

Arriving home to discover himself "keyless," Bloom devises a Ulyssean stratagem—jumping from the street level down to the basement level in an areaway in front of his house. "Did he fall?" asks the patient catechist.

> By his body's known weight of eleven stone and four pounds in avoirdupois measure, as certified by the graduated machine for periodical selfweighing in the premises of Francis Frœdman, pharmaceutical chemist of 19 Frederick street, north, on the last feast of the Ascension, to wit, the twelfth day of May of the bissextile year one thousand nine hundred and four of the christian era (jewish era five thousand six hundred and sixty four, mohammedan era one thousand three hundred and twentytwo), golden number 5, epact 13, solar cycle 9, dominical letters C B, Roman indication 2, Julian period 6617, MXMIV [sic]. (pp. 668–669)

This question seems to have been doubly evaded, first by the discussion of Bloom's weight and then by the specification of the conditions of his last weighing. In fact, the question of falling has been treated as a problem of gravitation—"weight" is defined as the gravitational attraction of any bodies, in this case of Bloom and the earth. Given the fact that Bloom had weight—had a body—he fell. (We cannot here pursue the implications of this tautology in Joyce's version of the paradisal Fall elsewhere in *Ulysses*.) The question becomes: how much did Bloom weigh? This can be answered only by experiment: the record of the last experiment in determining his weight is required. In formal scientific fashion, the description of the experiment includes a specification of the equipment employed—here, ludicrously, it is a specific drugstore scale—and of other conditions, especially the time of weighing. The time in this case does not affect the outcome of the experiment but has a bearing on the application of its data: the fact that Bloom last weighed himself more than a month before limits the probable accuracy of the data as evidence for Bloom's weight at the time of his jump. We are brought up against the sobering reflection that, for all our information about Bloom, we shall never know him completely —we can never know his exact weight on Bloomsday. We can, however, have greater success in fixing the time of his weighing, but only by the pedantic process of specifying its position in a number of calendars. Does the variability of the date according to various systems of reckoning enforce the notion of the relativity of time? Only in the sense suggested in our discussion of relativism: these reckonings are all conventional—most are religious—systems and exhibit the same subjectivity as all culturally determined perspectives.[14] Bringing together these partial views, Joyce suggests, establishes a socially objective (i.e., widely agreed on) time for the event.

Elementary physical terminology is employed to describe Bloom's entry into his kitchen and his lighting of the stove and a candle. But a more sophisticated account of the same events is given in the immediately following exchange:

> What discrete succession of images did Stephen meanwhile perceive?
> Reclined against the area railings he perceived through the transparent kitchen panes a man regulating a gasflame of 14 C P, a man lighting a candle, a man removing in turn each of his two boots, a man leaving the kitchen holding a candle of 1 C P. (p. 669)

The four men Stephen sees are, of course, one, but the strict empiricism of the question has already established that we do not see things but only images of things, not actions but only stages of action. The contents of Stephen's mind, then, include no sense of continuity, much less of the identity of the actor, Bloom. It is we, the normal observers, who interpolate a concept of action performed by a single, identifiable actor. The matter is treated lightly: the fussiness of the strictly empirical description is crowned by specifying the candle's power as 1 candlepower. Yet, if science is gently mocked here, it manages to give an accurate impression of the state of Stephen's mind: in his somewhat dissociated and fatigued condition, he does not have an intimate sense of Bloom as another human being and tends to register Bloom's acts passively, making little attempt to engage with him as a person. With equal passivity, he collects discrete images from his memory in the pages that follow.

If the candle-lighting passage is a *reductio ad absurdum* of scientific objectivity, the description of the flow of water in Bloom's tap is an enlargement to the absurd:

> Did it flow?
> Yes. From Roundwood reservoir in county Wicklow of a cubic capacity of 2,400 million gallons, percolating through a subterranean aqueduct of filter mains of single and double pipeage constructed at

an initial plant cost of £5 per linear yard by way of the Dargle, Rath-down, Glen of the Downs and Callowhill to the 26 acre reservoir at Stillorgan, a distance of 22 statute miles, and thence, through a system of relieving tanks, by a gradient of 250 feet to the city boundary. . . . (p. 671)

The emphasis here is not on science but on technology, and the local-color details (both in the quoted and in the omitted portions of the extended sentence) reflect Bloom's absorption in gimmickry, in the practical and civic. But the larger scope of his mind is rendered in the following exchange:

> What in water did Bloom, waterlover, drawer of water, watercarrier returning to the range, admire?
> Its universality: its democratic equality and constancy to its nature in seeking its own level: . . . the restlessness of its waves and surface particles visiting in turn all points of its seaboard: . . . its climatic and commercial significance: . . . its capacity to dissolve and hold in solution all soluble substances including millions of tons of the most precious metals: . . . the simplicity of its composition, two constituent parts of hydrogen with one constituent part of oxygen: its healing virtues: . . . its properties for cleansing, quenching thirst and fire, nourishing vegetation: its infallibility as paradigm and paragon: its metamorphoses as vapour, mist, cloud, rain, sleet, snow, hail: . . . its ubiquity as constituting 90% of the human body: the noxiousness of its effluvia in lacustrine marshes, pestilential fens, faded flower-water, stagnant pools in the wandering moon. (pp. 671–672)

Here, too, the contents of a mind overflow but, unlike Stephen's passive accumulation, these are the disjecta membra of a hobbyist, amateur scientist, pragmatist, projector, and poet of the pools of the moon. Bloom's curiosity is a form of imagination; his inquisitive energy goes out to water as it does to everything around him, and in the qualities of water he finds his own character reflected. Stephen, on the other hand is "hydrophobe," "distrusting aquacities of thought and language" (p. 673): for all his keenness, he is locked up in his own subjectivity and only on his walk on Sandymount strand does he engage with the watery flux of things. Quasi-scientific information is used in Bloom's case as data for a psychology of character: the narrator's collection of data includes the makings of a character structure. But the objective respondent limits himself to assembling the evidence; it is left to the reader to pick about the midden for fragments of a self.

After preparing cocoa—with appropriate remarks on "the phenomenon of ebullition"—Bloom joins Stephen in drinking it: "Bloom, having the advantage of ten seconds at the initiation and taking, from the concave surface of a spoon along the handle of which a steady flow of heat was conducted, three sips to his opponent's one, six to two, nine to three" (p. 677). We are given a foretaste of two schoolboyish exercises in which Bloom is fond of engaging, both of which will soon be developed into major issues. The first is the contest: Stephen is labeled the opponent, and later their friendly sport will turn to micturition. The other is the series: the elaboration of the ratio of three sips to one is only a simple case of the speculation that is to ensue on the relative ages of Stephen and Bloom (p. 679). While one mathematical series shows them through the years diminishing the ratio of their initial disparity of age, the other envisions them always in the same ratio as at Stephen's first birthday—climaxing in a Bloom of 83,000 years.[15]

These games establish relationships in Bloom's mind, while none develop in their conversation. A later passage introduces a subject of great sensitivity and further separation:

> What, reduced to their simplest reciprocal form, were Bloom's thoughts about Stephen's thoughts about Bloom and Bloom's thoughts about Stephen's thoughts about Bloom's thoughts about Stephen?
> He thought that he thought that he was a jew whereas he knew that he knew that he knew that he was not. (p. 682)

Again, the childish game (in this case a parody not of science but of logic) expresses the basic relationship and divergence of the characters: Bloom's capacity to intuit the consciousness of another is brought up against the other's splendid isolation and the immutable differences between them.

At this point, the narrative departs temporarily from its predominantly scientific mode. As Bloom's reflections on his own Jewishness and his companion's possible anti-Semitism continue, we learn something about the heroes' similarities, e.g., that Bloom was baptized a Catholic by the same priest who baptized Stephen. After they attempt to further their unity by discussing the linguistic relationships of Hebrew and Celtic, Stephen shatters the growing communion by singing an anti-Semitic ballad. Despite his renewed loneliness, Bloom pursues his project of bringing Stephen into his family to substitute for his lost son. But Stephen refuses the invitation to spend the night and the two men go outside to part.

There begins an extended meditation on "the heaventree of stars hung with humid nightblue fruit"—a threshold moment in the scientific reference of "Ithaca":

> With what meditations did Bloom accompany his demonstration to his companion of various constellations?
> Meditations of evolution increasingly vaster: . . . of our system plunging towards the constellation of Hercules: of the parallax or parallactic drift of socalled fixed stars, in reality evermoving from im-

measurably remote eons to infinitely remote futures in comparison with which the years, threescore and ten, of allotted human life formed a parenthesis of infinitesimal brevity.

Were there obverse meditations of involution increasingly less vast?

Of the eons of geological periods recorded in the stratifications of the earth: of the myriad minute entomological organic existences . . . : of the universe of human serum constellated with red and white bodies, themselves universes of void space constellated with other bodies, each, in continuity, its universe of divisible component bodies of which each was again divisible in divisions of redivisible component bodies, dividends and divisors ever diminishing without actual division till, if the progress were carried far enough, nought nowhere was never reached. (pp. 698–699)

Presented with a superb image of Pascal's two infinites, Bloom, like that mathematician, is frightened by the eternal silence of the infinite spaces. But Bloom's heroism lies in his willingness to explore mentally the infinities: evolution and involution are conceived as ongoing processes, adventurous enterprises, journeys to the exotically remote. Bloom as Ulyssean mariner is caught up in the quest for scientific knowledge, and in his "demonstration to his companion of various constellations" he expresses the spirit of the Dantean Ulysses:

> fatti non foste a viver come bruti,
> ma per seguir virtute e canoscenza.

Bloom adumbrates, in effect, the symbol of Ulysses as scientific discoverer: ". . . as a competent keyless citizen he had proceeded energetically from the unknown to the known through the incertitude of the void" (p. 697). And Joyce pins the symbol down by pronouncing: "What two temperaments did they individually represent? The scientific. The artistic" (p. 683).

The scientific implications of Bloom's worldview are further developed:

> Did he find the problem of the inhabitability of the planets and their satellites by a race, given in species, and of the possible social and moral redemption of said race by a redeemer, easier of solution?
>
> Of a different order of difficulty. . . . an apogean humanity of beings created in varying forms with finite differences resulting similar to the whole and to one another would probably there as here remain inalterably and inalienably attached to vanities, to vanities of vanities and all that is vanity.
>
> And the problem of possible redemption?
> The minor was proved by the major. (pp. 699–700)

Given the constancy of (human) nature and the doubtfulness of supernatural intervention in the natural order, Bloom's universe is a secular-scientific one. His skepticism of human perfectibility is accompanied by a tolerant interest in feasible ameliorations of the human condition. Yet his view of human nature is touched by a more profound emotion that one can call *tragic* (despite the comic mode of the novel): we hear the note in his *vanitas vanitatum* conclusion, and we feel it in his subsequent confrontation with the void.

The next pages enlarge this sense of the eternally sorrowful, as a mighty listing is made of Bloom's reflections on the constellations. After accounts of astronomical discoveries, stellar sightings at the time of the births of Shakespeare, of Bloom, of Stephen, and of Rudy, and other scientific and poetic lore, the meditation ends with "the attendant phenomena of eclipses, solar and lunar, from immersion to emersion, abatement of wind, transit of shadow, taciturnity of winged creatures, emergence of nocturnal or crepuscular animals, persistence of infernal light, obscurity of terrestrial waters, pallor of human beings" (p. 701). Since this strong suggestion of human transiency in the scale of cosmic evolution pervades *Ulysses*, we are prepared to accept the further application of this view of life to the cosmos itself. This extension is made in the next exchange:

> His (Bloom's) logical conclusion, having weighed the matter and allowing for possible error?
> That it was not a heaventree, not a heavengrot, not a heavenbeast, not a heavenman. That is was a Utopia, there being no known method from the known to the unknown: . . . a mobility of illusory forms immobilised in space, remobilised in air: a past which possibly had ceased to exist as a present before its future spectators had entered actual present existence. (p. 701)

This literal reading of utopia—nowhere—marks a major theme of *Ulysses*: the traditional form of the quest for a promised land is rendered comically in this novel, and here toward its conclusion it is renounced. There are no more utopias, and Bloom—for all his plucky meliorism—is reconciled to things as they are.

The succeeding passages acknowledge the possibility of maintaining an esthetic attitude toward a universe thus bereft of supernatural or other consoling attributes. But art is not Bloom's metier, as we have seen: he pays lip service to the "reiterated examples of poets," but his deeper interest lies in myth. When he turns to the affinities between the moon and woman, his imagination expands into a prescientific realm. From this point to the conclusion of "Ithaca," scientific implications are sporadic, as Bloom performs his preparations for going to bed and takes stock of his day, his accounts, his expectations and hopes in life, his feelings about his wife's adultery. The transition from a scientific to a mythic ambience is accomplished at the point of highest tension in the chapter, when Stephen has left him:

Alone, what did Bloom feel?

The cold of interstellar space, thousands of degrees below freezing point or the absolute zero of Fahrenheit, Centigrade or Réaumur: the incipient intimations of proximate dawn. (p. 704)

This turn from the absolute nothingness of existence to the archetypal sign of revival and resurrection is extended in the subsequent description of the dawn:

More active air, a matutinal distant cock, ecclesiastical clocks at various points, avine music, the isolated tread of an early wayfarer, the visible diffusion of the light of an invisible luminous body, the first golden limb of the resurgent sun perceptible low on the horizon. (p. 705)

Eventually, Bloom is seen as the eternal wanderer, "Everyman or Noman," who will range beyond the limits of the human world and will reappear in the heavens as a star in the constellation of Cassiopeia, an archetype in an eternal myth (pp. 727–728). It is therefore consistent with the larger movement of the section that Molly Bloom is introduced at the end "in the attitude of Gea-Tellus, fulfilled, recumbent, big with seed" (p. 737). This introduction to Molly as earth goddess—as the earth itself, it is developed in the "Penelope" section—is fully in keeping with the astronomical dimensions that have been implied throughout "Ithaca" and which have been assimilated into our conception of the hero. If Bloom is a wandering but ultimately fixed and eternal star, his wife is a lesser body, Venus or Earth, settled in its fecund cycle of procreation and sensation. If Bloom is the scientist, the modern mind and its secular attitudes, Molly is the object of science, the realm of nature—or, if that seems to dehumanize her too much, she may be considered the prescientific mind, moving slowly in its elementary egoism without the sophistications of a relativistic perspective.

"Ithaca" has followed no consistent scientific development, much less a consistently relativistic one, but in its conclusion there is an unmistakable reference to the Einsteinian universe that is merged with its mythic pattern. The eternal return of the wanderer, the sailor, the child, home to haven, bed, womb—this is the dominant motif. The reversion to origins is emphasized by a biological-mythical note: the "roc's auk's egg" (p. 737) suggests a retracing of the evolutionary process back to its primeval origins. But the conception of Bloom and Molly as a planetary or astral bodies suggests something more: the closing of cosmic space. The curvature of the universe according to Einstein's conception of space has been expressed by Arthur Eddington in a way that is strongly suggestive of the theme of *Ulysses*:

I think Einstein showed his greatness in the simple and drastic way he disposed of difficulties at infinity. He abolished infinity. He slightly altered his equations so as to make space at great distances bend round till it closed up. So that, if in Einstein's space you keep going right on in one direction, you do not get to infinity; you find yourself back at your startingpoint again.[16]

Bloom becomes a hero of the human imagination which, for all its absurdities and limitations, has the courage to expand with the infinite universe, project itself beyond its narrow experience, and go out to other human beings—the most dangerous and difficult motion of the self. Yet ultimately this heroic quest is comic, for it ends with a return to self, to the intimate things of familiar surroundings, and to the persons by whom one's life is shaped.

The curvature of space entails another feature of the modern cosmic view: the stupendous multiplicity of bodies, in which our own planet is a satellite of a minor star in a small constellation of a moderate-sized galaxy which is one of an enormous number of such profusions of stars. Put in the words of a great astronomer:

> The teaching of all this is: Don't take man too seriously, even when orienting him among the animals and plants on this local planet; and certainly not when comparing him with possibilities elsewhere in the richly endowed Metagalaxy.[17]

The refusal of seriousness is, of course, based on an ironic sense of smallness and, perhaps, irrelevance in the total scheme of things. But, as we know from classical comedy, the comic view is a serious one, too: it gives us the form of human experience lived under conditions of disparity in our expectations and needs. Bloom lost in the abyss of space is a clown, but he is a noble clown—both in his tendency to return home and in his attempt to range beyond. The ultimate viewpoint of *Ulysses* on the human condition accords well with the attitudes that have been fostered by modern science on man's place in the universe. Joyce did not write "Ithaca" to tell a scientific tale, but his tale is instinct with the wisdom of the scientific temper.

11. Being and Nothing in
A Passage to India

Warum ist überhaupt Seiendes und nicht vielmehr Nichts?
–Das Nichts als das Andere zum Seienden ist der Schleier des Seins.
—HEIDEGGER

XCEPT for the Marabar Caves—and they are twenty miles off—the city of Chandrapore presents nothing extraordinary."[1] We are presented from the outset with the structure of a reality divided in two, the ordinary and the extraordinary. Chandrapore is typical of what is ordinary: it is the city, the place of human habitation, and has no things that can be called extraordinary. But outside the ordinary there is the *extra*ordinary; it is there in addition to the ordinary. The realm of human life is not only a presence of the ordinary but also an absence of the extraordinary. In this state of absence the ordinary realm "presents nothing." But it does so in an extraordinary way: "nothing" becomes a presence when presented. Primary reality, then, is both what is there and what is not there; it is something (something ordinary) and it is nothing ("nothing extraordinary"). As an exception to the ordinary, the city also presents the caves, which are extraordinary but which contain nothing. There is the same copresence of nothing and something as in the city, and this allows it to be said that the city presents the caves, even though they are twenty miles off. Yet the caves are an exception, different from the ordinary realm that Chandrapore presents.

"Edged rather than washed by the river Ganges, it trails for a couple of miles along the bank, scarcely distinguishable from the rubbish it deposits so freely." The circumference of this ordinary realm is the river, which topographically edges rather than hygienically washes the town. This river is both of and outside the city, both its boundary and an independent force along whose bank it trails. The city is "scarcely distinguishable from the rubbish": the rubbish comes from the city, mingles with the river, and then is deposited on the bank to form the base of the city itself. The rubbish is silt, excrement, and garbage presumably; both earth and human wastes. It is all one substance: mud—whether city or river, floating silt or solid land, waste or renewed earth. This is the matter of which ordinary reality is composed; there are distinctions among the phases of its cycles, and there are distinctions among various organizations of matter—individuals, communities, geographical entities. But the cycle of life and death in the organic body of mankind and in the daily life of the town breaks down and builds up the riverbanks in an apparently endless series, each organization mingling with the others, each phase of their cycles merging with the others. Like the mixture of nothing and something in the opening sentence's description of Chandrapore, the account of the Ganges and its relation to the city includes both negative and positive movements: there is elimination and decay but also a building up of substance.[2]

"There are no bathing-steps on the river front, as the Ganges happens not to be holy here; indeed there is no river front, and bazaars shut out the wide and shifting panorama of the stream." Here the realm of ordinary life is conceived as the marketplace of trade and other practical efforts to survive. The Ganges is not holy here: the ordinary realm is perhaps elsewhere surrounded by holiness but is here seen devoid of spirituality. Like the combination of polar elements in the initial descriptions of the city and river, the riverfront of the city is both a positive and a negative boundary; "there is no river front," for the town has no interest in defining its boundaries, yet "bazaars shut out . . . the stream," for the unplanned processes of trade create a boundary and limit people's awareness of their environment. "The streets are mean, the temples ineffective, and though a few fine houses exist they are hidden away in gardens or down alleys whose filth deters all but the invited guest." As in the previous sentences, there is a mixture here of presence and absence: a few esthetic values exist in this ordinary realm but are available only by invitation and with effort; they are surrounded by filth—identical to the rubbish deposited by the river—but in their hidden state they are kept safe, like a jewel in dung. Filthy alleys and private gardens mingle in the ordinary realm to surround the fine houses; both beauty and ugliness, upper- and lower-class life, form a continuous medium of ordinariness.

There follows a historical excursus, giving the social and political origins of the ordinary realm: "Chandrapore was never large or beautiful, but two hundred years ago it lay on the road between Upper India, then imperial, and the sea, and the fine houses date from that period. The zest for decoration stopped in the eighteenth century, nor was it ever democratic. There is no painting and scarcely any carving in the bazaars." The balancing of affirmative and negative values in the sentence structures indicates an extension of the doubleness of the opening sentences into matters of art and politics. India has a great history and culture, but it is limited by its social system (the end of its period of decorative art is associated with its lack of democratic distribution), and the great tradition of its imperial period makes little impact on the present ("no painting . . . in the bazaars"). The route to the sea has made Chandrapore important, but it is no longer a major one and the city has declined. Even at its apogee, the historical cycle makes no very significant departure from mediocrity, for "Chandrapore was never large or beautiful." The lines of movement in the history of the ordinary realm are, then, as limited as the cycles of the human and social organisms or those of the river.

"The very wood seems made of mud, the inhabitants of mud moving. So abased, so monotonous is everything that meets the eye, that when the Ganges comes down it might be expected to wash the excrescence back into the soil. Houses do fall, people are drowned and left rotting, but the general outline of the town persists, swelling here, shrinking there, like some low but indestructible form of life." All our observations of the ordinary realm are brought together here: its undifferentiated structure, in which flesh, wood, and earth are confused; its elementary composition ("mud") at a low stage of organization ("abased, . . . monotonous"); its cyclical rhythm, exemplified by the recurrent floods and the rise and fall of people and their habitations; its primitive ("low") yet immortal ("indestructible") vitality. Chandrapore is here made typical of the realm of ordinary life; its nature is to be meaningless in its internal lack of structure yet filled with meaning when taken in relation to other realms.

The ordinary is the material basis of human existence that underlies all the exotic features of Indian and colonial English civilization, as they are represented in the novel's characters and their actions; it is the primary level of being, which most novelists leave out of account. For Forster's novel becomes an image of being as a whole, described in a systematic structure of three levels. Most discussions of *A Passage to India* have taken up the tripartite structure of parts I, II, and III, which are named "Mosque," "Caves," and "Temple." The more explicit structure proposed in this opening chapter is made up of a base of ordinary reality, a thin layer or veneer of conscious life growing out of it, and finally a realm of mystery and unfathomable space, which lies above but may also be found localized within the other realms.

The middle realm is found in the upper levels of Chandrapore itself. "Inland, the prospect alters. . . . Beyond the railway—which runs parallel to the river—the land sinks, then rises again rather steeply. On the second rise is laid out the little civil station, and viewed hence Chandrapore appears to be a totally different place. It is a city of gardens. It is no city, but a forest sparsely scattered with huts. It is a tropical pleasaunce washed by a noble river. The toddy palms and neem trees and mangoes and pepul that were hidden behind the bazaars now become visible and in their turn hide the bazaars." In this description of the upper city, the second realm of being, what seemed undifferentiated and unitary on the lowest level now is revealed as having a variety of parts and therefore different aspects. There are two cities, upper and lower: the upper "appears to be a totally different place," but this appearance is probably illusory, since the realm of differentiated life is only an excrescence from the ordinary realm of mud with which we began. The bazaars, which from ground level shut out the "wide and shifting panorama of the stream," now function in a double way, both hiding and being hidden: they hide the trees which make up the "tropical pleasaunce" but are in turn hidden by those trees. The trees, in turn, are not only hidden by the bazaars but themselves hide the city, turning it into a "forest" with only scattered habitations. What was hidden now appears, but in coming into view it serves to hide other things; what was simple and uniform at the primary level is double and complex at this second level of reality. In this realm much of the novel's action takes place; it is the realm of personal relations and psychology, of imperialism and religion, of snobbery and noncommunication.

The trees "rise from the gardens where ancient tanks nourish them, they burst out of stifling purlieus and unconsidered temples. Seeking light and air, and endowed with more strength than man or his works, they soar above the lower deposit to greet one another with branches and beckoning leaves, and to build a city for the birds. Especially after the rains do they screen what passes below, but at all times, even when scorched or leafless, they glorify the city to the English people who inhabit the rise, so that new-comers cannot believe it to be as meagre as it is described, and have to be driven down to acquire disillusionment." The upward movement of the trees is a movement toward life, toward "light and air," away from the confinement of the native quarters and religious institutions. The trees exhibit this urge toward life with even greater force than do humans in emerging from the river (they have "more strength than man"); their movement is an upward thrust, they "soar above the lower deposit." They build a city in their own right, a "city for the birds"—a society of animal life which resembles man's second-level existence and which may be approachable by such efforts as Godbole's "song of an unknown bird." (Trees like these give Mrs. Moore a final bit of knowledge as they laugh good-bye on her homeward voyage.) But their surge upward is in its turn a form of illusion, for the branches "screen what passes below" and spuriously "glorify the city"—at least to English people who are prone to such illusions. The complementary movement of the tourist is down toward the native city and disillusionment. The implication of this contrast between the trees' vital striving and the inquisitive mind's tendency to return to the substratum of being is that life exists within a vertical hierarchy of reality, exhibiting both the movement upward that differentiates "higher cultures" from the primary monotony and the downward movement of regression and reassimilation with the sludge.

The upper city, for all its luxuriant foliage, is a realm that human beings have organized, given over to social forms and set apart from nature: "As for the civil station itself, it provokes no emotion. It charms not, neither does it repel. It is sensibly planned, with a red-brick club on its brow, and farther back a grocer's and a cemetery, and the bungalows are disposed along roads that intersect at right angles. It has nothing hideous in it, and only the view is beautiful; it shares nothing with the city except the over-arching sky." The rectilinearity of the city, its sensible planning, and its careful provisions for life and death ("a grocer's and a cemetery") indicate that this social realm is the British *modus vivendi*; a more or less deliberate effort to distinguish civilized life from the lower realm of undifferentiated substance. But, in its attempted divorce from the meanness of Indian life, the upper city joins with the lower under a realm of being that spans them both: ". . . it shares nothing with the city except the overarching sky."[3] Despite the rational plans which admit "nothing hideous," the cities share "nothing": their common term is a nothingness whose only exception is the sky, which they also share.

"The sky too has its changes, but they are less marked than those of the vegetation and the river. Clouds map it up at times, but it is normally a dome of blending tints, and the main tint blue. By day the blue will pale down into white where it touches the white of the land, after sunset it has a new circumference—orange, melting upwards into tenderest purple. But the core of blue persists, and so it is by night." There are indications that the realm of reality associated with the sky has similarities both to the ever-changing fluid and to the artificially divided social realms; like them the sky "has its changes" and is occasionally mapped into sections by clouds. But it is normally a unifying dome, a spectrum that includes all colors. In its contact with the earthly realm, this spectrum expresses itself in simplest terms as white—the most comprehensive of colors, taking into itself all the colors of the visible universe—but its upward regions become more markedly differentiated from the earth. There its predominant shade of blue is transformed into tenderest purple—hinting at an approach toward black or an absence of color at the violet end of the spectrum. This upward disposition toward colorlessness suggests that as the sky recedes from the earth it approaches a condition which lies at an infinite remove from both earthly realms.

At night "the stars hang like lamps from the immense vault. The distance between the vault and them is as nothing to the distance behind them, and that farther distance, though beyond colour, last freed itself from blue." The referent of the pronoun "them" is "stars": they hang in the vault or dome of blue but are measured against a farther distance beyond the extent of blue—"the distance behind them." The latter is "beyond colour" (though it is last to be freed from color)—and color is typical of the qualities of per-ceptible being. Thus, beyond the sky which unites both the willed efforts of civilization and the passive substratum of matter under its dome, there is a space which is unperceivable because colorless, an empty extension be-yond the star-filled space of sky. This apparently empty space is infinite, for measured against it the finite space between the perceivable vault and the stars is "as nothing," and only by comparison with an infinite term can a finite term equal nothing. In sum, the sky is both an encompassing and unifying dome over life and an emptiness that stands outside human concerns—even outside the primary and the middle realms of being. In either case, the sky is the same, and its doubleness must be considered a meeting ground between being and nothing.

"The sky settles everything—not only climates and seasons but when the earth shall be beautiful. By herself she can do little—only feeble outbursts of flowers. But when the sky chooses, glory can rain into the Chandrapore bazaars or a benediction pass from horizon to horizon. The sky can do this because it is so strong and so enormous." The sky has power to choose and to bless and has the qualities of strength and enormous size, but its power can work only in relation to something other than itself—the earth, which exists on a lower plane. We may say, from previous conclusions, that the sky as reservoir of being and of nothing tends toward contact with the earth quite as a matter of course and that, in turn, the earth needs this entry of the sky's twin nature in order to have its benediction.

"Strength comes from the sun, infused in it daily; size from the prostrate earth. No mountains infringe on the curve. League after league the earth lies flat, heaves a little, is flat again. Only in the south, where a group of fists and fingers are thrust up through the soil, is the endless expanse interrupted. These fists and fingers are the Marabar Hills, containing the extraordinary caves." This mythic account of sun and earth includes the only terms directly drawn from Indian religion; the strength from the sun, "infused" into a prostrate earth which "lies flat," comes as a male seed fertilizing a female, as a sun god coupling with an earth goddess in a cosmic pantheon.[4] The ascription of such mythic associations to an otherwise impersonal and stratified structure of being is, like Indian mythology itself, a concession to human notions. In the same manner the excrescences of the earth are personified as fists and fingers which "thrust up through the soil"—presumably with an upward aspiration toward the realm of the sky. Yet this pathetic fallacy or anthropomorphic projection marks the distinction of a certain part of the earth from the ordinary realm of material existence: there is a difference between the rock of the hills and the sludge deposited by the river. The rock itself, seen as fists and fingers, is that part of the earth which surges toward the sky and in its heaving upward from the flat plain creates a place of vacancy. The hollowness within the rock constitutes the "extraordinary caves," and it is the presence of this vacancy that distinguishes the extraordinary from the ordinary. What these openings in the earth have in them is the same as that which lies in the third realm; to go there is to go beyond the stars. This, too, is a meeting ground of being and nonbeing, and to make a passage into the caves is to come in contact with nothing and to recognize its identity with everything, in the note of "boum." That passage is enacted in the plot of A Passage to India.

Given the tripartite structure of reality in chapter i, the novel's account of complex emotional and moral experience becomes more firmly interpretable. In the key chapter (xii) which introduces the climactic action, the caves are described in historical-geological terms carried over from the concluding paragraph of the first chapter: the high places of Dravidia are not only old but have remained unchanged since the earth was formed; their outlines show the forms of the sun "before our globe was torn from his bosom." Moreover, their creation is described in personified or mythic terms ("flesh of the sun's flesh," etc. [p. 123]). "Yet even they are altering. As Himalayan India rose, this India, the primal, has been depressed, and is slowly re-entering the curve of the earth." The land that retained its sky origin in its forms is sinking into the undifferentiated continuum of primal matter. Within this mass, within its upward thrust of "fists and fingers," are the caves, which partake of both air and earth, the third realm and the first. "They are like nothing else in the world" (p. 124): there is no other thing like them and thus their very existence is negative—they are the negation of the ordinary realm, the extraordinary.

In the caves, being exists in intimate relations with—is even defined by —nonbeing. As in the negative definitions of gods in Western and Oriental theology, which point toward their existence by denying them all finite and limiting qualities, the caves are described by their lack of attributes: "Nothing, nothing attaches to them" (p. 124). In Godbole's earlier account of them, only negatives are used: the caves are not large, not holy, not ornamented, contain no sculpture, etc. (When the conclusion is drawn that the caves' reputation is an "empty brag," Godbole can "not quite say that" [vii, 75].) Yet this very lack of attributes marks the presence of a quality: the caves open up an extraordinary situation for the visitors because of the absence they find there. According to the qualities they bring, their contact with nothing creates a turning point in their life. For here their being comes into relation with its negation. The caves can contain everything—every kind of visitor, sound, moral event, etc.—but reduce it to the uniform state expressed in the all-absorbing "boum," which is the annihilating sound of nothing. But they are also variously as well as uniformly negative: they create illusions corresponding to the points of view from which they are seen.

"There is little to see" (p. 124)—in fact, there is nothing, but the qualification "little" suggests that the mirrorlike walls are there as the ground of the seen. All the elements of perception—the match or other light, the objects or faces seen, and the eye which sees—these are provided by the visitor. This realm of uncompromising objectivity itself contains no subjectivity —"no eye to see it" (p. 125) is built into the structure. But it does open itself to the subjective visitor, at least to the extent of becoming the field for self-projection. Some visitors, like the one Forster describes, light a match and project a fantasy of mating between a real and a reflected flame ("A mirror . . . divides the lovers" [p. 125]). Others come fresh from a groping and disturbed mating process and have a sexual hallucination; still others come with ideals of religious love and emerge disgusted with "love in a church, love in a cave. . . ."

There is, however, a place which is impervious and unapproachable to subjectivity: the chambers without entrances. "But elsewhere, deeper in the granite, are there certain chambers that have no entrances? . . . Nothing is inside them, they were sealed up before the creation of pestilence or treasure; if mankind grew curious and excavated, nothing, nothing would be added to the sum of good or evil" (p. 125). These chambers have "nothing . . . inside them," in contrast to the potentially all-containing caves; they do not invite a transaction between being and nonbeing but maintain their splendid isolation. They are inaccessible to "pestilence or treasure" or any other human value but, if their contents were uncovered, "nothing would be added" to the sum of what is. This description suggests a pure state of nothingness which is never directly encountered but stands as a speculative limit. The final image of this nothingness in its eternal equanimity is the interior of the bubble-shaped cave of the Kawa Dol, which "mirrors its own darkness in every direction infinitely" (p. 125). It is equally distributed in all directions and thus attains infinity although confined within a finite shape. Although no light is available to mirror what is not there, the darkness mirrors itself.

Ordinarily this realm of what is beyond the stars is unseen and disregarded, but at certain extraordinary points it touches the ordinary realms of being and is made accessible to a visit. This provides the occasion for a journey not only to nothing but to being, a journey which constitutes the plot of A Passage to India. The dramatic crisis derives from the encounter of two fairly naïve tourists with the "mystery"—the place where the ordinary realm touches the extraordinary and is likely to be confused or muddled with it. Their passage is indeed a passage to more than India; it takes in the whole of reality. The novel revamps the archetypal pattern of spiritual quest and heroic trial in a comic mode—the errors of naïve tourists —but the form of the fable is as universal as the classic myths.

The effects of encountering the mystery and finding it a muddle are well known: the encounter with nothing produces a destructive chain of events for Adela and a moral exhaustion in Mrs. Moore. Not so well known are the preconditions for the confusion. One of Adela's formative experiences is the bump in the dark that jostles her into contact with Ronny and precipitates their engagement; whatever it was that attacked the car—whether a hyena, a ghost, or Adela herself (as it appears from the tracks after she inspects them)—it is concluded that the accident was "nothing," or at least "nothing criminal" (viii, 97). Chapter xiv begins by insistently reminding the reader that "most of life is so dull that there is nothing to be said about it," that "there are periods in the most thrilling day during which nothing happens" (pp. 132–133). Adela and Mrs. Moore have been prepared to encounter this vacuity by means of Godbole's song and have "felt nothing acutely" for a fortnight (p. 133). Further, the narrator's remark that "nothing occurred" at sunrise during the train ride to the caves (p. 137) expresses the blankness of the world and suggests the appropriate response to it.

Yet Adela fails to acknowledge this neutrality of being: Aziz assures her before their entry into the caves that "nothing embraces the whole of India, nothing, nothing," but Adela insists that "there will have to be something universal in this country" (p. 145). This failure to perceive the presence of nothing in everything leads to her confusion in the encounter with the emptiness of the caves. Mrs. Moore interprets them to say: "Pathos, piety, courage—they exist, but are identical, and so is filth. Everything exists, nothing has value" (p. 149). This generalization about homogeneity on the primary and secondary levels of life is itself muddled—as much so as Fielding's interpretation of Godbole's metaphysics (see below)—but it has the virtue of intimately relating being and nothing, which Adela's naïve idealism refuses to do. Instead of universals, the Indian world presents many things, mixed together with nothing, but she wants to integrate them with moral and personal meanings and so muddles them and herself.

In place of this muddled view is a perceptual mode that helps people in their daily affairs adjust their behavior to the conditions of a world composed of both being and nothing. This mode of perception is the "double vision" to which the narrator elsewhere alludes: it is a simultaneous awareness of being and nothing, an awareness that may lead not to metaphysical truth but to the truth about one's own experience. With this vision Adela is enabled to tell what happened to her in the cave; this may not seem much but is the climactic moment of the action.

When the tourists first enter the caves the action is rendered from a point of view far removed from and above the scene, as though a movie camera was filming the incident from a distant vantage point: "Bending their heads, they disappeared one by one into the interior of the hills. The small black hole gaped where their varied forms and colours had momentarily functioned. They were sucked in like water down a drain. Bland and bald rose the precipices . . ." (xiv, 146). After Adela has upset Aziz by asking about his presumed polygamy, they enter another cave (or caves) and are each described from their own point of view: ". . . he plunged into one of them to recover his balance. She followed at her leisure, quite unconscious that she had said the wrong thing, and not seeing him, she also went into a cave . . . (xv, 153).

At the trial Adela is asked:

> "You went alone into one of those caves?"
> "That is quite correct."

"And the prisoner followed you.". . .

Her vision was of several caves. She saw herself in one, and she
was also outside of it, watching its entrance, for Aziz to pass in. She
failed to locate him. . . . "I am not quite sure." (xxiv, 228–229)

It is, of course, difficult for Adela to describe Aziz following her into the
cave because he has entered first and she has followed him into that cave
or another like it. What she does in the passage just quoted is to adopt the
external point of view of the long-distance movielike observer, seeing herself not only in the cave but going into it–as though she were observing
herself. From this remote perspective she would have been able to see Aziz
entering the cave, if he had indeed entered it after her, but as he has not
she cannot see him and therefore accepts the fact that he has not followed
her.

What does Adela see, then? Nothing. That is the reality of her situation:
nothing happened in the cave. Acknowledging nothing is a metaphysical
discovery: "Something that she did not understand took hold of the girl and
pulled her through. Though the vision was over, and she had returned to
the insipidity of the world, she remembered what she had learnt. Atone-
ment and confession–they could wait. It was in hard prosaic tones that
she said, 'I withdraw everything'" (xxiv, 230). What she has learnt is the
distinction between nothing and something, although it is "something that
she did not understand." In withdrawing everything, Adela is acknowledging nothing–what is left when everything is removed. And in seeing
that nothing happened in the cave she learns to distinguish that nothing
from all her desired ideals–freeing her mind (at least temporarily) from
the muddle of being and nothing acquired in the experience. As Mrs. Moore
concludes, "nothing had happened" (xxiii, p 208), but this nonevent is an
event of considerable significance, an active force in people's lives and relationships, and also a revelatory power for the mind.

Godbole's explanation of the affair to Fielding is a more expressive identification of the events in the cave as nothing, while acknowledging that in
the conventional sense "nothing happened." Godbole maintains that "nothing can be performed in isolation" (xix, 177); he means, of course, that
everyone is involved in any action, in an endless sequence of causes–that
an action expresses the whole universe. But his words also imply that Adela, who has lived in the isolation of her subjectivity, performed "nothing,"
i.e., made the nothing into an active force in life. Fielding protests that in
this view "everything is anything and nothing something," but Godbole
manages to both agree and disagree with this muddle: "Good and evil are
different, as their names imply. But, in my own humble opinion, they are
both of them aspects of my Lord. He is present in the one, absent in the
other, and the difference between presence and absence is great, as great as
my feeble mind can grasp. Yet absence implies presence, absence is not

non-existence, and we are therefore entitled to repeat, 'Come, come, come, come'" (xix, 178). Not only does this amusing and characteristic discourse play on the contradictions of Indian habits of mind, it also makes a valid metaphysical distinction between absence (or nonfunctioning) and nonexistence (or nothing). The absence and the presence in the cave—the presence of a disturbing force in Adela's imagination and the absence of a literal attacker—both are present and condition the outcome, just as Krishna's presence and absence in both good and evil constitute reality. It is Forster's genius to have interpreted a "mystery story" about an unknown attacker as a confrontation with the mystery of the double nature of reality.

With this structure of being in mind, we can interpret some of the vexed questions surrounding Mrs. Moore. She is the brave tourist who announces, "I like mysteries but I rather dislike muddles" (vii, 69), and her interpreters —taking the intention for the deed—generally assume that she manages to follow her taste. But her distress after the visit to the caves suggests that she does not: "Nothing evil had been in the cave, but she had not enjoyed herself . . ." (xiv, 148). When she takes the vision of "nothing evil" with her, her ideals of love and her maternal warmth matter less and less. "She had come to that state where the horror of the universe and its smallness are both visible at the same time—the twilight of the double vision in which so many elderly people are involved" (xxiii, 207). These famous lines do not say that Mrs. Moore's double vision is accurate but rather that she is in a late stage of perhaps once-accurate double vision. This condition resembles twilight in two senses: it is obscure and it comes at the end of a temporal span—in this case the twilight not of a day but of a life. She sees both the universe's smallness (being, at least on the primary and secondary levels) and its horror (nothing) but muddles the two. To see the mystery is to regard without horror the universe's greatness (being) and its nothingness; the mystery is the negation of the muddle of horror and smallness.

The categories of muddledom are general enough, but what exactly are the mental images of it which Mrs. Moore confuses? "If this world is not to our taste, well, at all events there is Heaven, Hell, Annihilation—one or other of those large things, that huge scenic background of stars, fires, blue or black air. All heroic endeavour, and all that is known as art, assumes that there is such a background, just as all practical endeavour, when the world is to our taste, assumes that the world is all. But in the twilight of the double vision, a spiritual muddledom is set up for which no high-sounding words can be found; we can neither act nor refrain from action, we can neither ignore nor respect Infinity" (xxiii, 207–208). "That huge scenic background"—conceived of as the realm of Heaven, Hell, Annihilation—represents the area of speculation in which Mrs. Moore's Christian conception of things moves. But that same place of "stars, fires, blue or black air" can be seen not mythologized as part of a religious world view but nakedly as the third realm of being—which shades off toward the extreme condition of nothing as the blue of the heavens passes into the black or the absence of color beyond the stars. Some forms of behavior (art, heroism) focus on the "background," the third realm; others (practical endeavor) on the first and second realms, the "world." When the background is mythologized and muddled with the world of active being, the vision of both becomes confused: both action and nonaction in the world are compromised, and both consciousness and unconsciousness—respect and ignorance—of "Infinity" (the third realm) are no longer possible. Mrs. Moore, encountering nothing in the caves, takes it as demythologizing her background and even as making nothing of her world. Thus she is unfitted for moral action regarding Adela and for contemplation regarding herself.

Mrs. Moore does not end in this twilight state; she attains a degree of clarity respecting being and nothing, world and background, in the course of leaving India. On the train and boat journey away from the scene of her confusion, elements of the landscape provide the occasions for an exercise of double vision of the same sort as Adela's at the trial. India contains not only nothing but something—a multiplicity of things. The disused antiquities of the primary level and the curtaining and curtained trees of the second level come forward to speak to her (in all irony, of course—Forster is not likely to fall into the pathetic fallacy unselfconsciously). First Mrs. Moore passes the fortress Asirgarh: "No one had ever mentioned Asirgarh to her, but it had huge and noble bastions and to the right of them was a mosque. She forgot it. Ten minutes later, Asirgarh reappeared. The mosque was to the left of the bastions now. The train in its descent through the Vindyas had described a semicircle round Asirgarh. What could she connect it with except its own name? Nothing; she knew no one who lived there. But it had looked at her twice and seemed to say: 'I do not vanish'" (xxiii, 209). This (nontwilight) double vision involves a twin perspective on the primary level, the surface of the earth: it implies a relativistic freedom from conventional reference systems, such as right and left, which are found to be relative to the geography of the Vindyas and the course of the train. The double vision also involves a simultaneous awareness of being and nothing: "What could she connect it with except its own name? Nothing . . . ," yet it declares, "I do not vanish." Its being is connected with nonbeing, yet the two are distinguished in Mrs. Moore's perception of its enduring identity as an individual object.[5]

A similar experience occurs when Mrs. Moore takes ship; the coconut palms speak: "'So you thought an echo was India; you took the Marabar caves as final?' they laughed. 'What have we in common with them, or they with Asirgarh? Good-bye!' Then the steamer rounded Colaba, the continent swung about, the cliff of the Ghats melted into the haze of a tropic sea" (xxiii, 210). Here topographical double vision again occurs at a moment of recognition: as Mrs. Moore learns the separateness of objects, she also observes the turning around of a continent, from her (and the ship's) point of view. The trees tell her that India requires a recognition not only of nothing (caves, echo) but of the discrete elements of being (trees, Asirgarh, etc.). Mrs. Moore sails out of India—and out of life—with her muddle challenged but not with sufficient resolution to allow her to act in the world again.

Aziz is probably right to conclude: "What did this eternal goodness of Mrs. Moore amount to? To nothing, if brought to the test of thought" (xxxiii, 312). Eternal goodness is one of the notions that are demythologized by this novel yet, while they amount to nothing, that nothing is a matter worth attention. Mrs. Moore's charismatic power would seem to derive from her intimacy with nothing; indeed, she raises nothing to an active role in human affairs. As Adela says, ". . . you do nothing but good, you are so good" (xxii, 205); it is possible to conclude that she does nothing in the action of the plot, but she does it well. Doing nothing, like knowing nothing, is itself an act of considerable import and has consequences in the moral sphere. By refraining from intervention, Mrs. Moore creates a nothingness around Adela which allows her to come out of her muddle. Adela later has an experience somewhat like Mrs. Moore's two moments of double geographical vision: an American missionary plays on the words "turn" and "return" in a meaningless way, which nevertheless sets Adela in motion to pick up her relations with Mrs. Moore's children (xxix, 265–266). Out of Mrs. Moore's and Adela's contacts with nothing come the turnings that allow for informed and (at least for the latter) ongoing personal relations.

The dominant impression of the novel's closing movement is a return to the unity of all things on the primal level of being, the matter or sludge that is carried in water as an undifferentiated continuum. Just as the Ganges flowing by Chandrapore reduces land, flesh, and excrement to a uniform color and destiny, so the ritual enactment of the Gokul Ashtami festival re-creates the process by emptying all the contents of the community at Mau into the tank.[6] The act is prepared for conventionally in the form of a clay model of the town of Krishna's birth and is completed when the participants in the festival join the town in falling into the water: "Thus was He thrown year after year, and were others thrown—little images of Ganpati, baskets of ten-day corn, tiny tazias after Mohurram—scapegoats, husks, emblems of passage; a passage not easy, not now, not here, not to be apprehended except when it is unattainable: the God to be thrown was an emblem of that" (xxxvi, 314–315). The negativity of the repeated entries of "nothing" into the language and action of the novel persists in this final image of unity. It is the same "not now, not here" which closes the novel, deferring India's independence, the meeting of East and West, and human fulfillment to some other time and place. But the "emblems of passage"—in religion and in literature—emphasize instead of negation a continual recurrence, surge, or movement of mankind between the poles of being and nothing, between the primary and the tertiary levels of existence, and between birth and death. This pattern of rise and fall, turn and return, double vision and double movement is the passage which the emblems symbolize and is the subject of *A Passage to India*.

12. Woolf and McTaggart

. . . who can tell
Which of her forms has shown her substance right?
Or maybe substance can be composite,
Profound McTaggart thought so, and in a breath
A mouthful held the extreme of life and death.
—YEATS, "A Bronze Head"

*I*F the operative philosophy behind the narrative experiments in modern English fiction may be called perspectivism,[1] Virginia Woolf would seem to be the perspectivist par excellence. Despite the vigorous debate on her supposed Bergsonism that has engaged many of her critics, the most satisfying account so far of the metaphysical assumptions underlying her work is Erich Auerbach's:

> The essential characteristic of the technique represented by Virginia Woolf is that we are given not merely one person whose consciousness (that is, the impressions it receives) is rendered, but many persons, with frequent shifts from one to the other. . . . The multiplicity of persons suggests that we are here after all confronted with an endeavor to investigate an objective reality, that is, specifically, the "real" Mrs. Ramsay. She is, to be sure, an enigma and such she basically remains, but she is as it were encircled by the content of all the various consciousnesses directed upon her (including her own).[2]

The epistemological notion that reality is unknowable except by combining a variety of individual and partial viewpoints on any single object, and the related ethical notion that the individual's isolation can be overcome by the unifying powers of certain gifted beings (usually women), can be found writ large in Woolf's major works. From the culminating party and its moment of awareness in *Mrs. Dalloway*, through the *boeuf-en-daube* dinner and achievement of a painting in *To the Lighthouse*, to the reunion dinners and concluding life summary of *The Waves*—the pattern of uniting fragments of experience or isolated selves is well established. Woolf seized on the mind's power to synthesize and the heart's power to unify as the human endowment which might defeat the chaos of phenomena and the transitoriness of relationships that so weighed upon her.

But, as J. Hillis Miller maintains in a definitive essay,[3] the synthetic movement of "building it up" which occupies Clarissa Dalloway's social life and expresses her unifying social sense is accompanied by a contrary movement toward isolation and emotional detachment. The climax of this movement is her moment of identification with the man who has pressed his isolation and detachment to a limit by his suicide. This climactic sympathy of selves which have never met is, in Miller's view, a dramatization of the community in which all the soliloquizing characters of the novel participate: the omniscient mind of the narrator, which presents these soliloquies in a uniform prose medium of indirect (and often "free indirect") discourse. In Woolf's vision of human life, the inadequacy of the mind to maintain its precarious syntheses and the urgent interruptions of life and death that shatter temporary communion are compensated by an esthetic unity which exists outside the action, in the framing narrative. Yet it is not enough to ascribe those enabling acts to the author's synthetic power: the dramatic fact of their occurrence is inside the frame of the work of art and must be explained in its terms.[4]

The Bergsonian critics, too, have stressed Woolf's grasp of the unity of consciousness that is potential in *lived* time but are inclined to overlook the steady beat of mutability, of dispersion, of *dying* time, that sounds in all her work.[5] Lacking an ordering intelligence, the moment of total experience is the moment of total confusion, chaos, or death which Woolf's characters often experience. Both the perspectival unities of the creative imagination and the involuntary moments of unity of the mind that dwells in *la durée* are unable to provide an order for sustained life and, on this pragmatic ground, are in Woolf's novels found wanting as philosophies of life. Nor is a viable alternative presented by the leap at another form of being, at a union with others in an undifferentiated world of death that Mrs. Dalloway temporarily finds in Septimus Smith's suicide. Woolf regarded her own suicidal yearnings with horror, for the flight from an inadequate form of existence offers no convincing promise of a better state beyond the grave or in the act of death itself.

Yet there is a tendency in the novels I have cited—and occasionally in her other writings—to envision a unity that persists in the here and now, a unity independent of the synthetic power of the mind and, apparently, even of the heart or any other human faculty. The characters of Virginia Woolf's fiction sometimes seem to be in touch with each other without direct perception—or their consciousness of each other yields greater knowledge than is conveyed by the data of their experience—and this co-presence seems impervious even to the shocks of death and the desultoriness of time. Her short stories (if such static forms can be called stories) suggest the possibility of communication without dramatic contact, in the unmediated and yet thematically consistent passage from one mind to another in "Kew Gardens"; in the complete intuition of the life history of another self at the moment of its ecstatic love, in "Moments of Being"; in the dim presence of the consciousness of past inhabitants to the present occupants of "A Haunted House." How are we to interpret passages like the following?

> Fanny Wilmot saw the pin: she picked it up. She looked at Miss Craye. Was Miss Craye so lonely? No, Miss Craye was steadily, blissfully, if only for that moment, a happy woman. Fanny had surprised her in a moment of ecstasy. . . . Julia Craye, sitting hunched and compact holding her flower, seemed to emerge out of the London night, seemed to fling it like a cloak behind her, it seemed, in its bareness and intensity, the effluence of her spirit, something she had made which surrounded her. Fanny stared.
>
> All seemed transparent, for a moment, to the gaze of Fanny Wilmot, as if looking through Miss Craye, she saw the very fountain of her being spurting its pure silver drops. She saw back and back into the past behind her. . . . She saw Julia—
>
> Julia blazed. Julia kindled. Out of the night she burnt like a dead white star. Julia opened her arms. Julia kissed her on the lips. Julia possessed it.[6]

The "solitary traveller" who moves through and around Peter Walsh's dream (and who is not related to Peter alone, for she also enters Septimus Smith's mind), the "little airs" that occupy the Ramsays' house in their absence, the narrative voice that speaks the prologues of *The Waves* and records the passage of a day and the cycle of life—these presences in the novels suggest a form of perception that can be identified neither with the direct experience of any character nor with the spiritual intuition of traditional mysticism.

There is no evidence—either in her fiction or outside it—to support a contention that Woolf was given to the flirtations with the occult that absorbed some of her most illustrious contemporaries. The Cambridge temper she inherited from Leslie Stephen was too strong, her indifference to religious phenomena too deeply ingrained, for belief in "psychic" communication. A system of thought that could account for the presence of minds that know each other without intermediary would have had to be broadly speculative and nontheistic to have attracted Woolf. And it would more readily establish itself with her if it were a Cambridge system. In order to account for the phenomenon in question, I am led to consider a philosophical analogue to her fiction which picks up where perspectivism and Bergsonism falter.

Without claiming personal contact—and without suggesting a transfer of philosophical ideas of the mysterious, indirect kind to be found in Woolf's fiction—it is possible to see one Cambridge thinker in this role. Of the Trinity philosophers who came to prominence in the years of her brother's and future husband's residence there, only G. E. Moore has attracted much attention.[7] Moore's habits of skeptical argumentation and the high ethical value he placed on friendship and esthetic appreciation were doubtless lively talking points in Edwardian Cambridge and subsequently in Bloomsbury. But J. M. Keynes has exposed the superficial relevance of most of Moore's thought to the values derived from it by the Bloomsbury set,[8] and his analysis holds for Woolf at least as well as it does for the more directly implicated E. M. Forster. Neither novelist held with Moore's definition of *good* as an irreducible quality, with his exclusive valuation of friendship and esthetic experience, or with his falling back on convention in most cases of ethical choice. While the presence of Whitehead and Russell, who were also Fellows at Trinity early in this century, remains to be traced in modern fiction, it may be predicted that Russell's thought will be found to be more closely akin to the empiricist skepticism of Conrad than to the timorous clutching at metaphysical credence by Woolf.

The *least* lastingly influential of the Trinity philosophers was John McTaggart Ellis McTaggart. Most students of Woolf's intellectual milieu dismiss him as an incomprehensible and rather comic fuddy-duddy,[9] and even memoir writers inclined to eulogize him are preoccupied with this aspect of his reputation. But recent professional opinion places McTaggart in a central place in modern philosophy, in structuring the current discussion of the nature of time.[10] It would be worthwhile to examine the main themes of his philosophy, to see it as an element of the intellectual realm in which Woolf shaped her vision of human communication free of time, of direct contact, and perhaps even of death.

That Virginia Woolf was aware of McTaggart's philosophical activity may be assumed from the long tale of their mutual friends, but her awareness of the relevance of his ideas to her central concerns can be established more firmly through one of those friends in particular: Roger Fry. McTaggart and Fry were lifelong friends, from public school through Cambridge and up until McTaggart's death. Woolf's biography of Fry was written later than most of her fiction, but it makes frequent and familiar allusions to McTaggart's career. Especially interesting is her account of McTaggart's funeral, to which she devotes extended attention by quoting a long letter of Fry's:

> ". . . partly because in a way I had loved him very deeply—no, not that for we were au fond too different in temperament and his was the warmer, less critical affection—but because he had been one of the most constantly familiar beings in my life and one with whom I always found myself happily at ease, I was very much moved." They played Beethoven's Hymn of Creation, Bach's Pastorale, and a Chorale of Bach, and then—"was read this from Spinoza, 'The free man thinks less of death than of anything else and all his wisdom is the contemplation of life' or very nearly that. So for once the right thing was said."[11]

Strangely, Virginia Woolf dates this letter January 21, 1935, apparently misreading the manuscript date 1925, when McTaggart actually died—and ignoring momentarily the fact that Fry died in 1934. When she comes to describe Fry's funeral, moreover, she not only points out that much the same music was played and that identical ceremonies of cremation were followed but adds the corrected quotation from Spinoza: "A free man thinks of death least of all things; and his wisdom is a meditation not of death but of life." The implication of this association—partly gratuitous—in Virginia Woolf's mind of Fry's and McTaggart's deaths and funerals is not only that the philosopher was strongly present to her imagination but that he was connected with the meditation on mortality which runs throughout her work: the liberation from the fear of, if not the fact of, death through intense involvement in personal relations, in life.

McTaggart was lecturer in moral philosophy at Trinity from 1897 to 1923. In these years he continued, with refinements, to enunciate a system which—for all its partial analogues in Hegelian philosophy, Christian doctrine, and mystical visions—won him a reputation for originality and profundity, even among many outside Cambridge. For McTaggart presented the situation of an atheist who sought to redefine God, Freedom, and Immorality in nontheistic terms and thereby to create a secular substitute for the highest aspirations of Christian eschatology and ethics.[12] While one group of his listeners, like Forster's friend G. Lowes Dickinson, was led to use his theories for a leap into Eastern doctrines of preexistence, automatic writing, and pantheism, others were captured by his discussion of selfhood, love, and time as categories of this-wordly experience. It is the contention of this essay that Virginia Woolf was among the latter and that her approaches to psychic communication are to be interpreted in the light of McTaggart's personal-idealist categories, not in the vaguer terms of the mystics who were multiplying around her in the British intelligentsia.

In the years around the turn of the century, McTaggart published three works on Hegelian philosophy, which was then prominent in England through the efforts of the Oxford neo-Hegelians T. H. Green, F. H. Bradley, and Bernard Bosanquet. While these had adopted Hegel as the philosopher of the state, in order to produce an ethics and a political theory to counter utilitarian individualism, McTaggart wrote two of his books on Hegelian logic. In the second of the three, *Studies in Hegelian Cosmology* (1901), he approached some of the social issues with which the Oxford neo-Hegelians were concerned (though McTaggart refused to glorify the organic state, his politics being Liberal Unionist). What is striking about the *Studies* is their fresh reformulation of the Hegelian doctrine of the individual as a concrete universal and their original speculations on the character of the Hegelian Absolute and the transcendence of the individual within it. These ideas McTaggart was to maintain and develop throughout his career, so that they reach full elaboration in his summa, *The Nature of Existence*, which was published in two volumes, one posthumously, in the twenties.

At the center of McTaggart's thought is the doctrine that "the universe consists of selves and nothing but selves, which form a set of parts of the universe. . . . Each self contains a set of parts which are perceptions . . . each of these perceptions has the quality of being an emotion. The direct perception of another self is the emotion of love."[13] This, the fundamental language of McTaggart's metaphysics, connects it with the world of Woolf's fiction, in which selves, perceptions, and emotions make up the metaphysical substance of the universe. Putting this unique idea in Hegelian terms in his early work, McTaggart modifies the collectivist tendency in the neo-Hegelian view of society and the individual, emphasizing the primacy of that concrete universal, the individual self:

> Each self can only exist in virtue of its connection with all the others, and with the Absolute which is their unity. But this is a relation, not of subordination, but of reciprocal dependence. . . . If the self has no meaning, except as manifesting the Absolute, the Absolute has no meaning except as manifested in that Self.[14]

But this Absolute is itself defined not as something above or apart from man but, rather, as the totality of the love of each self in the universe for all other selves.

The special character of McTaggart's metaphysics comes from his endowing of the universe's parts with the attributes of personality. When he speaks of selves he means real human beings in their unique identities. That is what makes his vision of a universe composed of selves not merely a variant on traditional idealism but closer to a Dantean order of souls who retain their personal character and in it know each other and reality.

One of the peculiarities of McTaggart's conception of the self is his hesitation to ascribe self-consciousness to it (indeed, his curious article on "Personality" in the *Encyclopaedia of Religion and Ethics* is almost entirely taken up with this apparently secondary question). Aside from the logical difficulties which stand in the way of such an ascription, the motive for McTaggart's fastidiousness seems to be his desire to make perception of *others* the primary activity of the self. To the question, what do selves do? McTaggart might have answered simply, they know each other. We are here close to the world of Woolf's novels, in which such moments of knowledge are the only events that count, while true self-knowledge is both rarer and less crucial.

Another streak of temperament colors McTaggart's doctrine of knowledge and even extends to his ethical consideration of volition: knowledge and volition are imperfect and even undesirable modes of the self's existence and are merely preparatory to its genuine life, which is love. The notion that to know another self is necessarily a step to loving it is clearly an article of faith, and McTaggart is realistic enough about the imperfections of human knowledge and love in our present state. He therefore projects an ideal condition in which selves will come perfectly to know each other and thereby to love each other, in which their knowledge and volition will be transcended and absorbed into their love, and in which the society of selves thus constituted will fully embody the Absolute, will become the universal unity in which each individual will have perfect existence. Nor does McTaggart maintain this ideal as merely a speculative one but as the logical limit of our present relations with other human beings; although he disclaims the ability to indicate how such a utopia could or will be brought about, he describes it as the end product of a series of partial improvements of personal relations. For McTaggart, the modern problem of transcendence is to be answered in the concrete experience of human beings in their relations with each other. His is the personal ethic of Bloomsbury raised to metaphysical generality.

Despite its many precedents in the history of English literature and philosophy, particularly at Cambridge, the doctrine of McTaggart that is likely to seem most curious is that of preexistence, which, taken together with his formulation of postexistence, makes up his theory of the immortality of the self. The poignant way in which he begins his speculations on immortality strikes a familiar note: "Our lives are so fragmentary that, in trying to explain them, we are almost tied down to two alternatives—either they mean nothing, or they are episodes in a long chain" (*Studies*, p. 48). We are here in a philosophic tradition that stretches back to Plato, not necessarily Eastward.

Like Woolf, McTaggart considers such immortality as a desperate alternative to utter negativity, and it remains for him a hypothesis *als ob*—much in the way Woolf toyed with the doctrine of metempsychosis in *Orlando*. For him it is a way of guaranteeing the relevance of personal experience: our present capacities are determined by our previous avatars, and our present actions in turn determine our future descendants. As Lowes Dickinson put it, glowingly: "If we have formed here a beautiful personal relation, it will not perish at death, but be perpetuated, albeit unconsciously, in some future life." But in this unconsciousness is the mark of a distinction from Woolf's entertainment of the idea of metempsychosis. When McTaggart excludes memory of its past from the revived self, he dispenses with one of the modes of continuity that give the heroine of *Orlando* her identity as the sum of her family's experience in history, i.e., her conscious tradition.

Despite this difference between their images of the survival of the self in successive ages, it is possible to see in McTaggart's account of his doctrine an underlying temperamental affinity: "Indeed, nothing is really lost by the loss of memory. Although it is inevitable that it should appear to us that something is lost." The peculiarity of McTaggart's thinking is that it projects an ideal human condition that is often ludicrously remote from our present situation, yet it remains fully cognizant of the limitations of our present awareness which prevent our self-transcendence. McTaggart's gift is to incorporate these worldly limits into his vision of transcendence: although we do not remember we long for the past. It may not be too much to say that McTaggart is the only idealist philosopher with a tragic view of life, and it is this tragic view that is his deepest point of connection with Virginia Woolf.

It is not only in his theory of memory that the tragedy of selfhood appears in McTaggart's philosophy. He is aware of the anxiety the individual experiences in confronting the plenitude of other selves—although he regards the progressive interconnection of each self with all other selves as the way in which the puniness of the individual is to be overcome (*Studies*, pp. 291–292). The demands of a total interconnection are so great that the difficulties encountered in our present condition must be expected to accompany us until the last stage of ordinary life, before we reach an ideal society of individuals transformed by universal love.

Beyond his broad description of this ideal and his discussion of the limitations of life as we live it, projected toward that ideal, McTaggart's chief interest for an understanding of Woolf lies in his doctrine of the illusion of time. In this, McTaggart appears to approach mysticism more closely than in any other phase of his thought—although he does not claim nontemporal experience for himself. "Nothing is in time," he states flatly, and he proceeds to elaborate a system of three "series" of events: an illusory past-present-future series (A series), an illusory before-and-after series (B series), and a real atemporal series to which the first two series illusorily correspond. McTaggart later refined his terms, distinguishing the series of erroneous correspondences (C series) from the real, quantitative atemporal series (the D series). Taken subjectively, the number of time-series is considerably larger, for McTaggart believed that "there are as many time-series as there are selves who perceive things in time." And, from an absolute standpoint, there are no time-series at all:

> There is, on our theory, no time-series, for nothing is in time.
> There is no series of events, but a timeless series of misperceptions which perceive a series of timeless existents as being in time.
> Now every misperception, since it is a perception, must fall within a self, and no misperception can be common to two selves. Two selves can no more have the same misperception than the same fit of toothache. (*Nature*, II, 273)

The rejection of time, especially of shared, public time, and its replacement by a number of individual sequences of perception (or misperception), is a more accurate description of the mental states in Woolf's fiction than the standard Bergsonian theory of subjective, lived time. The timeless patterns of her characters' perception make up an order in the flux of experience and define a personality, which the time-filled process in Bergsonian psychology is unable to account for. Woolf deals with the "misperception" of time as a creative activity, rather than as a chaotic or streamlike flux, and thus these misperceptions in an unreal time become the source of the individuation of personality.

Another consequence of McTaggart's time theory is thoroughly Woolfian: whether time is real or not, selves perceive it primarily in all their common experiences. We are led again to the fundamental loneliness of the self in the world Woolf describes. McTaggart's real atemporal series is made up exclusively of perceptions by selves of other selves. This total absorption breaks down their separateness, for such exhaustive perception constitutes perfect love. Yet each self must, up to the final stage of integration, maintain time-series different from those of the selves it perceives. There is, short of the Absolute, no common ground of existence for the selves, and McTaggart joins Leibnitz in the monadological conclusion that the selves are total worlds which do not touch. This individualistic conclusion satisfies McTaggart's tendency to resist immersion of the self in the Absolute, with the consequent loss of personal identity, but its drawback is to leave the self sempiternally perceiving and even loving other selves with whom it can never fully join. This paradox is at the heart of the tragic view of life in Virginia Woolf and accounts for the peculiar structure of her major novels, in which communication *is* occasionally effected by selves without contact, only to fall back into radical isolation.

I wish now to show how such a set of ideas can help explain some of the special qualities of Woolf's fiction, especially in one novel, *To the Lighthouse*.

The primary activity in Virginia Woolf's major novels is the effort of selves to know other selves; there is remarkably little moral drama. (It is this that separates Woolf from the main tradition of English fiction, makes her anathema to Leavisite criticism, and establishes her centrality in the modern novel.)

Some conventional dramatic action, occurring in a temporal process, does take place in Woolf's universe, but such action can be seen as secondary and irrelevant to what really happens in her world, without time. To take the case of the famous transitional part of *To the Lighthouse*—titled, with deceptive simplicity, "Time Passes." Time indeed passes somewhere: the world war transpires and people are killed in it, and simultaneously Mrs. Ramsay and her children Prue and Andrew die of various causes. But, while time passes outside, inside the unoccupied Ramsay vacation house nothing happens—no action is recorded but that of the little airs which move through it according to no temporal order. It is not entirely accurate to say that nothing happens in the section, for what happens is the airs. The little airs are the selves McTaggart defines as endowed with perception but not self-consciousness. In the novel they are later described as some "secret sense, fine as air, with which to steal through keyholes and surround her," which the artist Lily Briscoe wishes for when she finds fifty pairs of eyes insufficient to know Mrs. Ramsay (III, xi, 303). This sense is a medium of pure consciousness: it "took to itself and treasured up like the air which held the smoke of the steamer, her thoughts, her imaginations, her desires" (p. 304). And, like the material air, it is not localized or personal to any individual: it is the substance of selves before they have reached identity, when they can pass from knowledge into love. Their knowledge is not a personal attribute attached to human beings who exist in time, and consequently their activity is not temporal. They do pass through the house but maintain themselves there as a possiblity of renewed passage, a permanent transitoriness. They correspond, very generally, to McTaggart's C series, the succession of real, atemporal events seen from the misperceptions of time. What passes in the "Time Passes" section is, then, the concept of time itself.

The airs, the disembodied selves of part II, stand between the group of human selves presented in parts I and III—before and after, when the novel is read in sequence. It is not, however, accurate to say that the Ramsays and their friends come together earlier and later than the airs (as in McTaggart's B series), for the airs take no part in their lives (although Lily intuits them) and cannot be located in time. Nor do the three parts represent a past-present-future sequence (McTaggart's A series), for these abstractions are not germane to the pattern of characterization in the novel. The characters do not develop in a linear sequence from one section to the other; neither time nor events in time (such as Mrs. Ramsay's death) demonstrably affect them—although they live and die in a deducible history. Lily Briscoe is (along with Mr. Ramsay) the exception, but her effort to come to grips with the illusion of time is an extraordinary effort in an otherwise time-free universe.

The effective structure of the novel is a static symbolic pattern of three moments—akin to the three strokes of the lighthouse's beam, which are not so much successive as the fulfillment of potentialities which complete a whole. In the first part we have Mrs. Ramsay's creation of unity by love, and in the last Lily Briscoe's creation of unity by art; in the first part there is parental opposition and Oedipal rebellion, in the last, family reconciliation; in the first the lighthouse exists in the imagination as potentiality, and in the last it becomes actuality—the minds of yachtsmen and artists reach the lighthouse. The novel is an arrangement of the aspects of unchanging things.

In poising this pattern on the central point of the "Time Passes" section, Woolf made the little airs the effective norms of selfhood. Measured against them, the human characters are partially realized dramatic equivalents. They represent the self engaged in the toils of body, personality, and time, but some are distinguished by the effort of their consciousness to extend itself universally in love. Of this effort, Mrs. Ramsay is the heroine, and her sometimes challenged excellence as a unifier must be seen as the embodiment of a philosophical ideal.

The more commonly found problems of knowledge on its way to becoming love are initially traced in Lily Briscoe's meditation on the Ramsays:

> They became part of that unreal but penetrating and exciting universe which is the world seen through the eyes of love. The sky stuck to them; the birds sang through them. And, what was even more exciting, she felt, too, as she saw Mr. Ramsay bearing down and retreating, and Mrs. Ramsay sitting with James in the window and the cloud moving and the tree bending, how life, from being made up of little separate incidents which one lived one by one, became curled and whole like a wave which bore one up with it and threw one down with it, there, with a dash on the beach. (I, ix, 76)

The mind already captivated by love is able to know not only the selves it loves but their interconnections with the flux around them. This vision is "penetrating and exciting" but "unreal," since it does not limit itself to knowledge of the only real beings, the selves. In consequence, the knowing self is exposed to a threat of destruction in the very act of its knowledge: Lily imagines the incidents of life, including those she is presently experiencing, as passing through a curve which ends with her diffusion among all other selves—as expressed in the image of watery dissolution which haunts this and Woolf's next major novel, *The Waves*.

The dangers of too widespread a knowledge having been recognized, its genuine scope is subsequently set out in Lily's meditation:

> Could loving, as people called it, make her and Mrs. Ramsay one?
> for it was not knowledge but unity that she desired, not inscriptions on tablets, nothing that could be written in any language known to men, but intimacy itself, which is knowledge, she had thought, leaning her head on Mrs. Ramsay's knee.
> . . . How then, she had asked herself, did one know one thing or another thing about people, sealed as they were? Only like a bee, drawn by some sweetness or sharpness in the air intangible to touch or taste, one haunted the dome-shaped hive, ranged the wastes of the air over the countries of the world alone, and then haunted the hives with their murmurs and their stirrings; the hives which were people. (I, x, 83)

Knowledge of selves, then, aside from its inexpressibility (lacking a human language), must operate on intangible data: the qualities which attract the knower, like the bee, are sweet and sharp but not known by the senses. The knower must haunt the hive to get the intimacy, or the intuition of the individuality of the self, that is the goal of knowledge. She must see the self whole, like a unifying dome, taking account of the multiplicity of phenomena in the self, the murmurings and stirrings; and she must also remain alone, ranging outside the hive, through the air "over the countries of the world"—presumably to avoid remaining a prisoner within the dome-shaped world of another.

This much the novel tells us, and dramatizes in its action, but what exactly is the process by which this knowledge is achieved? We are back to the question of perception without contact with which we began. McTaggart cannot give a direct answer here, because in his absolutist mood he does not admit the premise that we can know other selves: ". . . in present experience I perceive no self but myself." For him, true perception is direct, complete, and indistinguishable from love, and therefore all present experience must fall short of this ideal. But McTaggart describes in passing another form of perception, indirect perception, and though he does not make much of it it seems to describe the knowing process that takes place in Woolf's fiction:

> We can recognize indirect perception in our present experience. If I perceive my perception of a sensum, then this second and introspective perception, which is a direct perception of my perception of the sensum, can be an indirect perception of the sensum. But in our present experience the importance of such indirect perceptions is very small. For in present experience I perceive no self but myself, and so the only objects which I perceive indirectly are those which my own self perceives directly. . . . But it would be quite different when my perception extended to other selves, for then I could perceive indirectly things which those other selves perceived directly, but which I did not perceive directly. (*Nature*, II, 127)

From this standpoint, to perceive others means perceiving their perceptions: Woolf's knowing characters are able to perceive the objects of experience which they share with others not only as they appear to themselves but as they appear to others. This is not a mere adoption of a perspectival view which makes allowances for differences in the point of observation. Rather, it is an imaginative projection into the mind of others, effected through observation of others' experience. While this perception of another may occur only at a moment, the moment that other perceives an object, it opens to the perceiver of selves the whole self of the other, for that selfhood is made up of perceptions.

What the perceiver of selves gains is not knowledge of objects that she or he does not directly perceive (as in McTaggart's discussion of the benefits of indirect perception) but knowledge of another perceiving self. When one perceives the perceiver perceiving, one also has access to all the other contents of that mind, for that other self also perceives its own life history, its own existence. Woolf's knowing characters perceive other selves initially in the manner in which characters in other fictional worlds do, as objects who may become subjects to the perceiver through extraordinary acts of imaginative sympathy. What distinguishes her fictional world is a methodology, as it were, of imaginative sympathy. By perceiving others in the act of perception, Woolf's characters gain knowledge of them not only in that particular perceptual relation but in all the subject-object relations of their lives, i.e., in their essential selfhood.

The process by which isolated selves come to know each other through their observation of other objects can be traced in *To the Lighthouse* with some precision. The third section of the novel is taken up with Lily Briscoe's creation of a unified work of art while observing the Ramsay family reuniting itself in the achievement of a long-deferred goal, the trip to the lighthouse. What has been neglected in critical accounts of this process is the systematic achievement of communication between Lily and the poet Augustus Carmichael, in which knowledge of another self and the simultaneous recovery of Mrs. Ramsay's self come to be fully realized. In this process of selves' coming to know the contents of each other's minds—not by direct self-revelation but by mutual observation of a third object—the knowledge of selfhood becomes the highest achievement in the denouement of the novel. This metaphysical process is validated by—and makes possible—the dramatic action: Lily's completion of the process of making a timeless work of art out of the passing scene before her.

The painter's silent communication with the poet is deftly traced in repeated quotations from Lily's silent thoughts: "'D'you remember, Mr. Carmichael?' she was inclined to ask. . . . he was asleep, or he was dreaming, or he was lying there catching words, she supposed" (III, v, 263). "He lay on his chair with his hands clasped above his paunch not reading, or sleeping, but basking like a creature gorged with existence. . . . She wanted to go straight up to him and say, 'Mr. Carmichael! . . . About life, about death; about Mrs. Ramsay'" (III, v, 274). ". . . the whole world seemed to have dissolved in this early morning hour into a pool of thought, a deep basin of reality, and one could almost fancy that, had Mr. Carmichael spoken, a little tear would have rent the surface of the pool. And then?" (pp. 275–276). "A curious notion came to her that he did after all hear the things she could not say" (p. 276). "Mr. Carmichael suddenly grunted. She laughed. He clawed his book up from the grass. He settled into his chair again puffing and blowing like some sea monster" (III, xi, 294). "But this was one way of knowing people, she thought: to know the outline, not the detail, to sit in one's garden and look at the slopes of a hill running purple down into the distant heather. She knew him in that way" (III, xi, 299). And finally:

"He has landed," she said aloud. "It is finished." Then, surging
up, puffing slightly, old Mr. Carmichael stood beside her, looking
like an old pagan God, shaggy, with weeds in his hair and the trident

(it was only a French novel) in his hand. . . . "They will have landed," [he said] and she felt that she had been right. They had not needed to speak. They had been thinking the same things and he had answered her without her asking him anything. He stood there spreading his hands over all the weakness and suffering of mankind; she thought he was surveying, tolerantly, compassionately, their final destiny. Now he has crowned the occasion, she thought, when his hand slowly fell, as if she had seen him let fall from his great height a wreath of violets and asphodels which, fluttering slowly, lay at length upon the earth. (III, xiii, 319)

A full metaphoric analysis of this passage would account for Carmichael's association with the leech gatherer of "Resolution and Independence" (indeed, many elements of the scene recall Wordsworthian landscape and dialogue); a full symbolic reading would take up the mythological attributes with which the mana-laden prophet figure is invested—particularly his association with the underworld, from which he brings flowers of resurrection; a full psychological interpretation would explain the bearing of these facts on Carmichael's dislike of Mrs. Ramsay and his achievement of poetic stature only after the death of Andrew Ramsay in the war. But my present emphasis is on the achievement in Lily's and Carmichael's relationship of a unity not only in perception of the Ramsays, not only in memories of Mrs. Ramsay, but in insight into the larger shape of reality. It is this insight that precipitates the final stroke with which Lily completes her painting and achieves her vision in the closing lines of the novel.

Despite this triumph of perceptual communion, Woolf's fiction, like McTaggart's philosophy, is exposed to a paradox in conceiving its ideal of selfhood which effectively challenges it in its own terms. Underlying the perceptions of selves, which are their characteristic mode of behavior, is a form of activity which is more desirable and more real. This is the ubiquitous love of the self for all selves, of which Mrs. Ramsay is the highest exemplar in the novel. But the difficulty of the concept of love, as McTaggart was explicit in pointing out and as Woolf was painfully aware, is that it is all or nothing: perfect love by one self of another depends on the perfection of that self, on the love of other selves, and ultimately on the perfection of the love of all selves for all selves. Until that millennial state, human love is imperfect and the loving self is isolated amid a world which is not love—which is not, at least in appearance, self. Thus the self is thrown back upon itself and finds there the perfect object of love. It would be difficult to dissociate this conclusion from a metaphysical narcissism whose sterility lies in its very purity.

One might choose a number of moments in Mrs. Ramsay's meditations to illustrate this lonely narcissism, but I shall cite an occasion which reaches a logical limit. In a mirror that once reflected the members of the family, the light of another day finds nothing to illuminate, and yet it remains an agent of perception:

> Now, day after day, light turned, like a flower reflected in water, its clear image on the wall opposite. Only the shadows of the trees, flourishing in the wind, made obeisance on the wall, and for a moment darkened the pool in which light reflected itself. . . . So loveliness reigned and stillness, and together made the shape of loveliness itself, a form from which life had parted. . . . (II, iv, 200–201)

It is an image close to the view of McTaggart, who finds that in current life one perceives no self but oneself. It cannot be reduced to the laws of optics by saying that the mirror and the wall are bouncing the passive light back and forth between them. Woolf's language—"light turned . . . its clear image on the wall," "light reflected itself"—insists that the light is the activity of a self-directed being—a self which replaces the selves of the persons who have departed. This self without personality, the light, is sufficient to itself: it need not enter into subject-object relationships as the medium of vision but maintains itself indefinitely by giving back to itself its own image. This is both its grandeur and its misery: it needs no other self, but it loves only itself. It shapes a loveliness beyond other loveliness, but its form is lifeless, lacking humanity.

The weariness with others implied here has its positive side: it is not only a withdrawal from the effort of living but a condition of knowing, at least of confronting oneself. Mrs. Ramsay picks up one of Lily Briscoe's images of painting in her approach to herself:

> Not as oneself did one find rest ever, in her experience . . . but as a wedge of darkness. Losing personality, one lost the fret, the hurry, the stir; and there rose to her lips always some exclamation of triumph over life when things came together in this peace, this rest, this eternity; and pausing there she looked out to meet that stroke of the Lighthouse, the long steady stroke, the last of the three, which was her stroke. . . . and it seemed to her like her own eyes meeting her own eyes, searching as she alone could search into her mind and her heart, purifying out of existence that lie, any lie. (I, xi, 100–101)

Mrs. Ramsay moves from relaxation to a sense of unity, "when things came together," to a sense of her identity with an external phenomenon, to a use of that phenomenon as an instrument of self-discovery. It is a mirror of the self, to be sure, but it is independent still: "her own eyes meeting her own eyes" suggests a confrontation with oneself as if it were another being, not simply the use of an external object to act as a passive intermediary off which to bounce one's projected image. Although our knowledge of and union with others may be bounded by the limits of apparent temporality, we can achieve self-awareness by the acts of loving perception and of esthetic creation which Mrs. Ramsay and Lily respectively undertake in the novel.

It is in her attitude toward death that Virginia Woolf comes ultimately to break with McTaggart for, despite his awareness of our tragic limitations, his philosophy remains at heart an attempt to offer the atheist some consolation in expectations of an afterlife. She makes no effort to imagine postexistence, with or without memory of preexistence, presumably because even a transfer of life is an unmaking of the individual identity, and no other self can be the same. The firmness of Woolf's acceptance of the fact of death—as expressed with ultimate poignancy in the cries of Lily after the departed Mrs. Ramsay—is equaled only by the firmness of her attachment to the value of life. In the end, the struggle to maintain this dual vision became too exhausting, and she walked off into the water. But the ideal of a timeless life in apparent time, a transcendence to where we already really are, an identity completely composed of relationships with others, reverberates throughout her work. In her diary, she wrote, ". . . I am now and then haunted by some semi-mystic very profound life of a woman, which shall all be told on one occasion; and time shall be utterly obliterated; future shall somehow blossom out of the past. One incident—say the fall of a flower—might contain it. My theory being that the actual event practically does not exist—nor time either. But I don't want to force this."[15]

13. *The Magus* of the Wizard of the West

ORPHEE: *Quelle épreuve cruelle!*
—GLUCK/MOLINE

OME courage, if not heroism, is required of the critic of *The Magus*. Has not its author expressed his contempt of critics —especially American critics—with their "strangely pragmatic view of what books are. . . . Obscure books, for them, are a kind of crossword puzzle. . . . They believe, in short, that a book is like a machine; that if you have the knack, you can take it to bits."[1] Setting aside the metaphoric switches from pragmatic machinery to crossword puzzles, there is more than British provincialism or authorial defensiveness to this statement. John Fowles wants a residue of mystery to persist in his art; his own account of *The Magus'* genesis in a visit to a Greek villa concludes: "Its mysterious significance to me fifteen years ago remains mysterious." And his conception of metaphoric indirectness as a condition of any approach to reality insures that his means will be oblique: "Memorandum: *If you want to be true to life, start lying about the reality of it.*"

Given this much obliquity, even in a culture so professedly modernist as ours, it is inevitable that a novel from such a hand will be neglected or impugned. Marvin Mudrick's is the casual approach destined to insure the former results: ". . . a shrewd and lively, brilliantly visualized, continuously provoking and entertaining novel; above all, a prodigy of ingenuity. . . . *The Magus* may well be, when it sticks to its job of mystification, one of the best 'mystery stories' ever written."[2] Such praise is likely to bring out the crossword-puzzle solvers, or at best consign the work to the society of Nabokov, Barth, and Borges, where it might suffer by comparison. For *The Magus* is not another tour de force like *The Collector*, and it is a mystery only in the sense in which the Eleusinian rites were—and remain—mysteries.

The other approach to Fowles is well represented by Angus Wilson's review. After some sneers at cinematic success and a lengthy plot summary, it concludes with a hint of the novel's metaphysical and moral concerns: "These are big and interesting questions, but they are hardly new. Mr. Fowles propounds them with the maximum of elaboration and mystification, but since he does not illuminate them at all, they merely clutter up an over-ingenious fantasy."[3] One can imagine the same response in an

early review of *Paradise Lost*: "big and interesting questions . . . hardly new
. . . maximum of elaboration . . . does not illuminate them at all . . . over-
ingenious fantasy." It would be important to know how the book posed
these age-old issues before reaching those conclusions.

Consideration of *The Magus* properly begins with *The Aristos*, a book of
philosophical aphorisms written in the years during which Fowles wrote
the novel, although later heavily revised. (I use the original 1964 version as
representing Fowles at the time of *The Magus*.) It is the quarry from which
the fiction's philosophy is mined, though nothing of fictional art is suggested in its bare and somewhat awkward reasonings. *The Aristos* is a peculiar book, not only in substance but in motive: it seems outlandish that
a gifted young author should want to publish his notebook and express a
number of traditional and semioriginal ideas about life and the world in 246
pages. The aphorisms are modeled on the surviving fragments of the pre-
Socratic philosophers, particularly those of Heraclitus. Such early practitioners could set down an entire philosophy (granted its difficulties of interpretation) in what amounts now to only a few pages—presumably because they stood at the beginning of the Western world view. In taking up
this stance while placed near the end of the Western tradition, Fowles is
asserting a need to go back to origins, to reassert elementary ideas.

Fowles specifies, moreover, that he is not going to talk about the world
but about *his* world: he subtitles the book *A Self-Portrait in Ideas*. His
mind emerges as a synthesis of surprising contradictions: it presents the
image of a socialist, humanist, atheist existentialist with strong aristocratic
and individualist tendencies—rather of the Ayn Rand sort. The author
emerges as a man who wants to see the social order rationalized and yet
sees the deep irrationalities which are its splendor and its misery. He is
also a man with a particular gripe against the modern age, as an age of over-
civilization and of overkill, but who sees its spectacular possibilities for
mental and personal liberation. As in *The Magus*, the urgent fiat posed by
The Aristos is "thou shalt be free," and, as we come to discover, that is the
most outrageously difficult demand that could be made of us. Yet our special position as inheritors of all the ages gives us a strong chance to claim
such freedom, and the novel applies the myriad arts of the West to the task
of freeing a representative modern man.

"Aristos" is the name for the man who is first—that is, the excellent, the
aristocratic, the man of *areté*. The man of singular competence, power, and
freedom is, of course, a Greek ideal, and in *The Magus* the enactment of
an educational process (*paideia*) takes place in the isles of Greece, under the
aegis of a Greek who embodies many of the virtues he inculcates. In the
course of *The Aristos*, Fowles considers, among a number of ways of looking at the world, the so-called Divine Solution—the antidote people need
when they set themselves up as gods or when they erect a god for themselves. Fowles writes:

Appoint yourself a god; lay down the laws of a universe; become the master of a process.

You then find yourself in the predicament I call the Divine Predicament: to remain good governors good governors must govern, and gov ern all equally, and all fairly. But no act of government can be fair to all, in all their different situations, except one.[?]

The Divine Solution: govern by not governing in any sense that the governed can call being governed; that is, constitute a situation in which the governed must govern themselves. . . .

Put dice on the table and leave the room; but make it for the players that there was never a time before you left the room.[4]

The irony of this Greek or Pascalian god is that he does not govern, since laws are general and there exist only individuals. He gives us only the illusion that we are governed, and he condemns us to govern ourselves. The god of this world is an existential bettor with whom we are to play a fatal game; he is also a bit of a con man, not by loading the dice against us but by leaving us to play alone—and by disguising himself so that we think "there was never a time before [he] left the room." With such a playful and elusive god there are all kinds of possibilities for comic deception and self-mystification; here we find the root images of *The Magus*.

God's authority constitutes a peculiar anarchy because it parades under the banner of tyranny. From the ancient myths of the *kakos daimon* to the existential rebellions against all authority figures, there has been a tendency to erect a god of enmity and restraint as a projection of man's rage at his own unprotected and precarious state. Fowles' vision of the absent or dead god of modern theology and poetic tradition is a humanized one. In *The Magus*, a man has grasped that god—whatever his ontological status may be—leaves us free but that we insist on erecting a divine governance in order to escape from our own possibility of freedom. This man decides to play god for his contemporaries, commanding them to be free by first asserting and then gradually withdrawing his control of their lives. This is the god-game, as played in the novel. It rests on the notion that a man can teach another to be free by playing god and then revealing that he is not a god, that there are no gods, and that each must be his own god.

The Aristos further enlarges on Fowles' views of life and the afterlife and on the relation between them that might be called myth. It is only in the modern world that we have, potentially, the capacity to make this life—insofar as it is a bodily affair—decently human for all. "The great myth of the afterlife has stood between us and reality" (p. 32)—both as a confession of man's incapacities and as a stumbling block to our possession of our physical world. Yet are our illusions of the afterlife to be utterly dispensed with? A great many have entertained visions of this realm, have regarded it as a mystery, and have worshiped this mystery in occult ways. Heraclitus' attitude toward the myths and rites was the modern humanist's: "Mystery enough at noon; no need to multiply the midnight rites" (p. 94). Yet perhaps we can use the midnight rites at noon to organize the mystery of the world we *do* live in. *The Magus* is a retelling of classical myth—the Orpheus legend—according to a structure derived from the presumed pattern of the "mystery" religions. These cults aimed at making the Orphic legends operative in eschatological salvation; in *The Magus* an individual is morally saved by going through the process established in Orphic religion.

Why stop with Orphism, since it is instrumental, not doctinal? Fowles uses in this educational process a wide variety of occult lore, from the Tarot deck to the mystifications of de Sade. It is never clear how much one approach is to be believed—that is, all are to be played out and known by their fruits in personal growth. Such syncretism leaves Fowles open to the reviewers' charges that he has made a modish bouillabaisse of his mythical sources. Despite the enormous investment in mythical and other strains of imagery that flow into *The Magus*, Fowles' educational art is ultimately quite simple. He himself scorns avant-garde mystifications in other novelists and poets (see p. 135) and has expressed his approach to art in an account of a trip to the mythical realm of the Muses: "I climbed Parnassus once, and between the mundane village of Arachova . . . and the lovely summit, quite as lovely as the poets have always had it to be, there is nothing but a slope; no abysm, no gulf, no place where wings are necessary" (p. 209). The realm of art is, then, part of the human, not the occult, scene. Not only the artist but the ordinary man who is the subject of art needs to discover this humanly accessible, natural realm. The hero and the heroine of *The Magus* are shown making the same trip and experiencing Parnassus in an eminently mundane and winning way. It is not a sheer cliff, Alison and Nicholas discover, but a long climb. Man is on the mountain with the muses, with the great poets, with those who live at the top: there are no secrets of the trade, only the various forms of mental blindness by which we manage to obscure from ourselves our own freedom and the bountifulness of our world.

In *The Aristos*, Heraclitus is quoted to the effect that *"all men have one concern: to know themselves, and be sober"* (p. 233). In this process of self-education, the traditional aids to reflection are eschewed, again in Heraclitus' phrase, with Fowles' commentary: *"Nightwalkers* [lovers of obscurity], *Magians* [professional mystifiers], *priests of Bacchus and priestesses of the vat, and the initiated* [the elect who brag of their election], *are evil"* (p. 233). But such is our condition that we do not receive the truth directly, even from reliable sources; as Heraclitus was the first to admit, *"the Oracle at Delphi neither hides nor states, but gives signs"* (p. 234). Thus the novel—like life itself—is to be conceived not as a regression to an occult, religious, or mythic world view but as a symbolic experience, in which the characters learn to interpret the signs given by the world. The artist is not to descend to mystification but can learn to distill the core of truth from the traditional forms of self-obfuscation that humanity has chosen. The magic is useful only as something to be stripped away, and eventually we are to transcend those forms and come into the harsh light of reality where we can learn to live. Yet there will remain a sense of mystery, not added by the magus figures but built into the world and adding to its attraction for us.

We see from the outset that Fowles wants to initiate his reader in the same provocative and artificially mystifying way chosen by the magus figure who initiates the novel's hero. Underneath his name on the original title page Fowles put *"Aqua non unda"*–"the water not the wave"–which is later quoted in answer to the apparently homiletic question *"Utram bibis? Aquam an undam?* Which are you drinking? The water or the wave?"[5] He next dedicates the book "To Astarte"–perhaps referring to a real person, but by the name of the great mother goddess who dominated the ancient Near East in various guises.[6] There follows an epigraph from A. E. Waite's *The Key to the Tarot*, one of the favorite books of occult science that modern poets like Eliot and Yeats have thumbed in search of metaphors for poetry. Fowles clearly labels the Tarot lore as "TRUMPS MAJOR: Otherwise, Greater Arcana." We are to take it as supplying the various figures of the magus, together with his retinue of roses and lilies, who are to dominate the action of the novel.[7] The characters are to play a trick on the hero; and why not the author on the reader, too, with the Tarot deck as well as another?

The final piece of initiatory machinery is the first of a series of quotations from de Sade's *Les Infortunes de la vertu* which open each of the novel's three parts. I confess that I don't know quite how to take these: as an accurate psychological description (*"Un débauché de profession est rarement un homme pitoyable"* gives us the hero in a nutshell, but do we need it?); as an acknowledgment of the strong current of sadism that marks the novel's treatment of its hero/victim (and which marks *The Collector* even more grossly); or as another bit of trumpery to outdo such mystifiers as Lawrence Durrell, who uses quotes from de Sade to even more banal effect. There is no doubt, however, that the quotations provide the images of Black Mass and Orphic illumination for the activities of parts II and III: the former is called *"nos mystères"* (p. 61/65) and the latter is to *"jeter du jour sur l'obscurité des voies . . . et de tracer d'après cela quelque plan de conduite. . ."* (p. 515/567).

Although the hero eventually winds up in bondage and is variously stimulated in his masochistic and sadistic centers–the *pièce de résistance* being his opportunity to cudgel a willing female, a temptation he masters with flying colors–his experiences are mainly of a more familiar psychic order. A young Englishman, recent graduate of Oxford, placed in the middle state between the bourgeois and the bohemian, rebounding from a love affair in which he cannot or will not allow himself to love, takes a teaching job at a Greek boys' school and is told by one of his predecessors to "beware of the waiting room." In his first weeks on the Greek island,[8] he discovers that he is no poet, develops an apparently venereal disease, fails at a stagy existential suicide, and in despair begins "quietly to rape the island" (ix, 59/63). The "body of the island" is represented as "virgin" (vii, 46–47/50), and the hero's response to the Greek landscape is from the first a love affair, "as if Greece were a woman" (vii, 45/49); so it is inevitable that the site of his rebirth should be a landscape conceived as eternally feminine. The imagery surrounding the dramatic process enacted in the novel does not point, then, to a pattern of education through torment, through successive encounters with suffering—either one's own or that of others—although the hero gets a full treatment in these respects. It is rather a pattern of education through rebirth, returning to sources, discovering the meaning of one's name (Urfe, Orphée), and reordering the past—developing new transactions with what is already given in the self but not yet fulfilled. The orphaned hero acquires more intense feelings toward father and mother surrogates than he ever enjoyed with his parents; he learns how to love the woman who had already been given him, and whom he had let slip away; he comes to enjoy the freedom which he had always claimed and never exercised. That this is to be the outcome is intimated in the passage of "Little Gidding" (x, 65/69) left on the shore for him to find:

> We shall not cease from exploration
> And the end of all our exploring
> Will be to arrive where we started
> And know the place for the first time.

Returning to origins and discovering one's name and race traditionally require a journey in quest, and another passage marked for the hero in an idiom he will presumably understand is from Pound's Canto XLVII:

> Yet must thou sail after knowledge
> Knowing less than drugged beasts. *phthengometha thasson.*

The archetype, with its reference to Odysseus, marks the striving of the alienated—from the ancient Greeks to modern man—the effort to return home and come into one's own. Moreover, the advice is that of Pound's Tiresias, who challenges Odysseus' state of bondage to Circe, sex, and present pleasures; it is an injunction to deny oneself in order to find oneself, to lift the veil of illusion and see what is there, to fully raise oneself above the animal. All these things the hero undertakes to do in choosing to pursue the sender of the messages; source hunting here becomes a parody of the quest, and the interpretation of one's own nature becomes an advanced problem in literary criticism.

If the images of rebirth and quest are models for the experience the hero is to undergo, the enactment of this experiment is not a rebirth in the sense in which a psychic reformation, such as that in psychoanalysis, is a rebirth. Nor is it literally a journey, beyond the initial movement from England to Greece which precedes and is the precondition for the educational process. For the *paideia* of his *aristos*, this man made if not born excellent, Fowles has chosen an educational model from ancient rather than modern culture. While the upper-crust boys of the "Lord Byron School" are taught to model themselves on the British norms represented by the school's namesake, their teacher Nicholas Urfe is taught to live according to a traditional wisdom lost to modern England and Greece. With the early suggestion that Nicholas is "in hell" (viii, 54/58); by comparison with the leave-taking of his girlfriend, who knows how to make a passage without looking back (vi, 44/47–48; vii, 49/53); and most strikingly in the appearance of the "SALLE D'ATTENTE" or waiting-room signboard, we are trained to see Nicholas undertaking a pilgrimage to a place of mysteries, where religious and moral truth is taught by giving symbolic access into the underworld, where the foundations of such truths reside. The most famous of such mystery cults in the ancient world was that of Eleusis, and the Eleusinian mysteries become the primary—though not the exclusive—model for the ritual of education in *The Magus*.

The visitor to Eleusis today meets with a maze of foundations, stones, and columns, but it is still possible to pick one's way from the greater and lesser *propylaea* or waiting rooms, where the people of Athens and initiates from all Greece once gathered, past the two caves where Persephone descended to and reemerged from Hades—and on to the *telesterion* or sanctuary of the mysteries, where the initiation rites took place. To quote my Hachette guidebook: "What were these revelations? According to P. Foucart, they took the form of a *sacred drama* in which the legends of Core (Persephone-Proserpina), and of the union of Zeus and Demeter, were enacted. The *mystes* were then shown 'how the soul journeys in the underworld, and they were taught how this journey can be brought to a happy end.' . . . After the sacred drama the *mystes* were led by the hierophant and torchbearer on a sort of torch-lit voyage through the initiation hall, the different parts of which reproduced in stylised fashion the topography of hell. After this the sacred objects (*hiera*) were revealed to them, and the ceremony was doubtless completed by a visit to the temples of Demeter, Core and Pluto."[9]

The education of the ancient populace in the mysteries of life and death —based on a living mythology in which the seasonal cycle, the fecundity and terrors of the earth, and the possibilities of redemption and resurrection were made real to all—would hardly seem the appropriate model for the private education of a modern man, for whom the myths are literature and the gods unnecessary fictions. Insofar as Fowles and his readers share this skeptic and enlightened attitude with the hero, the Eleusinian mysteries and their underlying myths can serve only as formal analogues to the educative scheme. Nicholas shrugs off the intimations he receives, for example, at encountering a figure dressed as "Anubis, guardian of the underworld, who later became Cerberus": "Fascinating. But it explained nothing," he says (xxxvii, 230/partially omitted). Yet the island is early seen as a "site for myths" where "the mysteries began" (ix, 59/63); Nicholas has the feeling "of having entered a myth. . . . It was not in the least a literary feeling, but an intensely mysterious present and concrete feeling of excitement, of being in a situation where anything still might happen" (xxv, 152–153/157). And the magus himself encourages him to regard his experience mythically –but with a sense of humor not lacking in the Greeks, ancient and modern, toward their gods: after Nicholas has pumped Conchis' muleteer, named Hermes, for information, Conchis waggishly tells him, "If you interrogate Hermes, Zeus will know" (xiii, 76/80; this is also the speech in which he prefers his name to be pronounced with "the *ch* soft"–for a lovely pun on his psychic powers of enlightenment).

At the same time, Nicholas' skepticism, while it is one of the hindrances of his education, is also an appropriate stance before a world ultimately without gods. Man must live skeptically, in doubt, and attuned to the metaphoric illusoriness of myth and other cultural modes, as Fowles has indicated in *The Aristos*. Thus Nicholas reacts not only to the content but to the style of Conchis' tale, for example, that of the Axel or des Esseintes figure of de Deukans (another perhaps oversubtle pun) or the Kierkegaardian parable of Henrik Nygaard. Conchis not only reveals but emphasizes the symbolic and stagy nature of his enterprise, encouraging perception not only of the tenor but of the vehicle of his metaphors, as when he comments on a passage in a book on masques he has left for Nicholas to read, "It is only a metaphor. But it may help" (xxvii, 162/166). The appropriate educational (or critical) attitude is registered by an *objet d'art* left prominently on the scene, the bust of a deity but also a paradigm for human response to the world: "The little head watched our watching; bland, certain, and almost maliciously inscrutable. It flashed on me that it was also the smile that Conchis sometimes wore; as if he sat before the head and practiced it. At the same time I realized exactly what I disliked about it. It was above all the smile of dramatic irony, of those who have privileged information" (xxiii, 142–143/147). As Nicholas comes to recognize more of the behind-the-scenes trumpery of the magus' artifice, he is not the less but the more ready to acknowledge the home truths delivered in the course of its mystifications. Revelation and demystification come packaged together, just as truth and illusion usually come to us intertwined; sometimes by conscious design the illusion can act as a symbolic medium for the truth, but only when our skepticism is trained to operate selectively upon it.

While the tools of literary criticism are never far from hand in *The Magus*, the art most dramatically employed is that of the theater. Conchis is a master of not only interpretation but scenario—an "Empson of the event," as Nicholas says (lvi, 417/458). He is mountebank, impresario, master of revels, *psychopompos*, and movie director, if not puppeteer. While these images have been used to describe Fowles the novelist in his manipulation of character, Conchis has only scorn for fiction: "The novel is dead. As dead as alchemy. . . . Why should I struggle through hundreds of pages of fabrication to reach half a dozen very little truths?" (xv, 92/96). Incorporating Fowles' parody not only of his own art but also of contemporary reviewers' clichés, the passage is significant in mingling the arts in which Conchis is engaged: fiction, alchemy, and dramaturgy are all called upon, but the last, being most kinetic and efficient for education, is most in evidence. Conchis also comments on Forster's dictum, "Only connect": "Fiction is the worst form of connection" (xviii, 108/111); and Nicholas sums up his position as follows: *"Words are for facts. Not fiction"* (xxiii, 137/141). The vulgar interpretation of this position would be that language in fiction is twice-removed from reality and that reality must be imitated or expressed directly in action to have a cathartic effect. Only a little analysis is needed to show that theatrical art is as twice-removed as fiction; in drama there is usually an initial verbal mimesis and then a better or worse performance which acts directly on the audience. (*Pace* the modern attempts, from naturalism to the theater of the absurd, to break down the wall between stage and audience.) The ultimate comedy of Conchis' position is, of course, that it is spoken inside a novel; Fowles is not about to abandon his art, although he may chafe at his bondage to it and curse its limitations.

Conchis has, to be sure, an elaborate theory of dramaturgy which bears resemblance to the avant-garde contemporary stage; he aims at

> . . . a new kind of drama. One in which the conventional relations between audience and actors were forgotten. In which the conventional scenic geography, the notions of proscenium, stage, auditorium, were completely discarded. In which continuity of performance, either in time or place, was ignored. And in which the action, the narrative was fluid, with only a point of departure and a fixed point of conclusion. . . . You will find that Artaud and Pirandello and Brecht were all thinking, in their different ways, along similar lines. . . . The element that they could never bring themselves to discard was the audience. . . . Here we are all actors. . . . You think you are not acting. Just pretending a little. But you have much to learn about yourself. (lii, 366/404–405 [with modifications])

In this exposition of his new theater, Conchis comes round to one of the oldest topoi of the genre, the world-as-stage motif. The exclusion of theatrical conventions is not a way of making the theater more realistic but a step toward capturing the world for art—unleashing mimesis to take in life directly. One of the assumptions of this dramaturgy is that the world's a stage and all are actors—the only choice being to play one's own play or another's. Yet this assumption is comprehended in a more basic one: if role playing is seen to be a universal phenomenon, it becomes part of the foundations of the world and thereby a means of access to them. The ancient ties between religion and drama are here reasserted, as Nicholas' participation in a series of mock events is given meaning by their approximation to religious acts designed for the illumination, testing, and strengthening of the soul.

Yet Conchis' educative ritual bears the suspect odor that it does partly because of its absorption in theatrical modes. There is barely an effort made to prevent Nicholas from sensing "an air of stage management, of the planned and rehearsed. [Conchis] did not tell me of his coming to Bourani as a man tells something that chances to occur to him, but far more as a dramatist tells an anecdote where the play requires" (xvii, 105/109). The ground for Conchis' self-revealing technique is his intention to demystify, to reveal the ultimate absence of gods and other mythic equivalents of stage managers for human life; to do so, he must implant a distaste for manipulation on the occasions where Nicholas is manipulated for his own advancement. But there is also a flair for the theater in Conchis—fulfilling his role of magus as "Magician, or Juggler, the caster of the dice and mountebank in the world of vulgar trickery," as the epigraph from Waite's *Key to the Tarot* has it. It is with evident relish that he introduces his next theatrical mode: ". . . this evening I give you not a narrative. But a character" (xxvii, 166/170): the Lily-Rose *femme fatale* whose trappings were suggested by the same esoteric source. It is with equal relish that he pursues his metatheater, in which his characters are allowed to be *"mysteries to him as well"*—though he names his new mode with a conventional term in calling it a comedy (lii, 367/409 [modified]). But in the end this imitation of the baroque masque, with its deities, spectacles, and machinery, is returned to reality, or at least to the realm of the fictions by which we live: "The masque is a metaphor" (xlv, 290/omitted), as Conchis tells Nicholas. Through his response as audience and in his interpretive powers as actor, the hero will learn to be his own playwright, eventually composing the script of the final scene in which he wins his freedom and his perhaps beloved.

The sequence of episodes in the magus' mystery resembles the successive spectacles of the Eleusinian mysteries. First, there is the waiting room, corresponding to the *propylaea* where the initiates are gathered, then the appearance of the priestly figure of Conchis, hands raised in hieratic gesture, who announces, "Prospero will show you his domaine" (xiii, 79/83). Next, the novice is subjected to mock dismemberment, the ritual *sparagmos*, consisting in this case merely of the smell of decomposing flesh; its effect is powerful enough for Nicholas to conclude, "I had entered the domaine" (xxi, 130/134). At this point a fleeting vision of the gods is vouchsafed: the temptress Lily is called away by her "brother," Apollo (xxix, 176/181: this would establish her as Artemis), and Anubis, the Egyptian equivalent of the god of death, is shown in a tableau vivant: ". . . the figure was all in black, shrouded in the sun, and wearing the most sinister mask I had ever seen: the head of an enormous black dog, or jackal, with a long muzzle and high pointed ears" (xxxi, 195/199 [modified]). The next stage of initiation is more active: Nicholas is induced to help rebuild a garden wall, and the manual labor soon leaves him "sweating like a pig." Conchis explains that "labor is man's crowning glory"–facetiously quoting Marx but nonetheless confirming a stage in a purgative process–"you have earned your passage" (xxxv, 219/231 [second sentence omitted]). The "passage" is a temporary but grandiose trip: a drug-induced hallucination of a cosmic voyage, climaxing in a vision of reality akin to that projected by the statue's smile: "The indifference and the indispensability of all seemed one. I suddenly knew, but in a new hitherto unexperienced sense of knowing, that all else exists. . . . I simply wished to constitute it–not even 'wished to'–I constituted it. I was volitionless. There was no meaning. Only being" (xxxvi, 226/239).

There is this and much, much more to stimulate Nicholas' imagination in Conchis' domaine: there are masquelike tableaux illuminating, for instance, the characters in an obscure Puritan pamphlet; there are the intercalated narratives of Conchis' autobiography and the Huysmansian experiences of his friend de Deukans; there is the underwater spectacle of marine life, reached by snorkel and scuba gear. Nicholas tries to make some sense of his experience, looks up the gods in a handbook of mythology, and feels enriched as well as irritated by his election to receive this elaborate entertainment. The turning point of the action occurs with the reintroduction of Alison, the amour from whom Nicholas had escaped to Greece. Their weekend in Athens and their ascent of Mount Parnassus give him an opportunity to apply his lessons, to make something of his newly enriched self, to test education in practice. Needless to say–since this is at a point midway through the novel–he muffs it. Alison–the name is later defined as a flower, "from the Greek a (without) and lyssa (madness)" (lxvii, 514/566 [modified])–offers herself in a paradisal setting replete with biblical, folk, and classical associations, but Nicholas uses his absorption in the mysteries to withdraw from serious involvement: "This experience. It's like being halfway through a book. I can't just throw it in the dustbin" (xlii, 259/273). Alison's reply is an apt, yet oversimplified exposure of his psychic subtlety: "All that mystery balls. You think I fall for that? There's some girl on your island and you want to lay her. That's all. But of course that's nasty, that's crude. So you tart it up. As usual. Tart it up so it makes you seem the innocent one, the great intellectual who must have his experience" (xlii, 261/274). And so Nicholas returns to his island and the second part of his education.

This second phase is marked by greater suffering (much of it sadomaso-chistic) for the novice and greater freedom in the means employed: Nicho-las must not only know but feel, so that he can act on his knowledge. As one of the *femmes fatales* who persecutes him reveals, Conchis said "you were to be like a man following a mysterious voice, voices, through a forest. A game with two tyrannesses and a victim. He gave us all sorts of parallels" (xlvi, 315/338 [much modified]). The most obvious would be Orpheus searching after his lost Eurydice, and the connection of the education with the Orphic myth behind the Eleusinian mysteries becomes explicit at this point. Since Orpheus, despite his derelictions, had passed through the un-derworld and gathered its lore, his myth was readily connected with the eschatological instruction at Eleusis and in many other cults in the ancient world. Similarly, since Alison had been able to part from Nicholas without looking back, in contrast to his weak-willed behavior throughout their af-fair, she becomes an inspiration for the defective will of the latter-day Orpheus, who must be trained to love well and to recover his beloved. The main theme of the later Orphic cults, liberation from the cycle of reincarna-tion by learning the appropriate mystic lore, becomes in this demytholo-gized version the pursuit of liberation from the bondage of egoism and of modernity and the discovery of oneself, one's world, and the possibility of existential freedom in it. To anticipate: the final phase of Nicholas' learn-ing will take him to a woman who identifies herself as a Demeter figure, a mother who underwrites his rebirth, an earth he has come to know and possess. The connection of Conchis' mysteries with the Eleusinian worship of Demeter will be fulfilled at that point.

But first Nicholas must learn more of his world. To teach him the reality of the land in which he has been content to respond to the beauty of land-scape only, he must be brought by elaborate means to confront its people and their historical experience. With the introduction of a crew of German (and Swiss-Jewish) youths playing the roles of the Nazi occupying forces in Greece, "the masque had moved outside the domaine" (xlix, 336/373). Whether or not these events had, as Conchis claims, actually transpired at Bourani and with him as the central figure, they enact a modern tragedy, with the mayor as tragic hero. Not only is Nicholas brought face to face with the reality of human wretchedness and the bare fact of pain, he is in-vited to suffer the doubt and claim the freedom involved in Conchis' choice of the principle of *Eleutheria*, even at the cost of immense loss of life. (The later reenactment of this choice, when Nicholas is offered the chance to flagellate his tormentor during the disintoxication scene, is a somewhat formalized occasion for applying the lessons learned earlier.) The only dan-ger of this remarkable sequence is that it brings recent history so movingly forward that it tends to diminish the universality of the hero's experience; there is even a hint of the tendentious in Conchis' summary of the story: "Because the event I have told you is the only European story. It is what

Europe is. A Colonel Wimmel. A rebel without a name. An Anton torn between them, killing himself when it is too late" (liv, 399/439). Fowles has here introduced the side of modern experience which Anglo-Saxon literature has failed most flagrantly to confront.

The horror of the war and the supposed calamity of Alison's death bring Nicholas to the next stage of the mysteries, the most elaborate sequence of costumed masque scenes and the most flamboyant sadomasochistic fantasies. It is all a Black Mass, a descent into the underworld—introduced by Nicholas' imprisonment in a cave called the earth, as his beloved is carried off by violent hands. Then he himself is carried off by violence as he is finally about to capture the elusive Julie. In illuminated spectacles he is shown cabalistic emblems, Tarot figures, and even the magus himself: "A man in a black cloak on which were various astrological and alchemical symbols in white. . . . Black gloves, and a long white staff surmounted by a circle, a snake with its tail in its mouth" (lxi, 449–450: the latter emblem is the self-regenerating *ouroboros*). The experience and its personae are intentionally obscurantist yet have the effect of an initiation, leaving Nicholas with "a dim conviction of having entered some deeper, wiser esoteric society than I could without danger speak in" (lxi, 467/519).

The most obvious parallel to the educational process conducted through role playing is the therapeutic technique of psychodrama. While the ends of growth and liberation and the means of projection and catharsis are in many ways similar in the psychiatric and the fictional dramas, the distinguishing element here is artistry—and, perhaps, humor. Conchis is concerned to create a set of theatrical forms, coyly alluding to their artificiality but at the same time making them highly finished and refined. This consideration is expressed in the brilliant parody of a medical demonstration which occupies much of the climactic disintoxication sequence. As the actors run through their roles of experimental clinicians—parading the jargon and expertise of the psychiatric clan in wonderful style—their director makes a point of acknowledging the esthetic quality of their experiment: ". . . we mere amateurs in the new drama all owe a great deal for the successful outcome and aesthetic beauty of our . . . enterprise" (lxi, 454/505). Other elements of the disintoxication process point to the artful element at work even in this moment of apparent scientific objectivity, for example, the degradation of the "subject" follows the forms of the similar scene in the "Circe" section of *Ulysses*, in which Bloom is classified and flayed by psychiatric and medical categories:

"He has basic marriage-destructive drives?"
"Yes."
"Specifically?"
"Infidelity. Selfishness. Inconsiderateness in everyday routines. Possibly, homosexual tendencies." (lxi, 462/513)

In this sequence, *The Magus* approaches nearest to the realm of pop culture—so close indeed that it may be said to justify the scorn that the well-behaved critical mind will be likely to display toward it. The final stage of Nicholas' disintoxication is his forced witnessing of a blue movie in which his beloved is willingly displayed with a black (the fact that the male partner has been provided with doctoral credentials and is said to be a "very intelligent and charming man" does little to comfort the appalled spectator). The scenario is, like the preceding Black Mass and the mock-psychiatric diagnosis, a borrowing from the "Circe" section of *Ulysses*, that paradigm of all the arts arrayed under the aegis of apparently direct enactment. But the justification for this incorporation of a low form of a lesser medium is not a literary but a philosophic one: the title frame declares the producing firm to be "Polymus Films" (lxii, 469/521). Though Nicholas misses the point, in his highly aroused state, he later recalls and identifies the allusion to Olympus—although it may also serve as a subtle philosophical reference to Heraclitus' doctrine of *polemos*, the eternal discord out of which harmony must be won—as the aphorism has it, "Tension in harmony, as for instance the lyre and the bow."

Whatever his immediate feelings, it is announced that "you are now elect" (lxii, 479/531), and Nicholas awakes to find himself thrust back into the world, on the cold hillside—in this case, the Old City of Monemvasia, farther down the Peloponnesus. The sensation of being left alone with one's freedom is powerfully summarized at this conclusion to the second part of the novel: "What was I? . . . I dismissed most of the Freudian jargon of the trial; but all my life I had tried to turn life into fiction, to hold reality away; always I had acted as if a third person was watching and listening and giving me marks for good or bad behavior—a god like a novelist, to whom I turned, like a character with the power to please, the sensitivity to feel slighted, the ability to adapt himself to whatever he believed the novelist-god wanted" (lxiii, 487/539). The power of this passage derives from its reflex action on the novelist himself: as the hero learns to reject life lived as a character in fiction—a metaphor of all cultural constructs for a nonexistent external controlling force—so the novelist who writes the novel reveals at last that it is only a construct, and a particularly pernicious one in its power to delude the reader, though a necessary deviation on the path to truth. (From this standpoint, Fowles' later success, *The French Lieutenant's Woman*, is merely a series of footnotes to this keen perception of the mysteries and banalities of his art.)

Part III is the return to the upper world, to life, to England. Nicholas does his research at the British Museum, looks up the former victim/triumphs of Conchisness, even reads an early version of his own life story in his namesake's "seventeenth-century bestseller *L'Astrée*" (i, 11/15; lxx, 529/581). But he is on the way to intellectualizing his experience again: "the more I read, the more I began to reidentify the whole situation. . . . Tartarus was ruled by a king, Hades (or Conchis); a Queen, Persephone, bringer of destruction (Lily)–who remained 'six months with Hades in the infernal regions and spent the rest of the year with her mother Demeter on earth.' . . . And Tartarus was where Eurydice went when Orpheus lost her" (lxx, 531/581). In order not to fall victim to his conscious knowledge, the hero must meet the mother as well as the daughter, and Nicholas by his own efforts (?) discovers Mrs. Lily de Seitas at her house at "Much Hadham, Herts." (lxxi, 534/585). She fills him in on the true (?) details of Conchis' career, especially his theatrical enterprises, and on her daughters' role and motives in playing out his "godgame" (lxxv, 575/625). She also justifies their impositions on Nicholas by the claim of disinterested membership in a secret society for the benefit of humanity: "Maurice convinced us–over twenty years ago–that we should banish the normal taboos of sexual behavior from our lives. Not because we were more immoral than other people. But because we were more moral" (lxxii, 551/603). The world has seen so much of special pleading for highly immoral behavior that here, if not long before, a number of readers will throw up their hands at the godgame's implied ethics. We can readily stifle our indignation at the manipulation of the hero throughout his education by recalling that our identification with him brings us under the same rule of comic undercutting for ultimate rewards; but when we are asked to identify with the manipulators, and to justify their arrogation of the divine stance, we humanistically balk. But when we join Nicholas in his indignant refusal of Demeter's gifts–"I'll see Alison in hell before I come to you again" (lxxii, 554/605)–we wake up to the fact that this is only a novel, after all, and that we are being given a schema of the denouement according to its mythic prototype.

Nicholas does see Alison again, not in hell but on earth, in the middle of London, in Regent's Park. The finale, a triumph of dramatic timing and scene setting, is placed in the park as on an open stage (lxxviii, 597/649), with for audience only the statues of the gods on the façades of Nash's Cumberland Terrace. The gods, or their late classical human representations, look down as man and woman confront their own destinies, conscious that someone (Conchis?) may be up there observing them but nevertheless resigned to their fate, which is to be free:

> A wall of windows.
> A row of statues. Gods. Classical gods.
> Not the Outer Circle. The dress circle.
> Polymus. (lxxviii, 601/omitted)

Given only the bare materials of the earth for his salvation, acting out the pattern of his life as he alone can conceive it, acting as if there were gods or other spectators out there (there are, for they are we), the hero must become no longer actor but stage director, the character his own novelist: "'You will communicate with no one. You will take a taxi.' I hesitated, losing impetus, then found the right echo; and the right exit. 'You will take a taxi and go straight to Paddington Station. The waiting room'" (lxxviii, 603/omitted). At this point, criticism becomes superfluous, and the text yields up its Delphic spell:

> I gave her bowed head one last stare, then I was walking. Firmer than Orpheus, as firm as Alison herself, that other day of parting, not once looking back. The autumn grass, the autumn sky. People. . . . A flight of gray pigeons over the houses. Fragments of freedom, an anagram made flesh. And somewhere the stinging smell of burning leaves. (lxxviii, 604/656 [partially omitted])[10]

Postscript

Having begun with a disclaimer of strict thematic or methodological unity, I close by inviting the reader's attention to a pair of lines in the collage which emerged only after it was assembled. It is widely recognized that Victorian fiction represents a theater for imaginative protrayals of man in society, whereas the modern British novel, from Hardy to Golding, is an open field for speculation on man's place in the cosmos. Looking back on the subject matter explored in the preceding studies, I feel empowered to undertake a few brief and inexhaustive generalizations.

The examples of *Northanger Abbey*, *Vanity Fair*, *Little Dorrit*, *The Way We Live Now*, and *Daniel Deronda*, drawn from a body of major works, witness a persistent reenactment of the universal patterns of acculturation —and of the historically specific conditions of adaptation to an emergent technological and capitalist society. (In this grouping, the essays on *Wuthering Heights* and *The Return of the Native* suggest the continued presence of what the founder of modern anthropology, Edward Burnett Tylor, called "survivals"–cultural forms left over from earlier stages of development, which have lost their original functions and/or acquired new ones.) When *Under Western Eyes*, *Ulysses*, *A Passage to India*, *To the Lighthouse*, and *The Magus* are considered together, they register an impulse to connect the coded forms of living culture with differently coded statements about the order of things–whether those of science, metaphysics, or archeology.

That these two traces follow the decisive literary-historical tracks of their respective periods, it would be premature to say. We can only reaffirm an abiding sense of the power of fiction to engage the most elementary and the most intractable of issues confronting humankind in its inveterate efforts to situate itself within its do-it-yourself world–and to situate the latter within the world that is given, irrefragable, and silent.

Notes

1. Introduction: Fiction as Supplement

1. *The Literary Work of Art: An Investigation on the Borderlines of Ontology, Logic, and Theory of Literature*, trans. G. B. Grabowicz (Evanston, Ill., 1973; German: 1931), p. 117.
2. *Feeling and Form: A Theory of Art* (New York, 1953), p. 72.
3. *The Logic of Literature*, trans. M. J. Rose (Bloomington, Ind., and London, 1973; German: 1957), p. 136. For a keen estimate of the book's theory of tenses and its implications for representation, see Roy Pascal, "Tense and Novel," *Modern Language Review* LVII (1962): 1–11.
4. Sigrid Undset, *Kristin Lavransdatter*, trans. Charles Archer and J. S. Scott (New York, 1971; Norwegian: 1920–1922), p. 3.
5. The special character of proper nouns has not escaped the attention of recent theorists of language; Derrida attempts to remove their correspondential relation to individual things by emphasizing their differential meaning in a system of classification (the name means this one, because not that other one). Commenting on anthropological evidence of prohibitions on the use of proper names, Derrida connects this taboo with an original disparity or erasure in the origin of language: ". . . it is because the proper name has never been, as the unique appellation reserved for the presence of a unique being, anything but the original myth of a transparent legibility present under the obliteration; it is because the proper name was never possible except through its functioning within a classification and therefore within a system of differences, within a writing retaining the traces of difference, that the interdict [of using the name] was possible . . ." (*Of Grammatology*, trans. G. C. Spivak [Baltimore and London, 1976; French: 1967], p. 109). But the "original myth" which Derrida scouts is one of the persistent and salutary illusions by which culture operates; the human impulse to identify oneself with one's name—and the economic motivations of similar behavior with respect to private property—are, as Derrida suggests in his critique of Lévi-Strauss, not necessarily deplorable as imperialistic appropriations. By their myths shall ye know them; similarly, by their names, or will-to-be-named. For a number of sprightly observations on names and naming, see Geoffrey Hartman, "Christopher Smart's *Magnificat*: Toward a Theory of Representation," *ELH* XLI (1974): 429–454,

esp. pp. 450–452; the essay is collected in Hartman's *The Fate of Reading* (Chicago and London, 1975).

6. "Trollope: Facts and Fiction," paper delivered at the Johns Hopkins University, May 1975.

7. For the first proposal, see Ingarden, *The Literary Work*, p. lvi–from the translator's introduction, citing Ingarden's *Studia z estetyki* (as yet untranslated). For the second proposition, see Wolfgang Iser, "The Reading Process: A Phenomenological Approach," in *New Directions in Literary History*, ed. Ralph Cohen (Baltimore, 1974), esp. pp. 137–141 (also included in Iser's *The Implied Reader* [Baltimore and London, 1974]).

8. *The Logic of Literature*, p. 111.

9. *Feeling and Form*, p. 295; the subsequent quotation is from pp. 296–297. Claude Lévi-Strauss has also used this optical metaphor, referring to the theoretical subject which dimly perceives structures as a "foyer virtuel."

10. In a subsequent lecture, Langer has acknowledged the presence of referential language in fictional works, in the course of distinguishing between her conception of the art symbol and conventional definitions of the symbol, which enforce its denotative function. She assents to the fact that "many artists incorporate symbols in their works" (it would be interesting to discover which ones do not); but she goes on to claim that "symbols used in art lie on a different semantic level from the work that contains them" (*Problems of Art: Ten Philosophical Lectures* [New York, 1957], pp. 135–136). The difference of semantic level is not absolute, however, but rests on an additional function while maintaining the original one: symbols in art "function in the normal manner of symbols; they mean something beyond what they present in themselves," yet these meanings are not part of the artwork's "import, but elements in the form that has import, the expressive form." Thus, "those meanings, as well as the images that convey them, enter into the work of art as elements in its composition. They serve to create the work, the expressive form. The art symbol, on the other hand, *is* the expressive form" (p. 139). It is clear that this concept of the art symbol has its roots in the literary tradition stemming from Mallarmé, Yeats, and Eliot (as Frank Kermode has pointed out in *Romantic Image*). This is a legitimate use of the concept of symbol, no doubt, and Langer adds a useful clarification of the difference between the symbolic function of an entire work and that of its constituent parts. Moreover, one welcomes the forthrightness with which Langer accepts the continuing normal functions of symbols, which refer to other realities or concepts while embedded in works of art; and one willingly agrees that their role is not limited to such referentiality but becomes part

of a new reality, the artwork itself. Only the "different semantic level" remains troubling; the duality of reference and expressive form exists for the art symbol or the work as a whole, just as it does for the particular symbol within that work. Reference is never lost in expression, if it is present in its making.

11. *The Literary Work;* for a convenient summary see the translator's introduction. The subsequent quotations are from pp. 220–222 and 359.

12. It should be stated that the notions of the novel's mixed and inevitably referential functions as presented here do not necessarily underwrite the positions of Mary McCarthy, Lionel Trilling, and other novelist-critics who urge the novel's deep involvement with social realities, with the gritty substance of everyday existence. However, if we divide theorists of the novel into realists and artificialists, we find even the latter acknowledging the functions of literature in the real world. Hugh Kenner allows—indeed, invites—a homeopathic effect for the myriad counterfeits he traces in modern life and in satire (*The Counterfeiters: An Historical Comedy* [Garden City, N.Y., 1973 (1968)], pp. 167–168). And William H. Gass admits a quasi-romantic uplift, derived from transactions with the human world, in even the most inventive novels (*Fiction and the Figures of Life* [New York, 1972 (1971)], pp. 68–70). In the event, even the artificialists agree to a measure of representation in the autotelic universes they posit, and the issue shifts to the question of whether the real stands for fiction at the beginning as model or at the end as functional context. In sum, art is like language in its transactions with the world, and like symbolic forms generally: it deals with reality not directly but by constructing a syntax of symbols; it elaborates and refines their mutual relations, so as to operate as a system *sui generis;* but it is at the same time overflowing into daily life, naming new objects as they come into existence, tinkering with its machinery so as to react to changed realities, exposing its new structures, and reacting to the results.

13. Husserl, *Formal and Transcendental Logic,* trans. Dorion Cairns (The Hague, 1969; German: 1929), pp. 260–261.

14. *Speech and Phenomena, and Other Essays on Husserl's Theory of Signs,* trans. D. B. Allison (Evanston, Ill., 1973; French: 1967), p. 88; further citations will be made parenthetically in the text. I follow the accent and spelling of the translated texts here and in n. 15.

15. The common differentiality of symbol systems and of the world itself is one of the chief "metaphysical" implications of Derrida's philosophy and may be welcomed as underlining the deeply symbolic constitution of nature and history (in line with the work of Cassirer, as well as Nietzsche). But the distinction between them remains and should not be obscured by a common mode of thought in dealing

with them. Their interaction—and thus their distinction—emerges even in Derrida's efforts to moot the priority of the world: "No doubt life protects itself by repetition, trace, *différance*. But we must be wary of this formulation: there is no life present *at first* which would *then* come to protect, postpone, reserve itself in *différance*. The latter constitutes the essence of life. Or rather: *différance* not being an essence, it *is not* life, if being is determined as *ousia*, presence, essence/existence, substance or subject. Life must be thought of as trace before being may be determined as presence" ("Freud and the Scene of Writing," trans. Jeffrey Mehlman, in *Yale French Studies*, no. 48 [1972]: 80; the French text is in *L'Ecriture et la différence* [Paris, 1967]).

16. *Of Grammatology*, p. 73. I greatly regret that I was unable to make use of the recently published *The Semantics of Metaphor*, by Samuel R. Levin (Baltimore and London, 1977), in this discussion.

17. The theme crops up throughout Derrida's critique of Western philosophy; a key exposition of his metaphorical-critical method of putting a variety of texts from different disciplines on the same plane of investigation has been translated as "White Mythology: Metaphor in the Text of Philosophy," trans. F. C. T. Moore, *New Literary History* VI (1974): 5–74; the French text is in *Marges de la philosophie* (Paris, 1972).

18. *The Literary Work*, pp. 329–330. After summarizing the distinctions in his earlier work (two points of which I have omitted, along with a number of subsidiary arguments), Ingarden devotes a fresh discussion to "the understanding of the scientific work and the perceptive apprehension of the literary work of art" in *The Cognition of the Literary Work of Art* (trans. R. A. Crowley and K. R. Olson [Evanston, Ill., 1973; German: 1968; Polish: 1937], pp. 153–167). As might be expected from so subtle a phenomenologist of reading, Ingarden's account of the difference between the two leads to intimations of their fundamental similarity: "The scientific work does not actually fulfill its intended function if it does not bring about the necessary investigative attitude in the reader and does not help him attain to an existing reality beyond the work itself. This kind of assistance is simply absent in the case of a literary work of art, since there is no such corresponding ontically independent domain for that work. . . . In reading a scientific work, the reader does not fulfill the task before him if, after he has understood it as precisely as possible, he does not know how to go beyond it to the corresponding 'reality' and if he does not linger upon it with his investigating gaze in order perhaps later to return to the work and then accept it or reject it or else only then reach a correct and deeper understanding of it" (p. 162). It will be seen that, except for the argument's tight hold on an ontical-

ly independent "'reality'" (does the extra quotation mark betray an insecurity?), the sequence of this transaction between the work and the world exactly corresponds to an adequate reading of a literary work.

19. In *New Literary History* VI (1975): 319–332. Recent alternative viewpoints on the seriousness of fictional statements include Morroe Berger, *Real and Imagined Worlds: The Novel and Social Science* (Cambridge, Mass., and London, 1977), and Earl Miner, "That Literature is a Kind of Knowledge," *Critical Inquiry* II (1976): 487–518.

20. See Stanley Fish, "How to Do Things with Austin and Searle: Speech Act Theory and Literary Criticism," *Modern Language Notes* XCI (1976): 983–1025, and my own version of the tenuous distinction between historical and fictional truth in *The English Historical Novel: Walter Scott to Virginia Woolf* (Baltimore and London, 1971), chap. I.

21. One may consider elsewhere a comparable utterance on the visual arts' dealings with traces: "I do not know whether anyone would call a footprint an image of the foot, but I certainly think it will be helpful if we look at images as traces, natural or artificial ones. After all, a photograph is nothing but such a natural trace, a series of tracks left not in the sand but on the emulsion of the film by the variously distributed light-waves which produced chemical changes made visible and permanent through further chemical operations. In fact, what the audience of a lecture sees on the screen may be described as the track of a track of a track, all along a chain of mechanical transformations. The screen shows a track or a shadow of the inverted slide in the projector made in a series of operations from the track in printer's ink of the block made from the photograph, which was of course made from a negative which preserved the tonal gradients but not the absolute tones of the developed film or plate. We do not usually think of these intermediate stages, because we rely on their capacity to transmit the original trace, though we know that changes or distortions are possible at every stage. Photographs can be touched up or tampered with or . . . supplemented by artificial traces made not by light but by an artist's hand. Unlike the natural trace the artist's trace is made with the intention of being interpretable" (E. H. Gombrich, "The Evidence of Images," in *Interpretation: Theory and Practice*, ed. C. S. Singleton [Baltimore, 1969], pp. 36–37).

22. Derrida, "Freud and the Scene of Writing," pp. 95–96.

23. Jonathan Daniels, *The Devil's Backbone: The Story of the Natchez Trace* (New York, Toronto, and London, 1962), pp. 8–9; the following quotation in the text is from p. 14.

24. Eudora Welty, "A Still Moment," *The Wide Net and Other Stories* (New York, 1943), pp. 82–83. Another Welty tale which should be read as the tracing of a path of meaning by effort, will, and suffering is the

story of an old black woman's painful journey to get medicine for her grandchild; it has the even more evocative title of "A Worn Path."

25. See Victor H. Thompson, "The Natchez Trace in Eudora Welty's 'A Still Moment,'" *The Southern Literary Journal* VI (1973): 59–69, for the direct quotations from, and other references to, historical persons. The quotation from Audubon is only partially exact: ". . . the mocking birds are so gentle that I followed one along a fence this morning for nearly one mile" (cited in Thompson, p. 69). Clearly art enters here to transform historical language; it constitutes itself as the trace of a trace.

26. "An Interview with Eudora Welty," in *Writers and Writing*, ed. Robert Van Gelder (New York, 1946), p. 290. See also Welty's introduction to her collection of photographs, *One Time, One Place: Mississippi in the Depression: A Snapshot Album* (New York, 1971), pp. 7–8, for other considerations of the "still moment."

2. The Socialization of Catherine Morland

1. *The Novels of Jane Austen*, ed. R. W. Chapman (1923; rpt. London, 1965), V; chap. xv, p. 124. Further citations will be made parenthetically in the text, by consecutive chapter and page numbers. The Chapman edition retains the original two-volume numbering, in which volume I has fifteen chapters.

2. Cassirer's formulation of the ways in which human life is given its specific and varied character by the cultural symbol systems into which it is organized is probably so well known as to require no extended summary here. Unfortunately, Cassirer nowhere, to my knowledge, provides an account of the individual's acquisition of the symbols by means of which perception, thought, and action in a given society proceed. His formulation of the functions of language, myth, art, historiography, science, etc., in constituting the shape of reality within civilization is given in *The Philosophy of Symbolic Forms*, trans. Ralph Manheim, 3 vols. (New Haven and London, 1953–1957; German: 1923–1929). An abbreviated version of his thought is available in *An Essay on Man: An Introduction to a Philosophy of Human Culture* (Garden City, N.Y., 1953 [1944]). Social theorists, e.g., Sorokin, and other philosophers, e.g., Langer, have developed systems to describe the relation of the individual's mental world and the forms provided by his culture. Anthropologists, too, have addressed themselves to the derivation of ways of seeing from the models made available to the individual by society. A number of such studies are collected in *Socialization: The Approach from*

Social Anthropology, ed. Philip Mayer, Monographs of the Association of Social Anthropologists of the Commonwealth, vol. VIII (London, 1970); especially interesting is an account of the influence of art in Anthony Forge's "Learning to See in New Guinea," pp. 269–291.

3. The Chapman edition's notes and appendixes indicate additional literary allusions that play their parts in Catherine's education; they represent most of the major eighteenth-century authors—that is, the "best" near-contemporary texts to stock a young mind. Besides Pope, Gray, and Thomson there are Prior and Gay; besides the Gothic romances there are Fielding, Richardson, Sterne, Burney, and Edgeworth; and for style there are (presumed) references to the *Spectator* papers, Johnson's *Dictionary*, and Hugh Blair's *Lectures on Rhetoric*.

4. The view that thought and conduct are affected, perhaps determined, by the semantic structure of the language in which the behavior is conceived is so widespread that it has been called the Humboldt-Boas-Cassirer-Sapir-Whorf-Lee hypothesis; see David French, "The Relationship of Anthropology to Studies in Perception and Cognition," in *Psychology: A Study of a Science*, ed. Sigmund Koch (New York, 1963), study II, vol. VI, p. 392. The entire article is useful as a review of research in this field.

5. A number of considerations have been made of landscape theory in Austen; the fullest is Alistair M. Duckworth, *The Improvement of the Estate: A Reading of Jane Austen's Novels* (Baltimore and London, 1971).

6. The social influence on perceptions of facial resemblance has been observed not only by many a member of the younger generation receiving the prescriptions of family chroniclers but also by observers around the world. The classic—and at some points amusing—account of a cultural formula for arriving at judgments of likeness has been Malinowski's; see M. H. Segall, D. T. Campbell, and M. J. Herskovits, *The Influence of Culture on Visual Perception* (Indianapolis, 1966), p. 26.

7. *Jane Austen: A Study of Her Artistic Development* (New York, 1965), pp. 64–65.

8. *Bits of Ivory: Narrative Techniques in Jane Austen's Fiction* (Baton Rouge, 1973), pp. 80–81. See also John K. Mathison, "*Northanger Abbey* and Jane Austen's Conception of the Value of Fiction," *ELH* XXIV (1957): 147–149, which lists the primary ways in which the romances contribute to Catherine's orientation.

9. "Satire and the Form of the Novel: The Problem of Aesthetic Unity in *Northanger Abbey*," *ELH* XX (1955): 526–527.

3. *Wuthering Heights*: The Love of a Sylph and a Gnome

1. This view has recently been restated by Winifred Gérin in *Emily Brontë: A Biography* (Oxford, 1971), pp. 102 ff., while discounting most of the possible sources of her mysticism. Perhaps the most systematic account of Brontë's religion from a mystical standpoint is Rudolf Kuhlmann, *Der Natur-Paganismus in der Weltanschaung [sic] von Emily Brontë* (Bonn dissertation, 1926). A recent account, attentive to the bibliographical evidence of her reading and to contemporary religious trends, is Tom Winnifrith, *The Brontës and their Background: Romance and Reality* (New York, 1973), which posits the following tenets of Brontë's eschatology: "(1) Hell exists only on earth, and no souls suffer torment after death. (2) A soul that has suffered sufficiently on earth attains its heaven. (3) A soul that has not suffered is in limbo for a time, but is redeemed by others' sufferings if not by its own, after enduring the *poena damni*, deprivation of the desired heaven" (p. 64).
2. Quoted in Fannie E. Ratchford, *The Brontës' Web of Childhood* (New York, 1941), pp. 14–15; the complete text is included in the Shakespeare Head Brontë. Other references to the Genii are cited in Ratchford, pp. 65 passim.
3. *Five Essays Written in French*, ed. Fannie E. Ratchford (Austin, 1948), p. 9; further citations are made parenthetically. The French text of these essays is given in an appendix to the Gérin biography cited above.
4. Hans Jonas, *The Gnostic Religion: The Message of the Alien God and the Beginnings of Christianity* (Boston, 1963 [1958]), pp. 42–45; the entire book is a rich treasury of ideas, symbols, and historical processes which illuminate English literary texts at many points.
5. *The Complete Poems of Emily Jane Brontë*, ed. C. W. Hatfield (New York, 1941), p. 19 (in a prefatory arrangement contributed by Ratchford). Subsequent citations of the poems will be made by their numbering in this edition.
6. *Emily Brontë: Expérience spirituelle et création poétique* (Paris, 1955), pp. 214 ff.
7. *Love in the Western World*, trans. Montgomery Belgion (Garden City, N.Y., 1957; French: 1939), p. 240; the subsequent quotations are from p. 138. The Cathars and their relation to Gnosticism are described on pp. 7 ff. of this work.
8. See Muriel Spark and Derek Stanford, *Emily Brontë: Her Life and Work* (London, 1966), p. 174 and note. Bataille's essay is in his *La littérature et le mal* (Paris, 1957), Miller's chapter in *The Disappearance of God: Five Nineteenth-Century Writers* (Cambridge, Mass., 1963).
9. I cite the Clarendon edition, ed. Hilda Marsden and Ian Jack (Oxford, 1976), parenthetically by consecutive chapter and page numbers. The

Clarendon retains the original two-volume numbering, in which volume I has fourteen chapters. The present quotation is from chapter ix, p. 98.

10. In *Four Treatises of . . . Paracelsus*, ed. Henry E. Sigerist (Baltimore, 1941). Correlation of the protagonists with these dwellers in or embodiments of earth and air is tempting but, except for a titular formula, I have resisted the temptation.

11. Samuel C. Chew, *The Pilgrimage of Life* (New Haven and London, 1962), p. 3.

12. Titus Burckhardt, *Alchemy: Science of the Cosmos, Science of the Soul*, trans. William Stoddart (Baltimore, 1971; German: 1960), pp. 25–26, 68, 74, 96, 100–101, and 149 and 156.

4. A Napoleon of Heroines: Historical Myth in *Vanity Fair*

1. Quotations from *Vanity Fair* are from the edition of Geoffrey and Kathleen Tillotson (Boston [Riverside edition], 1963 [1847–1848]). Subsequent citations are parenthetical, by chapter and page numbers.

2. I have discussed these issues in *The English Historical Novel: Walter Scott to Virginia Woolf* (Baltimore and London, 1971), esp. pp. 3 ff., 146–148, and 225–227.

3. John Hagen, "A Note on the Napoleonic Background of *Vanity Fair*," *Nineteenth-Century Fiction* XV (1961): 358–361, gives the general facts of the case; Russell A. Fraser, "Pernicious Casuistry: A Study of Character in *Vanity Fair*," *Nineteenth-Century Fiction* XII (1957): 145, makes perhaps the first effort to describe Becky as a "miniature Napoleon."

4. Christopher A. Kent, "The Idea of Bohemia in Mid-Victorian England," *Queen's Quarterly* LXXX (1973): 360–369, gives Thackeray's uses of the term in other novels, his own encounters with the London Bohemian clubs (on a rather genteel level, for his shadier London and Paris contacts remain to be explored), and the general growth of the concept in his time.

5. The fullest study of the English sympathizers in the Romantic period is E. Tangye Lean, *The Napoleonists: A Study in Political Disaffection, 1760–1960* (London, New York, and Toronto, 1970), unfortunately disfigured by a polemical analogy with recent fellow travelers.

6. Pérès' *Grand Erratum: Comme quoi Napoléon n'a jamais existé* (1827) is usefully summarized in Albert Sonnenfeld, "Napoleon as Sun Myth," *Yale French Studies*, no. 26 (1960–1961): 32–36; the entire issue is indispensable to students of the Napoleonic myth.

7. Quotations from Thackeray's other writings are from the Biographical Edition of *The Works of William Makepeace Thackeray*, 13 vols.

(London, 1899); citations are parenthetical, by volume and page numbers. This quotation is from "Napoleon and His System: On Prince Louis Napoleon's Work," V, 107.

8. Thackeray's interest in Napoleon—and perhaps his perception of the power of myth—dates from his childhood when, on his voyage "home" from India, his ship stopped at St. Helena and his servant delivered the monitory description quoted in my epigraph (see Gordon N. Ray, *Thackeray: The Uses of Adversity: 1811–1846* [London, 1955], p. 66). As a young man at Cambridge, however, he rose to defend the emperor's image—and cursed himself for his temerity. While reading for his first article on Louis Napoleon, he became interested in the intensity of Romantic-Tory vituperation and later thought of "making a collection of the lies which the French had written against us, and we had published against them during the war: it would be a strange memorial of popular falsehood" (*The Letters and Private Papers of W. M. Thackeray*, ed. Gordon N. Ray [Cambridge, Mass., 1945], I, 395–396 and n.). During the period of his political "quietism" following the revolutions of 1848, he seemed inclined to accept Louis Napoleon's ascendancy—and even to resign from *Punch* in protest against a vitriolic cartoon of Louis—while indicating that the proper course was "not to chafe him but silently to get ready to fight him" (Gordon N. Ray, *Thackeray: The Age of Wisdom: 1846–1863* [London, 1958], pp. 250–251). The received ideas of Thackeray's conservatism have recently been corrected in Barbara Hardy, *The Exposure of Luxury: Radical Themes in Thackeray* (London, 1972).

5. Master and Servant in *Little Dorrit*

1. *The Phenomenology of Mind*, trans. J. B. Baillie, rev. ed. (London and New York, 1931), pp. 234, 236–237, and 239.

2. All quotations are from the Oxford Illustrated Dickens edition (which reprints the Charles Dickens and Nonesuch editions' text), and references will be made parenthetically, by volume, chapter, and page numbers. The present quotation is from vol. II, chap. xxxiii, p. 811.

3. It should nevertheless not be overlooked that Little Dorrit employs her father's aggressive-submissive psychological tactics when her own deepest interests are at stake. In her timid love for Clennam, she is an ingenious competitor for his affection, while consciously renouncing the possibility and even the propriety of winning him. Her own two letters from Italy are unmistakably love letters, and Dickens used them to close two installments of the periodical publication as romantic climaxes. They are reports of Pet's marriage calcu-

lated to disturb Clennam, perhaps into renouncing his love for Pet, but certainly into emotional dependence on the reporter of the disturbing news. So chilling is her report that she is forced to explain "why I have resolved to tell you so much even while I am afraid it may make you a little uncomfortable without occasion. . . . She is so true and so devoted, and knows so completely that all her love and duty are his for ever, that you may be certain she will love him, admire him, praise him, and conceal all his faults, until she dies" (II, xi, 552). Only later on in the same letter does she remember to add that Pet has had a baby! Still further on, she deftly informs him, "I have no lover, of course." Thus Amy can portray herself as a devoted friend serving Clennam, while actually manipulating his feelings in her own behalf. But these are lapses into the wiles of romantic love; Little Dorrit's powers in other forms of love are even more effective in pursuit of the loved one, and she has ultimately no need to revert to the ways of lesser mortals. The classic study is Anders Nygren, *Agape and Eros*, trans. P. S. Watson (New York and Evanston, Ill., 1969; Swedish: 1930).

4. "Introduction aux problèmes d'une sociologie du roman," *Revue de l'Institut de Sociologie* (Brussels, 1962–1963), pp. 225 ff. Reprinted in Goldmann's *Pour une sociologie du roman* (Paris, 1964).

5. Dickens alludes to a specific instance of this topos, probably Euphrasia: "There was a classical daughter once—perhaps—who ministered to her father in his prison as her mother had ministered to her. Little Dorrit, though of the unheroic modern stock, and more English, did much more, in comforting her father's wasted heart upon her innocent breast, and turning to it a fountain of love and fidelity that never ran dry or waned, through all his years of famine" (I, xix, 229).

6. The Wanderings of Melmotte

1. Warren Miller, *The Way We Live Now* (New York, 1958). For a contemporary Melmotte figure, see the newspaper reports on the suicide of Eli M. Black, chairman of the billion-dollar United Brands Company: New York *Times*, February 4, 1975, et seq.

2. Randolph M. Bulgin, "Anthony Trollope's *The Way We Live Now*: A Study of its Historical Background and Critical Significance," unpublished dissertation, Princeton, 1963, p. 123. Other ascriptions in this thesis are more convincingly documented.

3. "The Way They Lived Then: Anthony Trollope and the 1870's," *Victorian Studies* XII (1968): 177–200.

4. Ruth ap Roberts, *Trollope: Artist and Moralist* (London, 1971), chap. I.

5. I quote the World's Classics edition of the novel, as most generally avail-

able. Subsequent citations are made parenthetically, by volume, chapter, and page numbers. The recent edition by Robert Tracy (Indianapolis and New York, 1974) contains a valuable introduction, citing many of the historical and literary analogues.

6. An obvious model for Melmotte has not, to my knowledge, been sufficiently explored: the prime minister at the time of the novel's writing, Disraeli, fresh from a manipulative triumph in acquiring financial control of the Suez Canal from France. Another, more recondite exemplar is Edward Vaughan Hyde Kenealy, who in 1875 became the first elected member of Parliament to take his seat without being introduced—no member being willing to do so, after his scurrilous behavior in connection with a legal case; see the article under his name in the *Dictionary of National Biography*. Melmotte fares better, the prime minister himself taking him into the House.

7. For an approximation of the Chinese emperor's detached view of the proceedings at the banquet, see Goldsmith's *The Citizen of the World* (1762); for comparable traits of the two Rogers, see *The Spectator* (1711–1712); e.g.: ". . . his singularities proceed from his good sense, and are contradictions to the manners of the world, only as he thinks the world is in the wrong. . . . It is said, he keeps himself a bachelor, by reason he was crossed in love."

8. George K. Anderson, *The Legend of the Wandering Jew* (Providence, 1965); the subsequent quotation is from p. 189.

9. The literary study of the *pharmakos* figure has recently been augmented by Jacques Derrida, "La Pharmacie de Platon," in *La Dissémination* (Paris, 1972), and by René Girard, *Violence and the Sacred*, trans. Patrick Gregory (Baltimore and London, 1977; French: 1972).

10. See Leven M. Dawson, "*Melmoth the Wanderer*: Paradox and the Gothic Novel," *Studies in English Literature* VIII (1968): 629, for a clear statement of the oxymoron.

11. See Hope Crampton, "Melmoth in *La Comédie Humaine*," *Modern Language Review* LXI (1966): 42–50, for a survey of Balzac's other versions of the figure.

12. Anderson, *Legend of the Wandering Jew*, pp. 332–333.

13. *From Shylock to Svengali: Jewish Stereotypes in English Fiction* (Stanford, 1960); the subsequent quotation is from p. 196.

14. *Childhood and Society* (New York, 1963 [1950]), pp. 355–356. Erikson speaks with authority, as his later autobiographical revelations suggest; see *Life History and the Historical Moment* (New York, 1975).

15. Claude Lévi-Strauss, *The Savage Mind*, no trans. (Chicago and London, 1973; French: 1962), p. 150 n.

16. Bradford A. Booth, *Anthony Trollope: Aspects of His Life and Art* (Bloomington, Ind., 1958), p. 120.

7. "Daniel Charisi"

1. Carole Robinson, "The Severe Angel: A Study of *Daniel Deronda*," *ELH* XXXI (1964): 299–300. To complement this reading, see Jean Sudrann, "*Daniel Deronda* and the Language of Exile," *ELH* XXXVII (1970): 433–455.
2. *The George Eliot Letters*, ed. Gordon S. Haight (New Haven and London, 1955), VI, 317; 16 December 1876. The subsequent quotation is from VI, 379; 31 May 1877.
3. Edward Dowden, "*Middlemarch* and *Daniel Deronda*," *Contemporary Review* XXIX (1877): 348–369; the essay is partially reprinted in *A Century of George Eliot Criticism*, ed. Gordon S. Haight (Boston, 1965), pp. 112–123; my quotation is from p. 117.
4. I quote the Penguin edition of *Daniel Deronda*, ed. Barbara Hardy, in the absence of a definitive text. Further citations (parenthetical) will be by chapter and page numbers in this edition. The present quotation is from chap. xxxv, pp. 472–473.
5. I quote J. Dover Wilson's edition of *Culture and Anarchy* (Cambridge, Eng., 1963), iii, 101; subsequent quotations are made parenthetically. (An equally authoritative text is given in *The Complete Prose Works of Matthew Arnold*, ed. R. H. Super [Ann Arbor, Mich., 1965], vol. V.) Wilson's note to this passage is worth quoting in full: "*Philistines:* 'Philister' being originally applied by students to the townsman who was not a member of the university. Arnold himself first used it in his essay on Heine [1863]: 'Philistinism!—we have not the expression in English. Perhaps we have not the word because we have so much of the thing. At Soli, I imagine, they did not talk of solecisms; and here, at the very headquarters of Goliath, nobody talks of Philistinism. . . . Philistine must have originally meant, in the mind of those who invented the nickname, a strong, dogged, unenlightened opponent of the chosen people, of the children of light'" (pp. 228–229). Eliot refers obliquely to *Culture and Anarchy* in the same letter in which she describes her studies of Jewish history, in preparation for writing *Daniel Deronda* (*Letters*, V, 460–461; 17 November 1873). But she had no need of Arnold's essay to import the German term; in "The Natural History of German Life" (1856), she writes: "It seems presumptuous in us to dispute Riehl's interpretation of a German word, but we must think that, in literature, the epithet *Philister* has usually a wider meaning than this—includes his definition and something more. We imagine the *Philister* is the personification of the spirit which judges everything from a lower point of view than the subject demands—which judges the affairs of the parish from the egotistic and purely personal point of view—which judges the affairs of the nation from the parochial point of view, and

does not hesitate to measure the merits of the universe from the human point of view" (*Essays of George Eliot*, ed. Thomas Pinney [London, 1963], p. 297). This sounds like a program for writing *Middlemarch*; it is also one of the first statements by anyone to connect "the egotistic and purely personal point of view" with Philistinism. (The term was earlier introduced to England in Carlyle's "Present State of German Literature" [1827] and *Sartor Resartus* [1833–1834].)

6. I have outlined the organicist tradition in *Conrad's Politics: Community and Anarchy in the Fiction of Joseph Conrad* (Baltimore, 1967). chap. III. The notes and bibliography of this volume provide further documentation for Eliot's, Arnold's, and others' positions in this mode of thought. The most ample discussion of organicist and related modes of thought is Maurice Mandelbaum, *History, Man and Reason* (Baltimore and London, 1971).

7. Cf. Robert Preyer, "Beyond the Liberal Imagination: Vision and Unreality in 'Daniel Deronda,'" *Victorian Studies* IV (1960): 35–54, for a compatible application of Arnold's critique of liberalism to Eliot's. I have drawn inspiration from Preyer's entire enterprise in this essay. See also Brian Swann, "George Eliot's Ecumenical Jew," *Novel* VII (1974), esp. pp. 46–47.

8. "The Natural History of German Life," p. 287.

9. See *Religious Humanism and the Victorian Novel: George Eliot, Walter Pater, and Samuel Butler* (Princeton, 1965), pp. 136 ff. In an earlier chapter, Knoepflmacher elaborates on another connection between Eliot and Arnold—their turning to biblical tradition or "Hebraism" in an effort to reinvigorate modern culture. Yet here, too, the terminology can stand clarification: "*Literature and Dogma*, like *Daniel Deronda*, which appeared less than three years later, is an undisguised attempt to provide England with a religion" (p. 64); the words "substitute for" should be inserted before the last word.

10. C. B. Cox, *The Free Spirit: A Study of Liberal Humanism in the Novels of George Eliot, Henry James, E. M. Forster, Virginia Woolf, Angus Wilson* (London, New York, and Toronto, 1963), p. 33.

11. *Experiments in Life: George Eliot's Quest for Values* (Detroit, 1965), esp. pp. 193–198, which also discuss *The Spanish Gypsy* as a cognate expression of Eliot's positive view of nationalism.

12. My text is *The Writings of George Eliot*, 10 vols. (Boston, 1900), which appears to be the equal of the much used Cabinet edition; both are, of course, a scandalous reflection on the present state of scholarship —given the distribution of editorial efforts on lesser British authors.

13. Biographical material is to be found in the memoir that introduces the *Literary Remains of the Late Emanuel Deutsch . . .* , ed. Emily Strangford (New York, 1874). The role of Deutsch as a donnée for the

novel is suggested in Gordon S. Haight, *George Eliot: A Biography* (New York and Oxford, 1968), pp. 469–473.

14.*Letters*, V, 160–161; 7 July 1871.

15.*The Essence of Christianity*, trans. George Eliot (New York, Evanston, Ill., and London, 1957 [1854]), p. 113; on Judaism, see pp. 112–119.

16.*Rom und Jerusalem: Die letzte Nationalistätsfrage* (Leipzig, 1862); I quote an English translation, to provide opportunities for comparison with Mordecai's prose. Substantial excerpts are given in Mary Schulman, *Moses Hess: Prophet of Zionism* (London and New York, 1963); the subsequent quotations are from 99, 100, 102, 107, and 104 respectively. Hess' career and thought are reliably described in Walter Laqueur, *A History of Zionism* (New York, Chicago, and San Francisco, 1972), pp. 46–55. The question of Lewes' (and thus Eliot's) acquaintance with Hess is raised in Haight, *George Eliot*, p. 471 n.; his conclusion–"There is no evidence that Lewes ever saw Hess or knew his book"–seems sweeping but actually leaves the question open.

17.The primary text is, of course, Isaiah, which had been presented to English readers from a Higher-Critical standpoint by Matthew Arnold in 1872 and again in 1875; his later and fuller version, with an important introduction, is in *The Complete Prose Works*, vol. X.

18.Haight, *George Eliot*, p. 469, mentions Eliot's reading of Pictet's *Origines des races aryennes*; I have not been able to see this but quote his later work, *Les Origines Indo-Européennes, ou les Aryas primitifs: Essai de paléontologie linguistique* (Paris, 1877). Haight, p. 472, also mentions Renan's *Histoire des langues sémitiques* as quarry for Eliot; I quote a lecture that summarizes his views: *De la part des peuples sémitiques dans l'histoire de la civilisation* (Paris, 1875), pp. 28, 31–32.

19.Pictet, *Les Origines Indo-Européennes*, III, 535–536.

20."George Eliot's Readings in Nineteenth-Century Jewish Historians: A Note on the Background of 'Daniel Deronda,'" *Victorian Studies* XV (1972): 463–473; the subsequent quotations are from pp. 471 and 472. Baker has expanded his research in *George Eliot and Judaism*, Salzburg Studies in English Literature, no. 45 (Salzburg, 1975).

21.Baker, *George Eliot and Judaism*, pp. 170 ff., adds another potential source of her organicist imagery: the medieval Jewish poet Judah Halevi's *Kuzari*, in which Israel is figured as seed, heart, and other vital members of larger collective bodies. Additional material is in Baker's *Some George Eliot Notebooks: An Edition of the Carl H. Pforzheimer Library's George Eliot Holograph Notebooks*, vol. I, Salzburg Studies in English Literature (Salzburg, 1976).

22.Freud's question is the title of a chapter in *Moses and Monotheism* (his answer is that Moses was an avatar of the monotheistic pharaoh, Akhenaten). The paradigm of the hero's nurture among an alien nation, a variant of his alienation at birth from his true home or parentage, is presented in Otto Rank's *The Myth of the Birth of the Hero* and in many syncretic handbooks of mythology.

23. Princess Halm-Eberstein (née Leonora Charisi) is introduced in a chapter headed by an epigraph of Eliot's invention: "She held the spindle where she sat, / Erinna with the thick-coiled mat / Of raven hair and deepest agate eyes . . ." (li, 686); she is then characterized: "Her worn beauty had a strangeness in it as if she were not quite a human mother, but a Melusina, who had ties with some world which is independent of ours" (li, 687–688); described in action: "You might have imagined her a sorceress who would stretch forth her wonderful hand and arm to mix youth-potions for others, but scorned to mix them for herself, having had enough of youth" (liii, 723).

24. *The Dartmouth Bible*, eds. Roy B. Chamberlain and Herman Feldman (Boston, 1950), p. 346. The subsequent quotation is from p. 712. I have used the text and notes of this edition in my interpretations.

25. *Paradise Regained*, II, 266–278. The subsequent quotation is from *Modern Painters*, vol. III, chap. xiv; it is given in the Cook and Wedderburn edition of Ruskin's *Works*, vol. V, p. 25. It should be pointed out that the *-th* ending transliterates the Hebrew letter *sof*, pronounced [t] by Sephardi and [s] by Ashkenazi Jews; the biblical word for the brook is כְּרִית, which may thus be pronounced *k'rís*. As with the noun previously described, "Charisi" would be the possessive form.

26. See Baker's article, p. 468: Eliot made notes on the poetry of return by Judah Alcharizi or Charizi in her copy of Franz Delitzsch's *Geschichte der Jüdischen Poësie*.

27. *Essays*, p. 326; the text is from a review here titled "Three Novels." References to Scott abound in *Daniel Deronda*, as may be seen from Professor Hardy's notes.

28. Graham Martin, "'Daniel Deronda': George Eliot and Political Change," in *Critical Essays on George Eliot*, ed. Barbara Hardy (New York and London, 1970), pp. 147–149. The most radical challenge to the ending was delivered by an anonymous American novelist who wrote a sequel entitled *Gwendolen* (Boston, 1878), in which Daniel returns from the East, reaffirms Christianity, and marries the girl named in the title; see Robert A. Colby, "An American Sequel to 'Daniel Deronda,'" *Nineteenth-Century Fiction* XII (1957): 231–235.

29. Eliot used both Stanley's *Sinai and Palestine: In Connection with their History* (London, 1864) and Milman's *The History of the Jews from the Earliest Period down to Modern Times* (London, 1830), according to Haight, *George Eliot*, p. 472.

8. The Buried Giant of Egdon Heath

1. "The 'Poetics' of *The Return of the Native*," *Modern Fiction Studies* VI (1960): 214; Paterson has also published a monograph on the composition of the novel: *The Making of "The Return of the Native,"* University of California English Studies, no. 19 (Berkeley and Los Angeles, 1960). The folkloric aspects of the novel have been recognized at least since Ruth A. Firor's *Folkways in Thomas Hardy* (Philadelphia and London, 1931), esp. pp. 265–268.
2. For a map that shows these positions clearly, see F. E. Halliday, *Thomas Hardy: His Life and Work* (New York, 1972), facing the acknowledgments page. More detailed maps of the region are to be found in F. B. Pinion, *A Hardy Companion: A Guide to the works of Thomas Hardy and their background* (London, New York, etc., 1968), pp. 313, 411 ff. Hardy's own sketch map of the fictional heath is reprinted in many editions.
3. The paper is reprinted in *Thomas Hardy's Personal Writings: Prefaces, Literary Opinions, Reminiscences*, ed. Harold Orel (Lawrence, Kan., London, etc., 1966), pp. 191–195; in this volume, see also "Shall Stonehenge Go?" "Maumbury Ring," and other pieces on Dorsetshire antiquities. Also see Richard M. Dorson, *The British Folklorists: A History* (Chicago and London, 1968), pp. 202 ff., for the vigorous activity in folklore and mythological studies during the period of Hardy's creation of a virtual county history in his fiction.
4. "A Tryst at an Ancient Earthwork," in *A Changed Man and Other Tales* (Wessex edition [London, 1912 ff.], vol. XVIII, p. 174). For a succinct description of Maiden Castle, see *Atlas of Ancient Archeology*, ed. Jacquetta Hawkes (London, New York, etc., 1974), p. 34.
5. The story is told in part I, act II, scene v, in a setting specified as "Rainbarrows' Beacon, Egdon Heath."
6. *Collected Poems of Thomas Hardy* (New York, 1964), p. 370; other quotations of the poetry are from this edition.
7. I quote the New Wessex edition (London, 1974) as most generally available (although not a definitive text), by book, chapter, and page numbers, parenthetically. The present quotation is from bk. I, chap. i, p. 33.
8. Perry Meisel's *Thomas Hardy: The Return of the Repressed: A Study of the Major Fiction* (New York and London, 1972) makes its Freudian point by its very title; also, for references to the Promethean theme, see p. 78.
9. Cf. J. Hillis Miller, *Thomas Hardy: Distance and Desire* (Cambridge, Mass., 1970), p. 91: "The heath is neither a character in itself nor merely a dark background against which the action takes place. The heath is rather the embodiment of certain ways in which human be-

ings may exist. Diggory Venn and Eustacia Vye rise out of the heath as versions of two of these ways, Diggory the detached waiting and watching expressed by the heath, Eustacia the tragical possibilities of violence and infinite longing the heath contains."

10. *Thomas Hardy's Notebooks* . . ., ed. Evelyn Hardy (New York, 1955), pp. 65–66; entry dated 12 September 1888. To this variant, compare the version recorded by the folklorist Gomme, reprinted in *A Dictionary of British Folk-tales in the English Language*, ed. Katherine M. Briggs (Bloomington, Ind., 1971), pt. B, vol. I, p. 611. Also see Robert Hunt's *Popular Romances of the West of England* . . . (London, 1865), an attractively presented collection of legends that Hardy may well have known, for it is close to his topographical interests. Its first section is "The Giants" and includes the story of Corineus and Gogmagog (to be discussed below), as well as tales of giant passions highly accordant with his fictional themes.

11. Stith Thompson, *Motif-Index of Folk-Literature* . . . (Bloomington, Ind., 1955), vol. I, nos. A570, A580. For other instances directly related to Hardy's interests, see E. W. Baughman, *Type and Motif-Index of the Folktales of England and North America*, Indiana University Folklore Series, no. 20 (The Hague, 1966), under the same index numbers.

12. *The Life of Thomas Hardy: 1840–1928*, by Florence E. Hardy [sic] (London, etc., 1965 [1928; 1930]), p. 17. For other references to and quotations from Shelley in Hardy's works, see Pinion, pp. 213–214.

13. *Prometheus Unbound*, II, ii, 52. For a discussion of the geological and meteorological phenomena, see Earl R. Wasserman, *Shelley's Prometheus Unbound: A Critical Reading* (Baltimore, 1965), pp. 147 ff.; the subsequent quotation is from p. 163 (also included in his later *Shelley: A Critical Reading*).

14. Wasserman finds Demogorgon cast in the role of "Typhon and the other volcanic giants or Titans who, like Prometheus, rebelled against Jove" (*Shelley's* Prometheus Unbound, p. 159), but this by no means precludes his conventional identification with philosophical necessity or, as M. H. Abrams would claim, with "process."

15. Robert Graves, *The Greek Myths* (Harmondsworth, Eng., 1962 [1955]), I, 40 and 145–147.

16. *Milton*, bk. II, pl. 39; *Complete Writings of William Blake*, ed. Geoffrey Keynes (London, New York, and Toronto, 1966 [1957]), p. 531. The subsequent quotations are from pp. 578 and 609 of this edition.

17. See Edward B. Hungerford, *Shores of Darkness* (Cleveland and New York, 1963 [1941]), pp. 46 ff.; also Harold Bloom, *Blake's Apocalypse: A Study in Poetic Argument* (Garden City, N.Y., 1965 [1963]), p. 108.

18. *Jerusalem*, chap. iii, pl. 74, p. 715 (in the Keynes edition); cf. the penultimate plate of poem, where the "Triple Headed Gog-Magog Giant / of Albion" is again recalled, in the midst of a redemptive apocalypse.

19. *Fearful Symmetry: A Study of William Blake* (Boston, 1962 [1947]), p.
399. Gog and Magog, who combine elements of the legendary giant
of hills and heaths, the dead and buried but ultimately to return
hero, and the original British race—the earthborn and earthbound
dwellers in the land—are well known in English popular culture,
though perhaps better in their London than their West Country representations. The first is a ubiquitous figure of the Western imagination,
in time, place and cultural level—from the book of Genesis to Andrew Sinclair's recent novel, *Gog*. In ancient legends of Alexander
the Great, Gog and Magog are his enemies and, once conquered, are
sealed behind a wall in the Caucasus; indeed, Robert Graves has
suggested by analogy the equation of Gog with Prometheus (*The
White Goddess: A Historical Grammar of Poetic Myth* [London,
1962 (1948)], p. 237). But Gog's British fortunes seem more closely
linked with his bad reputation in both the Old and New Testaments
(Ezek. 38–39, Rev. 20), which colors his role in Cornish legend with
connotations of the forces of Satan. When Spenser and Milton retell
Geoffrey of Monmouth's story of Gog's and the other resident giants'
defeat by the Trojan conquerors of England, the legend certifies the
cultural triumph of a higher race over the autochthonous one (*The
Faerie Queene*, II, x, 6–11; III, ix, 49–50; *The History of Britain . . .*,
bk. I). Yet this morality has not prevented the giant statues of Gog
and Magog in the Guildhall of London from being carried in procession on the Lord Mayor's Day (usually November 9, close on the
Guy Fawkes' dying-and-reviving-year festivals enacted in *The Return*)—when they are not so much exhibits of conquered savages as
impressive old friends. The most recent effort to recover Gog's English traces, T. C. Lethbridge's *Gogmagog: The Buried Gods* (London,
1957, pp. 10 ff.; as this does not appear to be a scientifically verifiable investigation, it should be treated as suggestive, not decisive),
describes his pattern found in the Gogmagog Hills of Cambridge-
shire. In an expanded scene around the Cerne Abbas giant, Lethbridge detects a sacred combat for possession and renewal of the
earth. In this conjectural interpretation, the male figure is both Gog
and the Sun, the female is Magog and Epona (the ancient British
horse goddess), and the other male participant is the demon of darkness, winter, and death—the archetypal antagonist of Frazerian fame.
20. Terms used in Paterson, *The Making of "The Return,"* esp. p. 167; for
the next quoted phrase, see p. 164.
21. As in Derwent May's introduction to the New Wessex edition of the
novel (pp. 14–15): "Egdon's 'Titanic' form, as Hardy more than once
calls it, suggests first of all the brute, mindless strength of the earth-
giants; but he does not leave the suggestion there. At times, he says,
the heath, like the fallen Titans, seems to be waiting for what he

ambiguously calls 'the final overthrow.' Revolution, in short, is in the air. We quickly associate the idea with much that the countrymen artlessly say [about the Napoleonic Wars]. . . . Even in the lost villages of Wessex, that unprecedented event in modern history, the French Revolution, has left its faint trace."

22. The latest entries in this line are Jeremy Hooker's volume of poems on the Cerne Abbas figure, *Soliloquies of a Chalk Giant* (London, 1974), and George Barker's "Dialogues of Gog and Magog," in *Dialogues, etc.* (London, 1976).

23. Although it has yet to be demonstrated that Hardy included Vico in his studies of history and mythology, he could have found in *The New Science* an imaginative interpretation of the giant figure much in accord with his own habits of thought. For Vico, the underlying principle in Promethean and other myths of chained or buried giants is connected with the origins of authority: "Authority was at first divine; the authority by which divinity appropriated to itself the few giants . . . by properly casting them into the depths and recesses of the caves under the mountains" (*The New Science*, trans. T. G. Bergin and M. H. Fisch [Ithaca, N.Y., 1948; Italian: 1725–1730], ¶ 369 f.). One may follow out in *The New Science* the process by which the giants came to check their bestial habits, learned to bury their dead in the mountains—where "enormous skulls and bones have been found and are still found"—and developed the "heroic education" and "poetic morals" which are Vico's terms for civilization. How Joyce took possession of this giant lore is well known; given his interests in repressive authority and latent liberation, Hardy might well have done so, too.

9. Speech and Writing in *Under Western Eyes*

1. Quoted in Jacques Derrida, *Of Grammatology*, trans. G. C. Spivak (Baltimore and London, 1976; French: 1967), p. 144. Subsequent cruxes in Derrida's discussion of Rousseau occur at pp. 202, 280, and 314.

2. *Speech and Phenomena, and Other Essays on Husserl's Theory of Signs*, trans. D. B. Allison (Evanston, Ill., 1973; French: 1967), p. 76. Subsequent quotations are from pp. 77, 86, 87, and 104.

3. *Phenomenology of Perception*, trans. Colin Smith (London and New York, 1962; French: 1945), pp. 183–184. Subsequent quotations are from pp. 193, 184, 389, and 403–404.

4. For a discussion of another Conrad text which explores the conditions of personal crisis, spoken invention, and self-constitution in language, see Jerry Wasserman, "Narrative Presence: The Illusion of Language in *Heart of Darkness*," *Studies in the Novel* VI (1974):

327–338. It was this article that led me back to Merleau-Ponty's linguistic theory. A good treatment of the latter is in Alphonse de Waelhens, *Existence et signification* (Paris and Louvain, 1958).

5. All quotations are from the collected edition of Conrad published by Dent (London) and Doubleday (New York) at various periods (apparently identically). It is cited parenthetically by part, chapter, and page numbers.

6. On the seedlike dispersion and pregnant power of words, see Jacques Derrida, *La Dissémination* (Paris, 1972). For another view of the narrator's influence on the text and its implications for a theory of speech and writing, see Ronald Schleifer, "Public and Private Narrative in *Under Western Eyes*," *Conradiana* IX (1977): 237–254.

10. Science in "Ithaca"

1. Letter of February 1921; quoted in Richard Ellmann, *James Joyce* (New York, 1965), p. 516.
2. Mark E. Littmann and Charles A. Schweighauser, "Astronomical Allusions, Their Meaning and Purpose in *Ulysses*," *James Joyce Quarterly* II (1965): 238–246.
3. *James Joyce: A Critical Introduction* (Norfolk, Conn., 1941), p. 122.
4. *Fabulous Voyager: James Joyce's* Ulysses (Chicago, 1947), pp. 232–233.
5. *The Books at the Wake: A Study of Literary Allusions in James Joyce's* Finnegans Wake (New York, 1960), pp. 54–55.
6. E.g., his playful reference to the chemist Frederick Soddy and the destructive potentialities of atom smashing: "We vivvy soddy. All be doood"; cf. Atherton, *The Books at the Wake*, p. 280.
7. E.g., his marginal markings in Tolstoy's *Essays and Letters*; see *The Personal Library of James Joyce: A Descriptive Bibliography*, ed. Thomas E. Connolly (Buffalo, 1957), pp. 36–40.
8. See Kevin Sullivan, *Joyce among the Jesuits* (New York, 1958).
9. *The ABC of Relativity* (New York and London, 1925), pp. 12–13.
10. "Astronomical Allusions," p. 238.
11. See Giorgio Abetti, *The History of Astronomy*, trans. B. B. Abetti (London and New York, 1952), pp. 178–179 and 212 ff.
12. Quoted in Cornelius Lanczos, *Albert Einstein and the Cosmic World Order* (New York, London, and Sydney, 1965), p. 30.
13. All quotations are from the corrected Random House–Modern Library edition of *Ulysses* and are accompanied by page numbers in parentheses.
14. For most of the chronological terms mentioned, see A. E. Stamp, *Methods of Chronology* (London, 1933).

15. Robert M. Adams, *Surface and Symbol: The Consistency of James Joyce's* Ulysses (New York, 1967 [1962]), p. 183.
16. *The Expanding Universe* (New York and Cambridge, 1933), p. 31.
17. Harlow Shapley, *Of Stars and Men: The Human Response to an Expanding Universe* (Boston, 1958), p. 143.

11. Being and Nothing in *A Passage to India*

1. All quotations, hereafter parenthetically cited by chapter and page numbers, are from the Harcourt, Brace paperback edition of the novel, whose pagination is apparently the same as that of several other widely available editions. Since the quotations in the first part of this essay run consecutively through the first chapter, I have omitted citations for them altogether.

2. The only criticism, amid the welter of commentary, which makes an effort to describe the actual world picture given in *A Passage to India* is Wilfred Stone, *The Cave and the Mountain: A Study of E. M. Forster* (Stanford and London, 1966), pp. 312 ff., where the physical substances of earth, water, and air are qualitatively and mythologically discussed. Unfortunately, this book has become better known for its application of Indian religious philosophy and Jungian psychology to the novel; these are probably more relevant as intellectual contexts than others that might have been chosen but remain less compelling than the world picture presented in the language of the text. (It should be remarked at this point that the present essay assumes that existential philosophy exists but does not depend on it for interpretation—indeed, a close comparison of Forster's world and, e.g., Heidegger's is out of the question.)

3. A definitive statement of the moral order of the second or social realm is given in Mr. Sorley the missionary's attitude toward the comprehensiveness of the Christian redemption: "We must exclude someone from our gathering, or we shall be left with nothing" (iv, 38). Society depends on exclusions, which belie the all-embracing life of the primary realm in order to avoid the threatening vacuity of the third realm. (It is, of course, ironic that the Christian approach to life is placed at the middle range, social stratification, rather than in the heavenly sphere; but it is the implicit view of the novel that Christian and other religious myths are not genuinely of the upper realm but are adjustments to the "world," i.e., rooted in the lower realms [xxiii, 207–208].)

4. Despite the critical tact which requires freedom from any fixed set of intellectual or symbolic references in interpreting this novel, it is

undeniable that the monistic implications of the identity of being and nothing, the triadic structure of the world picture, and the fluidity associated with the concept of matter are to be found in Indian religious thought; e.g.: "The secret of Maya is this identity of opposites. Creation *and* destruction, evolution *and* dissolution, the dream-idyll of the inward vision of the god *and* the desolate nought, the terror of the void, the dread infinite" (Heinrich Zimmer, *Myths and Symbols in Indian Art and Civilization* [New York, 1962 (1946)], p. 46); "according to an ancient Vedic conception, the universe comprises three worlds (*triloka*), (1) the earth, (2) the middle space or atmosphere, and (3) the firmament or sky. These are called 'The Three Towns (*tripura*)'" (p. 185); "boundless and imperishable, the cosmic waters are at once the immaculate source of all things and the dreadful grave. Through a power of self-transformation, the energy of the abyss puts forth, or assumes, individualized forms endowed with temporary life and limited self-consciousness. For a time it nourishes and sustains these with a vivifying sap. Then it dissolves them again, without mercy or distinction, back into the anonymous energy out of which they arose" (pp. 34–35). But these conceptions are to be found elsewhere in religious and metaphysical thought and do not exhaust the embodying language of the novel.

5. Asirgarh is also mentioned by Aziz at Mau as being "forty miles away" but inaccessible for getting a doctor because "the Ringnod Dam [is] broken" (xxxvi, 310). What are we to make of that? The method of description chosen in this essay attempts to avoid external interpretive systems by staying close to the language of the text, but there are enough linguistic links falling outside the novel's chosen structure to suggest that description alone will not exhaust the novel. Frank Kermode has called these extra links "plotlets," and it was a desire to integrate more of these with the "plot" of the novel that led to the present essay. But the essay is also in "passage."

6. Among the studies of Hinduism in the novel from which I have profited are Glen O. Allen, "Structure, Symbol, and Theme in E. M. Forster's *A Passage to India*," *PMLA* LXX (1955): 934–954, and Michael Spencer, "Hinduism in E. M. Forster's *A Passage to India*," *Journal of Asian Studies* XXVII (1968): 281–295. The common trait of most such studies is to make Forster's religious implications more closely correspondent with Hindu myths and doctrines than his skeptical turn of mind could have permitted them to become. For a useful synopsis of the state of criticism on this novel, see June Perry Levine, *Creation and Criticism: A Passage to India* (Lincoln, Neb., 1971), p. 136 f.

12. Woolf and McTaggart

1. For a brief but classic account of this term, see José Ortega y Gasset, *The Modern Theme*, trans. James Cleugh (New York, Evanston, Ill., and London, 1961 [1931]), chap. x, "The Doctrine of the Point of View."

2. *Mimesis: The Representation of Reality in Western Literature*, trans. Willard Trask (Garden City, N.Y., 1957; German: 1946), p. 473.

3. "Virginia Woolf's All Souls' Day: The Omniscient Narrator in *Mrs. Dalloway*," in *The Shaken Realist: Essays in Honor of Frederick J. Hoffman*, ed. John B. Vickery (Baton Rouge, 1970).

4. This constitution of the world out of individual consciousness connects Woolf with the tradition of English fiction, as it has been described by Miller in the above-mentioned essay and at greater length elsewhere (*The Form of Victorian Fiction* [South Bend, Ind., and London, 1968]). The omniscient narrator is there seen as a general mind, representing the collective awareness of society; in passing from one to another of the characters, the omniscient narrator is in effect passing from one to another of its constituent parts. Such a view posits the independent existence of a cohesive general mind. It is, of course, a tenable description of a relatively cohesive culture like that of Victorian England. But Woolf's world lacked such cohesion, and her omniscient narrator has as fragile, lonely, and personal a consciousness as those of her characters. It passes from mind to mind, to be sure, but there is no set of assumptions, no public opinion, no "spirit of the age" beyond those minds to which it may adhere when it is not among them.

5. The most rewarding of Bergsonian interpretations is the one carried out most flexibly: James Hafley, *The Glass Roof: Virginia Woolf as Novelist* (Berkeley and Los Angeles, 1954). The most effective refutation of Bergson's relevance is Jean Guiguet, *Virginia Woolf and Her Works*, trans. Jean Stewart (London, 1965; French: 1962), pp. 391 ff. Guiguet points out that the Bergsonian *durée* as an all-inclusive moment of experience remains part of a temporal sequence or flux: "But Virginia Woolf's 'moment' has no before, no afterwards: it is, as it were, instantaneously and totally. Hence the static character of the novels, of which no critic seems to have taken account. . . . the 'moments' lived by Clarissa, Peter Walsh or Septimus—or by Mrs. Ramsay or Lily Briscoe—constitute neither a sequence, nor a true process-of-becoming." Cf. also Guiguet's discussion of Woolf's short stories as "moments of being," pp. 331–342.

6. "Moments of Being: 'Slater's Pins Have no Points,'" *A Haunted House and Other Short Stories* (London, 1967 [1944]), pp. 107–108. All references to Woolf's fiction are to the Hogarth Press collected edi-

tion; citations of *To the Lighthouse* are by part, section, and page numbers.

7. Leonard Woolf, in *Sowing: An Autobiography of the Years 1880–1904* (London, 1960), describes the atmosphere at Trinity as one in which first Moore then Russell broke away from McTaggart's influence (pp. 132–133).

8. Cited in Frederick Crews, *E. M. Forster: The Perils of Humanism* (Princeton, 1962), pp. 45⁻46; Crews mentions McTaggart's indirect influence on Forster's ideas of friendship (pp. 41–42). The fullest study of Moore and Woolf is S. P. Rosenbaum, "The Philosophical Realism of Virginia Woolf," in *English Literature and British Philosophy*, ed. S. P. Rosenbaum (Chicago and London, 1971), pp. 316–356.

9. Only Irma Rantavaara, in *Virginia Woolf and Bloomsbury* (Helsinki, 1953), has developed the similarities of McTaggart's thought and Woolf's fiction, though she emphasizes the mystical side of McTaggart, filtered through G. Lowes Dickinson (p. 107), and the ethical value placed on friendship—which leaves him indistinguishable from Moore (pp. 28–30). He is also discussed in J. K. Johnstone, *The Bloomsbury Group: A Study of E. M. Forster, Lytton Strachey, Virginia Woolf, and Their Circle* (London, 1954), first as a parallel to Dickinson in the mystical line (p. 13) and later as a humanist, lumped together with Leslie Stephen (p. 375).

10. Cf. Richard M. Gale, *The Language of Time* (London, 1967) and *The Philosophy of Time: A Collection of Essays* (Garden City, N.Y., 1967), pp. 65–85.

11. *Roger Fry: A Biography* (New York [and London], 1940), pp. 277–278; the subsequent quotation is from p. 298.

12. E.g., as Yeats cited him in "A Bronze Head," to bolster his own doctrine of the antiself as a union of opposites, by means of McTaggart's peculiarly inclusive definition of substance as the conjunction of any existents in perception by a self. A quite unmystical portrayal of the philosopher is dramatized in Dorothy Richardson's *Deadlock* (the sixth novel in her *Pilgrimage* sequence), where he is shown "a perfect *darling*" when lecturing on his nontheistic metaphysics.

13. *The Nature of Existence* (Cambridge, 1927), II, 329; hereafter cited parenthetically in the text as *Nature*. The best short presentation of the metaphysical grounds for McTaggart's denial of matter and affirmation of selves is S. V. Keeling, "McTaggart's Metaphysics," in G. Lowes Dickinson et al., *John McTaggart Ellis McTaggart* (Cambridge, Eng., 1931), pp. 127–160. The most thorough work is C. D. Broad, *An Examination of McTaggart's Philosophy*, 2 vols. (Cambridge, Eng., 1938).

14. *Studies in Hegelian Cosmology* (Cambridge, Eng., 1918 [1901]), p. 36; hereafter cited parenthetically in the text as *Studies*.

15. *A Writer's Diary: Being Extracts from the Diary of Virginia Woolf*, ed. Leonard Woolf (London, 1953), p. 102; 23 Nov. 1926.

13. *The Magus* of the Wizard of the West

1. "Notes on an Unfinished Novel," in *Afterwords: Novelists on Their Novels*, ed. Thomas McCormick (Evanston, Ill., 1969), p. 174. The quotations that immediately follow are from pp. 163 and 164.

2. "Evelyn, Get the Horseradish!" *Hudson Review* XIX (1966): 306–307.

3. "Fowles's Foul Fantasy," *The Critic* (1966): 51. Recent criticism has improved on these reviews; besides a spate of articles on *The Magus*, two books may be cited: W. J. Palmer, *The Fiction of John Fowles: Tradition, Art, and the Loneliness of Selfhood* (Columbia, Mo., 1974), and Peter Wolfe, *John Fowles: Magus and Moralist* (Lewisburg, Pa., and London, 1976).

4. *The Aristos: A Self-Portrait in Ideas* (Boston, 1964), pp. 14–15. Subsequent citations are given in the text.

5. *The Magus* (New York, 1967), xxix, 183/188. I quote the Dell paperback edition, as it is most widely available and retains its authority. Subsequent citations in the text are given by chapter and page numbers, followed by corresponding page numbers in the "revised edition" (London, 1977)—see below, n. 10.

6. Astarte reappears in chap. xxxiii, p. 202/205, as one of Lily/Rose/June/Julie's avatars ("I am Astarte, mother of mystery"); as an equivalent for the Artemis apparition, which Nicholas discovers in a handbook of mythology (xxxvii, 230/243); as the implied inhabitant of an empty box, one of a series of symbols displayed before Nicholas during his initiation rite ("We call her Ashtaroth the Unseen. Your training in literature will permit you, I am sure, to guess at her meaning," as the pseudoscientific celebrant explains [lxi, 454/505]); and in an identifying title frame of the pornographic movie that completes the hero's degradation: his illusory beloved is revealed as Isis, Astarte, and Kali, among her other personae (lxii, 470/521). Fowles' method here is typical of his approach to mythology throughout the novel: introduce the lore, assume its dismissive explanation by the learned modern mind (of which the literary critic's is only the most ludicrous example), and then withdraw the evidence by a jest that leaves the mystery intact. The purpose is not to preserve the mystery, or simply to scorn easy explanations of it, but to make mystery and the efforts at explanation structural in the human condition portrayed.

7. Fowles' source for the historical appearance of such figures may well have been E. M. Butler's scholarly study, *The Myth of the Magus* (Cambridge, Eng., 1948). A more general but highly suggestive intro-

duction to the iconography of the ancient rituals is Edgar Wind, *Pagan Mysteries in the Renaissance* (London, 1958).

8. "Phraxos," as it is called; from the Greek verb meaning "to devise a plan" or "to intend something for someone" (according to Robert Scholes in *The Hollins Critic* VI [1969]). The closest contender for a geographical model would be the island of Spetsai, where Fowles taught at a boys' school—but the novel does not encourage biographical speculation. Geography, too, is distorted in the interests of symbolic associations; that is, after giving considerable details of the character of the island, the hero misplaces it "only a look north from where Clytemnestra killed Agamemnon" (vii, 47/51), whereas it would be south of Mycenae in the Gulf of Argos.

9. Robert Boulanger, *Greece*, trans. M. N. Clark and J. S. Hardman (Paris, 1964), p. 348. The work by Foucart cited is *Les Mystères d'Eleusis* (Paris, 1914). For a recent authoritative treatment, see George E. Mylonas, *Eleusis and the Eleusinian Mysteries* (Princeton, 1961), which maintains a skepticism of Foucart's hypothesis while refraining from an alternative explanation of the still secret mysteries.

10. Fowles' extensively revised version is—like most attempts of the mature writer to rescind first-book errors—a mixed blessing. Some fine things (like the passages just quoted) have been cut, along with many mawkish ones, while the new matter rarely touches the thematic core of the work—as evidenced by the majority of my quotations, which remain intact. Fowles' main effort has been to make more mechanically plausible the godgame plot and more readable (i.e., more erotic) the double-temptress plotting. In this he has undoubtedly succeeded, but it remains an accomplishment on the professional writer's, not the artist's, level. A number of the mythological identifications have been sharpened (in the nymph and satyr masque and elsewhere); *The Tempest* is more often alluded to (e.g., pp. 184, 204, 341, 383, 458, and 481), becoming the subject of extensive quotation and discussion in chap. xxxiii (replacing the nursery-rhyme conundrum "A frog he would a-wooing go"); and the new foreword suggests the resonance of the often used term "domaine," not so much in masque as in Alain-Fournier's *Le Grand Meaulnes* (to an English translation of which, as *The Wanderer*, Fowles has written an afterword). He also mentions *Great Expectations* and Richard Jefferies' *Bevis* as analogues, but without great encouragement to source hunters. Otherwise, the foreword arrestingly confirms the author's personal sources for the setting on Spetsai (and proposes an alternative translation of its pseudonym, Phraxos); we shall honor his assurance that "no correlative whatever of my fiction, beyond the above [details of teaching at a boys' school], took place on Spetsai during my stay" (p. 9). More germane, perhaps, are

Fowles' revelations that an alternative working title was *The God-game*, that his intention was to have Conchis "exhibit a series of masks representing human notions of God" (p. 10), and that Nicholas takes on the representative face of "a partial Everyman of my own class and background" (p. 9). But about the author's contention that he has now "declared a preferred aftermath [of the ending] less ambiguously" (p. 7) we can only wonder.